# THE SPANISH ECONOMY 1959–1976

# THE
# SPANISH ECONOMY
# 1959-1976

Alison Wright

HOLMES & MEIER PUBLISHERS
New York

First published in the United States of America 1977 by
Holmes & Meier Publishers, Inc.
101 Fifth Avenue
New York, New York 10003

Library of Congress Cataloging in Publication Data

Wright, Alison.
  The Spanish economy, 1959–1976.

  Includes bibliographical references and index.
  1.  Spain—Economic conditions—1918–1975.
2.  Spain—Economic conditions—1975–  1.  Title.
HC385.W74  1977      330.9'46'082      77–3022

ISBN 0–8419–0290–9

Printed in Great Britain

In memory of my grandfather
HERBERT GEORGE TANNER

# Contents

# List of Tables

# Preface

Spain has enjoyed a decade and a half of rapid economic growth often characterised as a 'miracle'. My own interest in Spain's economic development was aroused by my first visit there. Travelling in different regions then and subsequently, I was intrigued by the juxtaposition of old and new in such a variety of contexts. Curiosity led to investigation. In particular I wanted to know more about what made the 'miracle' and how widespread the effects had been. How had growth affected specific sectors or regions? Were the development plans instrumental in stimulating growth? Had changes been uniformly spread? These and a host of other questions were by no means answered by the bare statistics of Spain's rapid growth. In so far as this book suggests answers, they are derived from more detailed (if not always consistent) data and from personal observation. It does not purport to explain Spain's growth in terms of a theoretical model.

I have been helped in innumerable ways by many people, whether in personal or professional capacities, both in England and in Spain. The publishers and I wish to thank Ernest Benn Ltd for permission to reproduce E. A. Chambers' map of Spain from the book *Spain* (*Nations of the Modern World*) by George Hills. Sadly, it is not possible to mention all those who gave me their time and attention. I would like, however, to acknowledge my especial thanks to Roy Bradshaw, José and Mari Carmen Estébanez Alvarez, Freia von Fischer Treuenfeld, Francisco Gascón Juste, Peter and Imogen Janke, Augustin Mainar Alfonso, José Perez Gallego, Pedro Schwartz Girón and Ralph Skillbeck. I should also like to thank Monsieur Chevalier, the Director, for the hospitality of the Casa de Velázquez during my stay in Madrid. My family have been a great support throughout. I am especially indebted to my husband for his unfailing patience in face of the book's impositions and for his criticisms of the text. Finally, I should like to record my gratitude to Mrs Jennifer Martin for deciphering Spanish and English alike and typing the manuscript. Without her encouragement and efficiency I very much doubt whether the project would have reached fruition. I am most grateful to all who have actively assisted me in one way or another and I acknowledge a considerable debt to those on whose work, published and unpublished, I have drawn; only I am responsible for the views expressed in this book.

*September 1976*                                         ALISON WRIGHT

Sin embargo, durante los últimos cuarenta años, las ideas modernas han tomado pie en España, y lo nuevo y lo antiguo se han ido contraponiendo con una viveza de contrastes típicamente ibérica.

Irving Babbitt, 1898.

No me comprometería a predecir el fin de este movimiento. Me ocurre que, a veces, para distraerme, leo las viejas novelas españolas que nos deparan todo tipo de aventuras. El drama que tengo ante mis ojos es igualmente complicado : ¿Cuál será su final? ¿Dónde se detendrá? Es algo que ignoro. Conozco bien varios personajes que se mueven sobre la escena, y podría decir que quieren lo que parecen querer. Pero veo pasar sombras sin cesar detrás del telón de fondo y esas sombras me preocupan.

Pascal Duprat, 1868

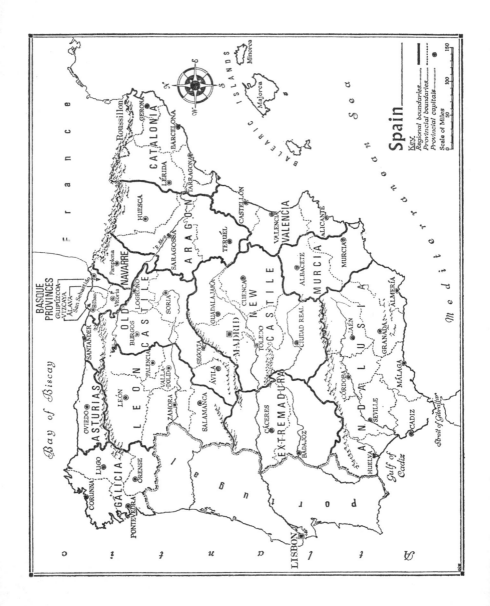

Spain

Key:
Regional boundaries............
Provincial boundaries............
Provincial capitals............

Scale of Miles
0    50    100    150

# 1 An Introduction

One of the most striking impressions when travelling in Spain is the mixture of old and new. Gleaming new factories and blocks of flats stand within a few miles of villages virtually unchanged for hundreds of years. The most up-to-date industrial processes exist side by side with the use of the Roman plough and traditional threshing methods. One can hardly fail, also, to be conscious of the abruptness with which change has hit many parts of Spain. Blocks of flats stand starkly on the edge of towns, surrounded by fields, with none of the subtle gradations from town to countryside which characterise a slower rate of change. Complementary to this is the common sight in Central Spain of unoccupied houses in villages and even on occasion whole villages left empty while their previous occupants seek a new style of life in the towns.

From the early 1960s, until 1974, when Spain felt the impact of the international recession, the Spanish economy underwent a period of very rapid expansion. Once the deflationary effects of the Stabilisation Plan of 1959 had been counteracted, and despite recessions of a cyclical nature, GNP grew at an average annual rate of 7·3 per cent in real terms between 1961 and 1973. In fact the foundation for the greater integration of Spain with other economies, which was the underlying principle of the Stabilisation Plan measures, had been laid somewhat earlier.[1]

The first overt sign of a lessening in international hostility towards Spain, in evidence from the end of the Civil War, was the Spanish/ US bases agreement of 1953. In 1958 Spain became an associate member of OEEC and a full member of the IBRD and the IMF.[2] It is arguable that rates of growth in the 1950s were not as dissimilar to growth rates in the 1960s as has often been assumed.[3] This book, however, is concerned with developments in Spain since the end of the period of economic autarky which lasted from 1939 to the end of the 1950s. In the following chapters reference is made to events prior to 1959 only when these had a direct bearing on the subject under discussion.[4]

Over the period covered, increases in population have been moderate.

In 1960 the population was 30·4 million. In 1975 it had increased to 35·4 million. While fewer children are now born, many more live. People also live longer and a breakdown of the Spanish demographic structure shows that the proportion of elderly people is increasing. In 1970 nearly 10 per cent of the population was over sixty-five years old. Over the century, despite great changes in the sectoral distribution of jobs, especially in the 1960s, the active population has not changed very much in relation to total population figures. In 1900 the total active population was approximately 35 per cent of the total population. In 1960 it was 38 per cent and had dropped very slightly to 37 per cent in 1974. This is below the average European level.[5] Perhaps the most fundamental change in the structure of the Spanish economy in the 1960s was the flight from the land. Table 1.1 gives a breakdown of the structure of the active population and shows how radical the shift away from the land has been. In 1960 41 per cent of the active population was employed in the agricultural sector while in 1970 this had dropped to 29 per cent. This had fallen further to 22 per cent in 1975. Table 1.2 shows the proportion of active population engaged in agriculture in different countries at various dates since 1900. From this table it can be seen that the turning point in Spain came after 1950.

Not all movement from the land has resulted in a swelling of population elsewhere in Spain. Since 1960 a great many Spaniards have sought work abroad. Between 1960 and 1973 over 1 million Spaniards were given official assistance in seeking work elsewhere in Europe.[6] In 1975 some 850,000 were working in other European countries. Internal migration within Spain, however, has also been on a sizable scale. This is no new phenomenon. What is new is the proportions that such movements have assumed since the end of the 1950s.[7] It is estimated that between 1961 and 1970 nearly 4½ million people moved on a permanent basis within Spain.

TABLE 1.1   Structure of the active population
(percentage of active population in relation to total population)

|  | 1960 | 1970 | 1975 |
|---|---|---|---|
| Agriculture | 41·7 | 29·1 | 22·2 |
| Industry | 24·7 | 28·7 | 27·3 |
| Construction | 7·1 | 8·6 | 10·3 |
| Services | 26·5 | 33·6 | 40·2[a] |

[a] This increase is in part due to a reclassification of some 250,000 from the industry to the service sector in 1972.
Source: Bank of Bilbao, *Informe Económico, 1975* (Bilbao).

TABLE 1.2   Changes in the active agrarian population in relation
to total population in various countries, 1900–66
(percentage of active agrarian population)

|      | USA | Sweden | France | Italy | Japan | Spain | USSR | Mexico |
|------|-----|--------|--------|-------|-------|-------|------|--------|
| 1900 | 38  | 54     | 42     | 59    | 70    | 68    | —    | 70     |
| 1910 | 32  | 46     | 41     | 55    | 63    | 64    | —    | 64     |
| 1920 | 27  | 41     | 42     | 56    | 54    | 59    | —    | 63     |
| 1930 | 22  | 36     | 37     | 47    | 49    | 47    | 80   | 68     |
| 1940 | 16  | 29     | 37     | 46    | 44    | 52    | 60   | 65     |
| 1950 | 12  | 20     | 28     | 44    | 48    | 50    | 56   | 58     |
| 1960 | 7   | 14     | 22     | 32    | 33    | 42    | 43   | 54     |
| 1966 | 6   | 10     | 16     | 25    | 24    | 30    | —    | —      |

Source: Fundación Foessa, *Informe sociológico sobre la situación social de España
1970* (Madrid) p. 162. Table compiled from many sources.

The massive outflow from the countryside has not had as marked an
effect on the agricultural sector as might at first be expected. Underemployment and actual unemployment were such widespread
characteristics of Spanish agriculture that the exodus has had little
effect on, for example, the system of land tenure.[8] However, there
are signs that excess labour in the agricultural sector is diminishing.
Pérez Díaz, in his book, *Estructura social del campo y exodo rural*,[9]
refers to the novel situation in Castile where farmers were actually
having to seek out extra casual labour at harvest time. Prior to this it
was common practice for agricultural labourers from Galicia, Asturias
and Andalusia to seek work elsewhere in Spain on a temporary seasonal
basis.

Internal migration is still strongly sustained by emigration from
rural areas. While in absolute terms, however, by far the largest con-
tingent of migrants are still labourers from the agricultural sector,
an increasing number of householders with a middle- and upper-class
urban background are also seeking jobs elsewhere. Another change
has been that, while traditionally it was men who sought employment
on a permanent basis away from their home towns, the balance of
sexes is now approximately equal.[10] It is difficult to assess the extent
to which the prospect of a better-paid job, more varied entertainment
and the general glamour of town life acts as the predominant motivating force in emigration. In the very poor areas, the desire to leave is
probably stronger than the attraction of any specific alternative way
of life. Living conditions in many villages are not conducive to remaining, when the prospect exists, even if illusory, of a better life elsewhere.

While each decision to emigrate must remain subject to the individual's desires and means, some geographical generalisations are possible on the pressures in various zones of high emigration. Where there have traditionally been large numbers of landless labourers employed on a casual basis, as in Andalusia, Extremadura and New Castile, the general standard of living is low and emigration gives the impression of a flight from misery rather than of a positive search for a better life. In parts of New Castile and in Old Castile, where property is more widely distributed and the standard of living higher, a traditional emigration pattern has been that of the sons of small proprietors to bureaucratic and administrative posts in the cities. Once a certain level of emigration has been reached in a particular village, the process is unlikely to be reversed. Those who stay are usually the older inhabitants, which has an effect on the tenor of the place and, more lastingly, on the birth rate. The amount of money spent within the village tends to drop and this creates an unfavourable atmosphere for small shopkeepers and craftsmen. In the dismal atmosphere of a village where a large proportion of the inhabitants have already emigrated, the urge for the remaining able-bodied to leave is intensified.

Despite a certain movement towards provincial capitals, the main focus of internal migration has increasingly been to the largest towns and, in particular, to Madrid, Barcelona and Bilbao. Until 1940 the most powerful magnet for anyone hoping to improve his situation was Barcelona. In the decade of the 1960s census figures show the population explosion to have been greatest in Madrid, Barcelona and the Basque provinces. Population figures increased by 45 per cent in Madrid, 47 per cent in Alava, 38 per cent in Vizcaya and 36 per cent in the province of Barcelona in the period 1960–70. While not all the increase was due to immigration, a very large part was. A survey in 1970 found that one-quarter of houseowners in Madrid and Barcelona had lived there for under ten years and only 35 per cent of the survey said that they had been born in either city.[11] This sudden influx has created difficulties in providing even basic amenities for the increased population. This is discussed in more detail in Chapter 5.

The shift to the three largest towns has created a situation in which the densely populated metropolitan area is often surrounded by almost deserted countryside. This is particularly striking in the case of Madrid. Spain overall has a low density of population by Western European standards, with an average density of sixty-seven inhabitants per square kilometre. However, Madrid, with a density of over 470 inhabitants per square kilometre, is surrounded by regions where the population is under thirty inhabitants per square kilometre.[12] Efforts to spread the massive increases of population into what are effectively dormitory suburbs, *polígonos*, after the failure of the development poles to dim the attraction of Madrid and Barcelona, are discussed in Chapter 4. Between 1960 and 1970 the percentage of the population who lived in towns of 50,000 or more had increased from 35 per cent to 44 per cent, while the proportion who lived in villages of under 2000 fell from 14 per cent to 11 per cent. Spain has in an extraordinarily short period become a predominantly urban society. By 1980 it is estimated that one-half of the population will live in 'metropolitan areas' of more than 100,000 inhabitants.[13] In the provinces the distribution of population is usually between a fairly large provincial centre and a large number of scattered and very small villages. The continuing lack of basic amenities in these small villages is commented on in Chapter 5.

The trends discernible in the flows of internal migration in the 1960s and early 1970s are broadly speaking an intensification of earlier tendencies. Since 1940 the majority of provinces have remained consistently either exporters or importers of population. Perhaps the biggest change in recent years has been the decrease in movements within provinces, usually to the provincial capital, and a corresponding increase in flows between provinces. As already mentioned, in geographical terms the main centres of attraction are Barcelona, Madrid and the Basque country. Other areas which have a net balance of immigrants are the coastal strip running from the French border to Valencia, the Canary and Balearic Islands and provinces such as Zaragoza and Navarra which constitute a link between the Basque country and the above coastal fringe. The pull is to the north-eastern parts of Spain and also to Madrid. Virtually all other areas are, in varying degrees, zones of emigration.

I have dwelt at some length on internal migration in Spain because developments, both social and economic, resulting from the magnitude of these movements, constitute a vital element in the changing structure of the Spanish economy in the 1960s. Other more familiar phenomena, such as the rates of growth of particular sectors, growth in national income, the rise in living standards and regional planning, cannot be considered in isolation from this. That there has been an economic 'miracle' in Spain is indisputable. The spectacular GNP growth over the 1960s and early 1970s, the doubling of *per capita* income from $594 in 1965 to $1160 in 1972 and rising levels of consumption all point to a far more affluent society. Consideration of the 'miracle', however, prompts not only the question, What changes have taken place? but also, How far does this signify a break with past tradition? While it has clearly been impossible in this book to enter into any great detail, I have attempted to draw attention to areas where there has been little or no change as well as where there has. Looking at the Spanish economy in the last fifteen years, one is also prompted to speculate on how far developments have been the result of conscious government decisions and, more specifically, on how closely changes in the structure of the economy have been related to the development plans. The most sceptical approach is to say that Spain's growth rate was so high in the 1960s because the starting point was low and that a fortunate influx of tourists provided the necessary financial resources. Obviously developments in the 1960s cannot be wholly accounted for by such a simplistic explanation. However, it is a healthy antidote to the assumption that the Spanish government has assiduously guided and controlled development, more particularly through the various planning devices employed. In the chapters that follow I have attempted to look at various sectors of the economy with these differing but related questions in mind.

A gap of which I am conscious is the lack of any account of political developments since 1959 and, in particular, the effect of any political group on the handling of economic affairs. This is not because I consider political events to be irrelevant. Far from it. Even in the most general terms it would be difficult to see, for instance, how planning would have become so well established without the backing of the Opus Dei, which constituted the most powerful political force throughout most of the 1960s. Because political parties have not been legally recognised in Spain until very recently, political groupings have had far looser connotations than in many other Western European countries. For this reason, while many economic decisions are intensely political in nature, they are usually directly attributable only to a particular individual and his response to a specific situation, and not to any long-term group policy decision. This means that any attempt to relate political to economic decisions must call for some degree of explanation in relation to each specific case in order to be intelligible. This is clearly impracticable, and I have therefore chosen by and large to omit political references rather than risk misleading generalisations.[14]

A formidable difficulty which bedevils any study of the Spanish economy is the extreme unreliability of statistics. Not only do figures relating to supposedly the same activities in the same years differ wildly according to different sources, but publications from within the same government department may also be quite contradictory. It is usually not possible to get to the bottom of this type of problem for two reasons. First, figures may sometimes be more the result of political wishful thinking than of empirical investigations. Second, there is often indifference or resignation in the face of incompatible sets of figures or the situation in which the sum of the parts is markedly different from the whole. Neither attitude is conducive to successful probing. However, while the best figures may be unpublished or unpublishable, use has to be made of what is available. As the Bank of Bilbao puts it, referring to industrial production, *Las diversas fuentes estadísticas sobre la evolución de la producción industrial en 1972 muestran disparidades que, al menos, ponen en evidencia la escasa fiabilidad de las informaciones estadísticas, pero que permiten intuir las auténticas tendencias registradas.*[15] ('Different statistical sources on industrial production in 1972 show disparities which, at the very least, demonstrate the unreliability of statistical information, but which nevertheless give an idea of the underlying trends.') Despite any initial aspiration to come to terms with the minutiae of the Spanish economy, most observers are eventually forced to content themselves with what they feel to be the *'auténticas tendencias'*.

# 2 Agriculture

The state of Spanish agriculture has long been the target of protagonists of reform in Spain. This continues to be true today, although criticisms of contemporary agricultural conditions and policies have gradually shifted in emphasis. Few people now believe that significant improvements could be brought about simply by a redistribution of land. Emphasis is increasingly on improving the use and the yield of the land.

In physical terms Spain does not, in most areas, offer an easy living.[1] The second highest country in Europe, temperatures vary over much of Spain from extreme cold in winter to scorching heat and often drought in summer. Only the northern fringes enjoy a temperate climate and plentiful rainfall. In the rest of Spain rainfall is often inadequate and tends to be concentrated in two fairly short periods of the year, which exacerbates the problem of soil erosion. Overall, soil in Spain is of poor quality. By Mallada's calculation only 10 per cent of the land can be described as being of really good quality.[2] The most fertile areas are to be found in Galicia, the cereal lands of New Castile, parts of Catalonia and the fruit- and vegetable-growing areas around Valencia and Granada. In comparison with other European countries the proportion of land used for agricultural purposes in relation to total terrain, approximately 43 per cent, is low. Agricultural land, including pasture, totals 45 million hectares, of which nearly 20 million are actually cultivated.[3]

In Spain, for a variety of historical reasons, there has never been any widespread development of small tenant farmers, and medium-sized holdings are widespread only in Alava, Navarra and the Catalan provinces.[4] The dominant forms of agricultural property have traditionally been large estates, *latifundios*, and very small holdings, *minifundios*, and this still remains the case in the 1970s. Figures given in the 1972 agrarian census show that almost one-half of all agricultural land is held in estates of over 200 hectares and this accounts for some 1·5 per cent of all agricultural holdings. At the other end of the scale, plots of under 5 hectares represent over 50 per cent of holdings while amounting to only 6 per cent of agricultural land. The extent of the *minifundios* is perhaps more clearly illustrated by the fact that 27 million plots of land are under 1 hectare in size. Often a farmer may own or rent several very small plots of land scattered over a considerable area, which involves loss of time in getting from one to another as well as the potential 'losses' incurred in the small size of the actual holdings. Fragmentation of land also involves a loss of cultivatable land and the OECD has calculated that this fragmentation has cost Spain some 4 to 5 per cent of agricultural income.[5] While *minifundios* are prevalent all over Spain they are especially characteristic of the north and the north-west. In the south, *latifundios* are the main form of holding. There are also large estates in central and western parts of Spain but to a lesser extent. In the decade between the first and second agricultural census the most notable change has been a diminution in the number of plots of land of less than 1 hectare. The number fell from 39 to 27 million between 1962 and 1972.

Since the beginning of the 1960s, the most important single change in the structure of agriculture in Spain has been the massive flight from the land. In 1960 41 per cent of the active population was employed in the agricultural sector. In 1975 the active population in agricultural employment accounted for only 22 per cent. Altogether 1,800,000 people left the land between 1960 and 1973 to seek work either in Spanish towns or abroad.[6] Since it is usually the younger generation who are first to leave, this has meant that the average age of those left in the villages has risen considerably. Of the current active agrarian population 55 per cent are over forty-five years old. In the early years of the 1960s the exodus did not have as much effect as might have been expected on incomes in the agricultural sector. This was because of the very large pockets of unemployment and underemployment which had long characterised Spanish agriculture. In the latter part of the 1960s, however, the relative scarcity of certain types of labour began to make itself felt and this, in conjunction with government policies to support prices of various agricultural products, resulted in a rise in income in the agricultural sector. Between 1960 and 1970 income in the agricultural sector grew at an annual rate of 6·8 per cent. It should be borne in mind, however, that in the same period the annual increase in manufacturing rose by 11·1 per cent and for industry and services jointly by 9·6 per cent.

The flight from the land has caused a fall in the number of very small plots of land but in overall terms has not brought about any substantial changes in the pattern of land ownership. Between the 1962 and the 1972 agrarian censuses the amount of land owned directly appears very slightly to have diminished while other forms of landholding, such as renting and sharecropping, have increased slightly. Neither the census of 1962 nor that of 1972 gives information on the proportion of cultivated land worked by tenants as opposed to owners. However, since renting and sharecropping is more common in holdings of cultivated land, estimates have been made that this may be as high as 60 per cent.

The declining share of agriculture in the economy is demonstrated in the fact that while in 1970 agriculture accounted for 15 per cent of GNP, in 1973 its share had fallen to below 13 per cent. Gross domestic capital formation in agriculture has also fallen, accounting for 9 per cent in 1968 and 7 per cent in 1972.[7] Despite repeated emphasis in the development plans on the importance of improving the lot of those still working in the agricultural sector, investment by the public sector in agriculture rose only from Ptas 5 billion to Ptas 13 billion between 1960 and 1969; investment by the private sector increased from Ptas 5 billion to Ptas 23 billion.

Government policies towards the agricultural sector have effectively centred on increasing the amount of irrigated land, promoting larger holdings, intervening in the distribution and sale of products and the regulation of prices for a wide range of agricultural products. In theory the government has also been interested in improving the quality of farming on the large estates, but a law passed in 1953 to this end has never been seriously implemented.

It is an irony of history that Spain, once so rich in irrigation techniques, should now find it necessary to undertake large-scale irrigation schemes. Only in the area surrounding Valencia has the tradition of irrigating land lasted unbroken since the expulsion of the Moors. Successive Spanish governments have tried to induce a greater interest in the benefits of irrigation but only after the Civil War was a large-scale programme set in motion. The principal law forming the basis of contemporary policies was passed in 1949. Under this law certain zones were to be chosen as suitable for irrigation and these were to be settled by 'colonists'. Having decided to irrigate a particular area, the Instituto Nacional de Colonización (INC),[8] usually in co-operation with the Dirección General de Obras Hidraulicas, agreed on a plan which included irrigation works and also provided for the settlement of the future 'colonists' or 'settlers'. This often necessitated the building of entire new villages. Briefly, the mechanism by which this was achieved was as follows : once a zone was declared of 'high national interest', it was decided how much land would be allowed to remain in the hands of the original proprietors and how much would be divided up amongst the new 'settlers'. Preference was given to tenant farmers and share-croppers resident in the immediate district, although farmers from other areas could also apply for resettlement. The newly settled farmers are initially under the tutelage of the INC and remain under general surveillance of the Institute even when they have paid off the initial costs and interest in the period laid down by the INC. Property once paid for is held in the farmer's name but cannot be subdivided in the future. In theory the Institute can acquire the property compulsorily if various norms are not satisfied but there is little concrete information on how strictly this is applied.

It can therefore be seen that irrigation policies have combined a mixture of social and economic aims. They have also proved extremely costly and it is doubtful whether the returns have always justified the initial outlay. Any detailed analysis of costs is virtually impossible due to the scanty information available on particular projects. The World Bank report of 1962 criticised the excessive number of uncompleted projects. In that year seventy-one projects were already under construction while a further seventy-nine were in the planning stage. The number of projects was subsequently reduced but the viability of particular projects still remains obscure. Moreover the amount of land under irrigation increased only slowly in the 1960s. In 1962 2 million hectares of land were under irrigation and in 1972 this had risen to 2·4 million hectares, of which almost one-fifth was subject to partial irrigation only and 140,000 hectares lay fallow. In the 1960s investment in government-sponsored irrigation works declined in relation to public investment in the agricultural sector as a whole and it is the private sector which in the early 1970s seems to have provided the impulse for increasing the area of irrigated land. While the INC can be criticised for having undertaken too many projects, many of which proved uneconomic, this might be justified in terms of the social benefits which have accrued from resettlement in the newly irrigated areas. Here, too, however, there is room for scepticism. The number of farmers who have actually been resettled in newly irrigated land has remained small,[9] due in part to the slowness with which the INC has proceeded with compulsory purchase. In practice, much of the land subject to such purchase has remained in the hands of the original proprietors. In the Plan Badajoz, in many ways the showpiece among irrigation projects, the 'settlers' owned only 32 per cent of the irrigated land by 1970. Between 1960 and 1970 the proportion of land held by newly settled farmers actually declined quite substantially.

A criticism which can also be levelled against the INC is the lack of practical training and help provided for the 'settlers' under the Institute's supervision. The initial five years in which the settlers are directly under the INC's tutelage gives them very little responsibility or incentive, for example to be more adventurous in what crops they grow when they enter the second phase and, within the limits of general surveillance, may grow what they choose. 'Safe' crops such as cotton and maize tend to predominate and only a small minority specialise in the fruit and vegetable crops which are especially suited to irrigated regions. In the initial five years' tutelage period machinery and animals provided by the INC have to be paid for. In the second stage, which may last twenty-five to thirty years, the farmer has gradually to pay for the property itself. At the most basic level, apart from the 10–20 per cent who become insolvent, most 'settlers' are better off in their new life than previously. However, their earlier experience is unlikely to have prepared them for the choices and decisions with which they are suddenly faced and many seem to live in a state of confused defiance in relation to the INC once the tutelage period is over. The 'settler' has to pay off a considerable debt before acquiring his property. It is therefore lamentable that many have no knowledge of their accounts or even the amount of the debt.[10] According to INC figures, only 11,907 out of 44,554 families working their land full-time under INC schemes actually owned their land at the end of the 1960s. The INC's projects have often been grandiose in conception but the benefits in either economic or social terms in relation to expenditure have been low.

The first development plan referred to small holdings as the 'greatest obstacle to agricultural development' and in the 1960s considerable publicity was given to the policy of *concentración parcelaria*, or consolidation of small holdings.[11] Consolidation of holdings is undertaken at the voluntary agreement of a village in which 60 per cent or more of the landowners who own at least a similar percentage of land petition the government to this effect In every village a 'minimum unit' and a 'typical unit' are chosen. The first represents the smallest size permissible and the second the most desirable, taking modern methods of cultivation into account. Those who initially do not own enough land to make up the minimum unit are able to obtain credit to buy what is necessary. Once consolidation has been legally effected, the plots cannot be divided in the future into holdings smaller than the agreed minimum unit.[12] While consolidation of holdings is the primary aim of *concentración parcelaria*, the process is undertaken by an organisation with wider powers for improvements in rural living, the Servicio Nacional de Concentración Parcelaria y Ordenación Rural (SNCPOR). This is concerned with matters such as improving access roads, construction of bridges, and more generally in improving facilities such as water supplies and sanitation. *Concentración parcelaria* in its widest interpretation is thus meant to improve agricultural productivity, to create a new structure of rural property and to raise the standards of living for the family unit.

Applications for consolidation rose dramatically in the 1960s and by 1973 the total of land covered by consolidation procedures amounted to 3·6 million hectares. The aims of the first development plan, that 1 million hectares should be consolidated within the years 1964–7, were not only fulfilled but surpassed. It has been estimated that in all some 8 million hectares 'benefit' from consolidation. On this assumption there still remains a good deal of work to be done. It is worth recalling the dramatic fall in the number of very small plots of land revealed by the 1972 agrarian census. This cannot possibly be accounted for solely by the official consolidation programmes. The exodus from the land is working in a complementary way to the government programmes.

A factor which has reduced the scope of the consolidation programmes has been the marked reluctance of the authorities to insist on the new holdings being united in one contiguous area. New 'minimum' or 'desirable' units are made up of plots of varying quality distributed around the relevant district. While this in a strict sense may be fair, it undoubtedly reduces the usefulness of the exercise. It may however be the only practicable method since the alternative would undoubtedly give rise to much ill-feeling. Both the consolidation programmes and the irrigation schemes, while admirable in principle, have been limited in scope and conception. In both cases the size of the new holding is small and in exceptionally few cases will the new holding be any more susceptible of mechanisation than the previous one. Moreover, little attention seems to have been paid to encouraging owners to experiment in less traditional but often eventually more advantageous crops. This has been particularly true in newly irrigated land. The restricted scope of both types of programmes stems from the mixture of objectives which the government has proposed and which have to some extent proved irreconcilable in practice. On the one hand the government has sought to set up, albeit on a very small scale, a new class of peasant farmer. This, however, has not been pursued wholeheartedly as to do so would have introduced an element of redistribution of property which in political terms would have been unacceptable. On the other hand these projects have been portrayed as increasing economic efficiency in the agricultural sector. While this has in some measure been achieved through the consolidation programmes, the possible extent of improvement has been limited.

A third factor which has in turn influenced the above programmes has been the nature and extent of the government's agricultural price-support policies. After the Civil War the main objective of agricultural policy was to ensure self sufficiency in various products, and especially in cereals. Spain's agricultural sector still reflects a high degree of control and protection,[13] and some 60 per cent of final agrarian product is subject to intervention and guaranteed prices. Until 1968 price and related policies were administered by a variety of bodies usually dealing with one specific product, i.e. wine, or a group of related products such as cereals. In 1968 the Fondo de Ordenación y Regulación de

Productos y Precios Agrarios (FORPPA) was set up as an autonomous agency affiliated to the Ministry of Agriculture, although its General Council includes representatives of the Ministries of Commerce, Finance and Industry. FORPPA was to provide for greater co-ordination in the administering of price policy. Generally speaking it has continued to use agencies, such as the Comisaría General de Abastecimientos y Transportes (CAT), to implement policies and this has weakened its potential to achieve any radical reorganisation. Moreover, strong pressure groups have developed within FORPPA which tend to reinforce the protectionist pressures in respect of traditional crops.

Over 60 per cent of cultivated land is still given over to cereals and fallow. Over 35 per cent is used in cereal cultivation, although cereals now account for only 18 per cent of total agricultural production. Moreover olive groves and vineyards occupy the largest amounts of cultivated land after cereals. Taken together olives and wine account for less than 12 per cent of total production. The large tracts of land still devoted to the cultivation of cereals give cause for concern for two related reasons. The most important is that, despite official policy to reduce the amount of wheat grown and to encourage instead more extensive cultivation of maize and animal foodstuffs, the process of change has been very slow and Spain is currently importing maize in large quantities. In 1972, of the 2·5 million hectares under irrigation, 196,200 hectares were destined for wheat. Second, yield per hectare in wheat, barley, rye and oats is extremely low in terms of international comparisons. The high cost of subsidising cereal production is underlined in FORPPA's Financial Plan for 1972 in which over 50 per cent of 'losses', for which compensation was required, were accounted for by the cereal sector. Moreover, in the distribution of credit and other subsidies the cereal sector has continued to be the chief beneficiary of FORPPA's activities.

The continued emphasis on cereals, especially wheat, and to a lesser degree wine and olives, reflected in the price-support schemes and other subsidies has led to a corresponding neglect of large-scale development of fruit and vegetable production and also of livestock. It would be wrong to infer from this that no advance has been made in either of these fields since the early 1960s. On the contrary, most fruit and vegetable products are now grown over a wider area and higher production levels are being reached. Tomatoes and citrus fruit have been particularly successful products; the latter continues to be a successful export despite increasing competition from Israel and Morocco. Citrus fruit exports have benefited from the introduction of grading for quality and size, laid down by the Ministry of Commerce. Table 2.1 shows the state of agricultural output in 1964–5,

1969–70 and 1973–4. This table shows the slight increase over the decade of livestock in relation to total agricultural output. Between 1964–5 and 1973–4 the share rose from 36 to 39 per cent. However, this increase has been minimal in relation to the change in Spanish eating habits. In the last fifteen years, in line with the overall increase in prosperity, there has been a shift away from carbohydrates to proteins and especially animal proteins. In 1964 meat consumption *per capita* was 25 kilograms and milk consumption 63 litres. By 1974 meat consumption had more than doubled to 59 kilograms and milk consump-

TABLE 2.1   Net agricultural output at current prices
(Ptas billion)

|  | *1964–5* | *1969–70* | *1973–4* |
|---|---|---|---|
| Agriculture | 177·7 | 254·4 | 299·4 |
| cereals | 59·2 | 87·4 | 48·4 |
| lentils, chickpeas, etc. | 13·5 | 19·8 | 25·0 |
| wine and products | 15·7 | 14·1 | 40·0 |
| olive oil and products | 3·9 | 14·3 | 26·3 |
| vegetables | 22·6 | 32·5 | 52·8 |
| fruit | 31·4 | 46·8 | 71·1 |
| sugar, cotton, tobacco | 9·1 | 12·4 | 16·8 |
| other | 22·3 | 27·1 | 19·0 |
| Livestock | 115·7 | 174·1 | 233·8 |
| meat | 44·3 | 83·9 | 128·4 |
| milk | 20·7 | 34·5 | 44·0 |
| eggs | 14·4 | 16·9 | 20·8 |
| other | 36·3 | 36·8 | 40·6 |
| Forestry | 13·6 | 18·7 | 18·4 |
| Fishing | 12·4 | 22·3 | 46·6 |
| Total | 319·4 | 469·5 | 598·2 |

Sources: Ministry of Agriculture and the National Institute of Statistics.

tion had risen to 96 litres. Obviously the increase in livestock registered in Table 2.1 has been quite insufficient to cope with the rise in demand and meat imports are increasing rapidly. In 1975 meat imports cost Spain some Ptas 6·5 billion and milk and eggs a further Ptas 7·7 billion.

Various incentives and subsidies have been introduced by the government in the last fifteen years to encourage greater production of livestock, but these have been small in relation to the need and some schemes, such as the joint action plans for cattle, have suffered from the inertia of officialdom.[14] The main obstacles to increasing and improving livestock still lie in the reduced size of holdings, the insufficient quantity of cheap forage, the prevalence of disease and the lack of intensive selective breeding. Moreover, little interest has been shown so far in farming projects which would integrate the production of animal foodstuffs and livestock in the same area. The World Bank has provided loans for livestock projects but not on a scale to effect a radical transformation of livestock projects in the near future. Cattle primarily reared for producing milk predominate in the north and north-west of Spain, while the small number of cattle reared primarily for meat are to be found in western Andalusia. In the March 1975 livestock census 4·4 million cattle were registered, 16·2 million sheep and 7·8 million pigs. The comparable figures for 1965 were 3·6 million cattle, 20·2 million sheep and 4 million pigs, showing that the most marked increase in livestock has been in pigs. Under the direction of FORPPA and through the agency of the CAT prices are fixed for the carcases of cows, sheep, pigs and hens. All meat offered is bought, provided certain conditions are complied with. The CAT also acts as a buffer stock for meat and eggs. 'Orientation' prices are set and stocks are released or withdrawn according to the behaviour of prices in the market. The incentives offered have not, however, been sufficient to combat the difficulties of substantially increasing livestock production and, despite frequent exhortations by the Ministry of Agriculture to this effect, the priority actually given to such activities has been low. In 1972 only 14 per cent of subsidies allocated through FORPPA went to the livestock sector and only 12 per cent of all loans.

Despite the considerable space allotted in the development plans to the betterment of agriculture and reference to many laudable if imprecisely worded improvements, government policy has continued to centre on price-support schemes. While joint-action schemes for particular sectors,[15] consolidation of holdings and irrigation programmes have all played their part, it is the use of price-support policies which has been by far the most important government device in influencing developments in the sector. Up to now it has also been an inflexible and often clumsy device. Despite the rapidly changing demands made on the Spanish agricultural sector, price policies have continued on balance to favour the traditional crops, and this has become an expensive preference. The failure to develop a stronger livestock sector or the wherewithal to feed existing stock has resulted in costly imports of meat and of animal foodstuffs. Similar failures of adjustment have resulted in imports of oil seeds and cotton in considerable quantities. In the early 1960s there was a slight surplus on the agricultural trade balance. By 1975 the deficit was in the region of $1 billion.

It is not possible here to consider in detail policies currently in operation in the many different sectors.[16] However, it is worth looking more closely at government policy in one or two of these. Tobacco is the crop which is subject to the most stringent supervision at all stages of its production and distribution. This is because of the importance of tobacco as a source of revenue. A farmer wishing to grow tobacco must first obtain permission from the Comisión Nacional del Servicio de Cultivo y Fermentación del Tabaco and, if this is granted, both the varieties grown and the conditions of cultivation are stipulated by this body, which is attached to the Ministry of Agriculture. Seeds from any other provenance than the Comisión Nacional may not be grown without express permission. An annual ruling by the Ministry of Agriculture governs the amount and the location of different types of tobacco to be grown within nine prescribed zones. Once grown and dried the tobacco is bought at fixed prices according to grading by the Comisión Nacional. Processing and sales of tobacco are then carried out by the Compañía Arrendataria del Monopolio Tabacalera SA, which is in turn controlled by the Treasury. The Bank of Spain has long been a principal shareholder in the Tabacalera and following the nationalisation of the Bank of Spain in 1962 the State now has majority control of the company. Only the Canary Islands are exempt from the Tabacalera monopoly. Tobacco growers on the Canary Islands are, however, subject to quota limitations on their sales to the peninsula. While it is not surprising to find a State monopoly governing the sale of tobacco, given the fiscal benefits accruing from such sales, the existence of two bodies and indeed a third, the Junta Superior Coordinada de Política Tabaquera (which as its name implies is supposed to co-ordinate the work of the Comisión Nacional and the Tabacalera) has meant that tobacco growers are subject to a proliferation of irksome regulations. Certainly in return they are assured a sale at a fixed price. However, there is increasing evidence that despite policies apparently designed to stimulate production actual implementation of these may serve as a disincentive to increased production. Paradoxically tobacco growers complain that they would like to grow more tobacco, while the Tabacalera continues to import tobacco from outside sources.[17]

Sugar production, of which beet is more important than cane, is also subject to regulation of production. Each year the Presidencia del Gobierno announces the desired national harvest target and the base price. The Ministry of Agriculture then calculates the area to be planted and divides this between the eight sugar-producing zones. Prices for different grades of sugar are also fixed. The refining plants provide the farmer with seed at prices fixed by the Ministry of Agriculture. Before planting begins, contracts are completed between sugar-refining plants and the individual farmer. Should the farmer produce more than the amount stipulated in the contract, the refining factory is under no obligation to buy the surplus. Nor is it forced to buy produce with a saccharine content below the norm set by the Presidencia del Gobierno and the National Sugar Syndicate.

Spain has continued its post-war policy of attempting to achieve self-sufficiency in sugar production. This however has entailed large increases in production as dietary changes in Spain have resulted in a far larger *per capita* sugar consumption. Ten years ago *per capita* consumption of sugar was 19 kilograms a year. Today it has risen to 28 kilograms. Between 1963 and 1973 consumption rose from 584,000 tons to 929,000 tons. The aim of self-sufficiency in sugar has been achieved in various years, although on an irregular basis. Years of shortage tend to be succeeded by years of over-production.

Increases in production have been largely brought about by enlarging the area devoted to sugar production rather than increasing yields. This has been achieved by increasing the subsidies paid to both sugar producers and refiners. These subsidies, which are paid by FORPPA, amounted to Ptas 1·7 billion in the 1970–1 harvest. Yield per hectare in sugar beet is extremely low in Spain by European standards and the policy of increasing production by extending the area under cultivation has in practice often meant that land not especially suitable for sugar cultivation has been brought into use, with a corresponding overall decrease in yield. While it is understandable that Spain should wish to supply a considerable portion of consumption from domestic sources, the aim of self-sufficiency, if it continues to be pursued by similar methods to those of the past, will prove increasingly costly, especially as *per capita* consumption of sugar is likely to continue to rise. Protection from external competition has been secured by placing sugar imports within the compass of the 'regimen del Comercio del Estado', which means that only the State may import this commodity. The CAT is responsible for sugar imports. Since sugar is an important item in the cost of living index, a maximum price for the sale of various grades of sugar is fixed and the consumer price is subsidised by the CAT. Moreover the structure of the sugar-refining industry reinforces an inflexible approach to prices. The refining industry is in few hands and concessionary factories have an absolute monopoly. The scale of subsidies from FORPPA to both farmers and refiners and the emphasis on producing more sugar through increased acreage tends to encourage the use of marginal land rather than concentration on high-yield areas. The high cost of pursuing self-sufficiency in sugar is shown in the fact that the price of sugar in Spain has for a long period been over twice as high as the prices obtaining in the international market.

The extent of government intervention in the production of sugar and tobacco cannot be considered as typical. With the exception of wheat, no other crop is subject to such meticulous regulation at various stages of production. However, the way in which the market for these two products is organised has been described in some detail because several of the features touched on are relevant to the production of other crops. While prices are not fixed in such minute detail for other crops, nearly all products are subject to regulation of some kind. This degree of intervention has not however had the desired effect of adapting output to new patterns of demand. Indeed it is arguable that the price policies in the various sectors have prevented agricultural production from following a more rational course.

Another feature of Spanish agriculture is the low yields experienced in various crops. Yields per hectare in wheat, barley, rye, oats, maize and wine, as well as sugar, are still well below European averages, although there have been slight improvements in the last fifteen years. Maize yields have shown the most substantial increases but are still substantially inferior to yields in most European countries. Rice is an exception to the general pattern. Yields, even though they have varied little over the last twenty years, compare well with international levels and exports have been consistently good. Agricultural policy has attempted to increase production though increased acreage rather than increased yields. The degree of protection which the agricultural sector enjoys is difficult to assess since nearly all agricultural imports are not subject to ordinary trade barriers but are imported by the State through State bodies such as the CAT or the Tabacalera. The policy of achieving self-sufficiency in a variety of products has been reinforced by the State's treatment of competing imports and the result has been highly protective and often expensive to the Spanish consumer. In the case of cotton, the high cost of Spanish-produced cotton compared with international prices, in conjunction with rapidly increasing demand from textile firms, has allowed a certain freedom in imports in this sector. This is rationalised by saying that cotton imports are to be used for exports and are not therefore prejudicial to domestic supplies. Nevertheless, despite increased imports FORPPA continues to subsidise domestic production of cotton and domestic prices have remained substantially higher than those obtaining on world markets.

In 1974, in response to the increasing agricultural deficit, the Ministry of Agriculture announced that the supply of various products was to be increased, namely vegetable oils, sugar, animal foodstuffs, meat and milk products.[18] This was to be achieved by two methods: first, through a realignment of price-support policies which would increase the attraction of growing the products in question; second, through a better utilisation of resources; this would include subsidies on fertilisers and a greater use of irrigated land for the above products either through a change in the use of existing irrigated land or by creating new areas of irrigation. It was also hoped that the extent of land lying fallow, some one-fifth of all farming land, would be reduced. How far pursuit of these objectives will ameliorate the problems touched on above remains open to question. Much will depend on whether the recommendations will in fact be used as a basis for active implementation. A seemingly more radical innovation was the decision in 1974 to announce the intervention price for eighteen farm products simultaneously. This has been repeated in the following two years and should provide the farmer with better grounds for deciding what products to concentrate on. It should therefore mean that the government can exert a more rational influence on the farmer's choice.

While these recent measures may help to lessen the agricultural trade deficit, they will do little to tackle other fundamental problems in the agricultural sector. A major problem is the low level of capitalisation. In 1965 OECD figures showed that average investment per hectare in Spain was approximately 20 per cent of the average in OECD countries. As seen earlier, investment by the public sector has played a decreasing rôle in total investment in the agricultural sector. Between 1960 and 1969 public-sector investment fell from 50 per cent to 35 per cent of total investment and this trend was not reversed in the early 1970s. Roughly speaking, one-half of this has gone to hydraulic projects sponsored by the Minister of Public Works. Of the remaining projects which are financed by the Ministry of Agriculture, between one-half and one-third has been spent on the Instituto Nacional de Colonización and its resettlement and irrigation schemes referred to earlier in the chapter. The remainder is spread between land consolidation, improving livestock, reafforestation, conserving soil, insect control, etc. While public investment slightly more than doubled in the 1960s, investment by the private sector increased by more than four-fold from Ptas 5 billion in 1960 to Ptas 23 billion in 1969. Of this, the most substantial increases in the 1960s came from investment in machinery of various sorts. Between 1971 and 1973 private investment appeared to increase by the remarkably high average of 23 per cent per annum. The motivating force behind this increase seems to have come from investment in joint-action plans, rural dwellings and to some extent irrigation rather than further mechanisation.

Despite the very low scale of mechanisation at the beginning of the 1960s and its increasing desirability in the face of less plentiful labour, investment in mechanical aids has, apart from odd years such as 1961, 1962 and 1966, shown slow growth. In some years, namely 1964, 1967, 1970, 1971 and 1973, investment actually dropped. The number of tractors registered on an annual basis was with few exceptions substantially below the targets foreseen by the development plans. The small size of many holdings and the roughness of terrain in many parts of Spain has served as a brake to faster expansion. Both these factors are reflected in the uneven rates of increase in different regions. By 1970 there were one hundred tractors for every thousand farmers in Aragon, Catalonia, New Castile and western Andalusia. In other regions there were often only forty to fifty tractors per thousand farmers. The increasing use of fertilisers is a hopeful sign and between 1960 and 1973 consumption has doubled. Here, too, there is room for considerable expansion.

Closely connected with the continuing low although gradually improving level of capitalisation is the paucity of credit available to the agricultural sector. Rates of increase in mechanisation might well have been greater had financing been easier. In a study of the market for agrarian credit, investment in machinery was first or second in the list of priorities in Old and New Castile, Leon, Catalonia, Aragon, Navarra, the Asturias and Rioja regions, Santander and the Balearic Islands.[19] The same survey attempted an estimate of the varying levels of self-financing in different regions of Spain. This ranged from some 33 per cent in the Asturias/Santander regions to 16 per cent in New Castile, 11 per cent in the area around Valencia, down to 5 per cent in Extremadura and only 2 per cent in western Andalusia and Galicia. The small size of many holdings and the high proportion of land rented rather than owned is not conducive to high levels of self-financing. Credit facilities are of great importance.

Official credit is allocated through State banks, of which the most important is the Banco de Crédito Agrícola,[20] and various government bodies such as the Instituto Nacional de Colonización and FORPPA. The Banco de Crédito Agrícola makes loans directly to farmers and also through collaborating bodies such as the Cajas de Ahorros (the savings banks) and the Cajas Rurales. Direct loans amounted to some 40 per cent of total loans by the Banco de Crédito Agrícola at the beginning of the 1970s. The share of loans by the Banco de Crédito Agrícola in relation to total official credit rose slowly from 43 to 46 per cent between 1962 and 1971.[21] During this period official credit to the agricultural sector increased nearly eight-fold, while credit from other external sources only doubled. In 1971 official credit accounted for 56 per cent of the Ptas 183 billion of credit disbursed for agricultural purposes in 1971.

For those seeking credit, the proliferation of sources can be bewildering, especially as there is little specialisation by any institution in specific types of loans. The one exception to this is the Banco de Crédito Agrícola, which prefers longer-term investment projects. Both the private and the State credit institutions make over one-half of their loans available in relation to particular harvests or short-term storing facilities. Generally speaking interest rates charged on loans from the private sector have been double those charged on govern-

B

ment-backed loans. Here, too, the situation is not clear-cut. Nineteen rates of interest have been charged within the range of 2·75 per cent to 7·5 per cent. Nearly all loans by the commercial banks are short-term, in line with their general policy on lending matters. Those wanting medium- or long-term loans have had to look to the public sector and in particular to the Banco de Crédito Agrícola, although even here long-term loans are often of shorter duration than the life span of the related project. Both private and public sector credit institutions tend to show more interest in the collateral offered as guarantee to the loan than in the viability of the proposed investment, or even sometimes actual capacity to repay. The Banco de Crédito Agrícola has often required a banker's guarantee from a prospective borrower which may in itself create problems. The slowness with which requests for credit are met may be an inhibiting factor to prospective clients. An example of this has been the length of time taken by the Banco de Crédito Agrícola in approving applications for participation in the joint-action plans for livestock. In the survey referred to above, the nature and length of the bureaucratic procedures necessary to obtain credit were the main reasons cited by those who were in a strong position to solicit credit but failed to do so.[22] As one observer put it, 'The farmer knows when he asked for the loan, but has no idea when he will get it.'[23] Although amounts of credit disbursed have risen considerably in absolute terms and relatively to agricultural production, there is still room for expansion, especially in the field of long-term credit. The defects of existing institutions as suppliers of credit are illustrated by the fact that loans from moneylenders continue to be an important source, probably still accounting for approximately one-quarter of all loans to the agricultural sector.

An added dimension to the general problem of inadequate and often expensive short-term credit is the rôle played by the Cajas de Ahorros – the savings banks. Traditionally more attractive to the small saver than the commercial banks, especially in rural areas, deposits have risen strongly over the last few years. The use of the greater part of the Cajas' funds, however, is strictly controlled by government regulations and since 1967 only 10 per cent of funds have been specifically directed to agricultural activities. The Cajas have in fact channelled savings from the agricultural sector to the industrial and services sector through mechanisms described in a later chapter.[24] While in relation to overall economic growth and development this may not in itself be considered detrimental, no other source has compensated for the drain of savings away from the agricultural sector. Unless a wider-reaching and more flexible credit network evolves, it is difficult to see how the many improvements constantly enumerated in the development plans can be achieved. Even the present system could probably be used to greater advantage if there was a clearer understanding of existing choices and opportunities. One of the problems caused by the exodus from the land has been that it is usually the less adventurous or the older members of communities who stay in the villages and they are likely to be cautious in their approach to innovations. Agricultural extension services which might, amongst other activities, act as a bridge between small farmers and the lending institutions do exist, but on a minimal scale and their impact has been negligible.

The agricultural sector could benefit considerably from an expansion of specialised firms processing and preserving fruit and vegetables. The fragmented nature of the existing industry is shown in the fact that in 1972 there were still 665 establishments concerned in processing vegetables, excluding olives. The basis of most firms is a family one and the workforce is small. Of the total of 743 establishments extant in 1970, 405 had an average of nine employees per factory. As would be expected, the distribution of firms roughly corresponds with traditional 'market-gardening' areas of Spain, namely Logroño, Murcia, Navarra and Valencia. Even in a good year employment is seasonal, consisting of the equivalent of intensive work over perhaps a hundred days a year. 80 per cent of the 51,000 people employed in the industry are women. These small establishments persist principally because of low costs and the availability of labour at the appropriate time. Because of the desire to spread employment as much as possible, there is little incentive to specialise and many firms deal with several kinds of fruit and vegetables. The present structure of the sector does not encourage change. Since firms are mostly small, they cannot afford to specialise. Even if they were prepared to try and could find the necessary finance, this might well curtail employment, which in the context of a family business would be undesirable. Similarly, the family basis of many enterprises does not encourage mergers. Another factor which has inhibited faster growth is the lack of co-ordination between the growers and the processing firms, which are usually distinct groups. There is mutual suspicion between buyers and growers, and buyers have usually been unable to persuade growers to contract price or quantities in advance. This is accentuated by the large numbers of producers involved. The lack of co-ordination between growers and the canning and freezing industries has been very marked for instance in the Plan Badajoz.

The market for canned fruit and vegetable products expanded fast both in Spain and abroad in the 1960s and early 1970s, and constraints on further expansion seem to arise from the structural difficulties mentioned above rather than lack of demand.[25] Incentives have been introduced by the Ministry of Industry to encourage canning firms to act collectively under joint-action schemes. There is still, however, a long way to go in creating a more rational structure in the industry. At the end of 1975, sixty-six firms were participating in the joint-action plan and those accounted for under one-quarter of all production in the sector. It is possible that in future a greater proportion of Spain's citrus crops may be directed into juice-making. Although exports of Spanish fruit juice have multiplied seven times over the past eight years, only 12 per cent of the total crop is put towards juice. Such a change would however involve considerable costs and could be a lengthy procedure, since at present less than one-half of Spain's citrus crop is suitable for industrial processing. These are difficulties which could also beset any large-scale expansion plans for processing of other types of fruit. While potential for the expansion of processing and conserving industries is considerable, the structural changes in present production and distribution methods required are likely to make this a lengthy process.

Since the end of the 1950s changes in the agricultural sector have very largely been the result of the massive flight from the land rather than of government policy. Gradually, the number of very small holdings has been reduced; decreasing supplies of labour have speeded mechanisation and also helped to raise wages in the agricultural sector. Although there has been a wide variety of activities promoted by the government, these have mostly been on a small scale and throughout the period the most important State activities have remained the land consolidation programmes, plans to increase the amount of irrigated land and price-support policies. All three have been characterised by a high degree of inflexibility. Irrigation schemes have tended to concentrate almost exclusively on increasing amounts of irrigated land and neglected wider considerations of what benefits could best be derived from the increase. Similarly, land consolidation programmes have been geared to an arbitrary view about the size of holdings rather than to the use to which new and larger holdings could be put. Price-support policies and credit to the agricultural sector have both tended to reinforce the strong position held by the traditional crops of wheat, wine and olives within the sector. This has been costly and is explicable in terms of the success of various pressure groups rather than any more coherent overall policy. In this respect the largest single break with past practices came in 1967 when excess supplies of wheat finally forced support prices for other cereals to be raised in relation to wheat. A thorough reappraisal of price-support policy has not yet followed. It may be, however, that the size of the agricultural trade deficit may force the government into a radical revision of its present policies.

Although Spain is not generally favoured with good agricultural conditions, the variety of climate and terrain and the existing tracts of irrigated land make it possible for a wide variety of crops to be grown. While it may be unrealistic and possibly not even desirable in terms of comparative cost to expect Spain to be self-sufficient in, for example, meat, much could be done through more purposeful use of existing incentives to improve the present situation. Moreover, less support for wheat and olives, which are uncompetitive in world markets, and greater concentration on the production of fruit and vegetables and associated processing enterprises, in all of which Spain is advantageously placed, would be beneficial.

Until recently the flow of labour from the countryside and the consequent short-term improvements in the agricultural sector have placed the government under little pressure to reconsider its agricultural policies. The benefits conferred by the shrinking of the agricultural labour force are, however, limited. Few farmers have the resources or have access to sufficient finance to allow greater experimentation with different types of crops or livestock or greater use of fertilisers and mechanical aids. Moreover, existing government policies do little to facilitate such activities. A more prosperous agricultural sector is unlikely to evolve without considerable changes in government policies. There is also a related point. Government initiatives under various schemes such as Ordenación Rural have been on a very small scale and have barely touched the extremely low standards of living still in evidence in many parts of rural Spain. Wages in the agricultural sector may have risen in the past few years but housing conditions and educational and medical facilities in many areas remain at a minimal level.[26] Building up a more dynamic agricultural sector must include substantial improvements in rural living standards.

# 3 Industry: Structure and Growth

The years following the stabilisation measures of 1959, or more precisely 1962, by which time the harsher effects of the Stabilisation Plan had been largely relieved, were those of 'take off' for the industrial sector. Before, however, examining the changes which have taken place since the early 1960s, a brief survey of earlier industrial developments in Spain follows, in order that the events of the 1960s and early 1970s should not be wholly divorced from their historical context.

Industrial activity on any appreciable scale began later in Spain than in Western Europe generally and then only in very limited geographical areas.[1] Catalonia was the first region to boast an industrialised economy, based on textiles, and trade with the Spanish colonies. By the 1870s, a new industrial centre was developing in the Basque provinces—centred on the export of iron ore, sold in return for cheap British coal. Spain was well endowed with iron ore and minerals such as zinc and copper but did not have a good supply of coal at competitive prices. In addition Spain lacked capital to exploit available resources. By the end of the nineteenth century both Catalonia and the Basque provinces were firmly established as industrial areas and Madrid, Barcelona and Bilbao had become the centres of banking. Foreign capital financed the mining of zinc, copper pyrites and other minerals, as well as the development of the railways.[2] There was also foreign interest in financing State or local corporation concessions on public utilities. By the 1920s the basis for heavy industry was well established and shipbuilding and metallurgical industries were developing close to the iron and steel works in the Basque provinces. A decade later, the Basque province of Vizcaya produced about three-quarters of the steel and one-half of the iron in Spain.[3] As cheap Spanish coal was not available, the development of hydro-electric power was of paramount importance in providing the power essential for further industrialisation and at the turn of the century this was already under way. Light industry began to develop and in particular the cement, paper and chemical industries.[4]

From 1892 onwards Spanish industry developed behind the shelter of high tariff barriers.[5] Protection in its turn stimulated the desire to make industry self-sufficient. This found expression in the law of 1907 which made it compulsory for all companies connected with the State to buy national products, and again in further supporting laws. A natural corollary of such policies was a high degree of State intervention in the economy which, in the pre-Civil War era, reached its apex in the 1920s under the dictatorship of Primo de Rivera.[6]

The devastation of the Civil War and the subsequent isolation of Spain, due to the outbreak of the Second World War and to ideological factors, resulted in a high degree of protection and far more direct State intervention in the economy. This is commonly known as the period of autarky which in varying degrees lasted until 1959, although it is arguable that the mentality and beginnings of autarkic behaviour were in evidence by the end of the nineteenth century. Neither the desire to achieve self-sufficiency nor the interference of the State in private concerns could be considered a novel feature in Spanish life; both represented a continuance of historical tradition. Whether the period 1939–59 is seen as a totally distinct era or as an intensification of an earlier process, it represented a distinctive epoch in the development of the Spanish economy. Protection which had previously been maintained almost entirely by high tariffs was now very largely reliant on severe quantitative restrictions on imports and strict export licensing, which constituted a far more effective control. After 1939 it was practically impossible to buy a product from abroad if the equivalent was obtainable on the Spanish market.

The industrial laws of 1939 and the setting up of the Instituto Nacional de Industria (INI) greatly extended the direct influence of the State in the economy.[7] The industrial laws sought through a series of benefits and concessions to establish a high degree of control in the private sector, enforceable by a stringent set of regulations which covered most aspects of economic life. State authorisation was required not only to set up new factories but also to expand the functions of existing ones. Output and prices were also subject to regulation. Industries connected with defence were to be strengthened. Government authorisation was necessary for industrial investment, a preferential category of industries 'of national interest' was established and government agencies and public enterprises were required to purchase all their supplies and equipment in Spain.[8] These policies were reinforced by the creation of the INI in 1941. The objectives of the Institute were to strengthen defence industries and to promote self-sufficiency in areas where private resources were insufficient. This was to be achieved either by specific INI investments or in collaboration with private capital. INI enterprises were automatically defined as being 'of national interest'[9] and they were required to use only articles made in Spain.

Government policy in this period laid a heavy emphasis on industrialisation. Industrial growth took place slowly in the 1940s and at a faster rhythm in the 1950s; in the fifties there was greater development of basic industries than in the forties. Up till 1950, however, the general level of production was below that of pre-war Spain. The rate of growth of industrial production between 1951 and 1959 was double that of Primo de Rivera's epoch. By the middle of the 1950s shortages of energy and basic materials, such as cement and steel, were less severe and there were signs that foreign hostility towards Spain was lessening.

In 1951 Spain was granted a loan by the USA and this was followed by the Pact of Madrid under which the USA gained permission to build bases in Spain in return for considerable economic aid.[10] As a result of rising living standards in many European countries and following the improvement in international relations with Spain, tourists were gradually making their way to Spain.[11]

Although growth accelerated in the 1950s,[12] the policy of self-sufficiency imposed severe strains on the economy and the effects were to last long after autarky was officially brought to an end by the implementation of the 1959 Stabilisation Plan measures. Industry had developed, but often based on small units whose high costs and inefficiency rendered them quite uncompetitive on world markets. As industrial growth had accelerated so, too, had the demand for products which could not be produced in Spain, and which could not be obtained elsewhere due to the very poor level of exports and the consequent strict implementation of import controls. This created shortages. In 1959 exports equalled less than 4 per cent of GNP – lower than the percentage for any OEEC country except Turkey. The system of multiple exchange rates created further distortions in prices and costs and had a damaging effect on the balance of payments. During these years Spain provided very little attraction for the foreign investor. Recurrent and accelerating inflation combined with the extremely delicate balance-of-payments situation[13] at the end of the 1950s, brought a new Cabinet into being which introduced the series of measures known collectively as the Stabilisation Plan.[14]

THE STABILISATION PLAN

The objectives of the Plan[15] were to introduce a degree of stability into the Spanish economy, while at the same time allowing a greater integration of Spain's economy with the international economy. Public expenditure was limited, bank rate was raised from 4·25 per cent to 5 per cent, limits were placed on rediscounting of bills, and all types of credit were severely restricted. 54·4 per cent of trade in private hands was liberalised and another 35·4 per cent was made subject to global quotas.[16] Prior to this only 9 per cent of trade in private hands was free; the rest fell mainly under bilateral agreements. An import deposit of 25 per cent was established and the peseta was devalued from 42 to 60 pesetas to the dollar. Multiple exchange controls were abolished, wages were frozen and at the same time a gradual dismantling of State fixing of prices began, causing various State organisations which dealt with aspects of economic intervention to be run down. Spain showed its closer ties with the Western world by obtaining associate membership of the OEEC. This was followed by membership of the International Monetary Fund and World Bank in 1958, and full membership of the OEEC in 1959, substantiated by credits from the OEEC, IMF and the USA.[17]

The Stabilisation Plan has been much criticised. On the one hand critics argue that the impact, which was severe, fell mainly on those least able to cope with it and that the stagnation effect produced was unnecessarily prolonged. Conversely, it has also been argued that while some action was unavoidable, the Plan was inadequate because it only touched the surface of Spain's problems and brought about no fundamental structural reforms. It was a change in policy but a conservative one.

Yet the effect of the measures was certainly dramatic. The deficit on the balance of payments was converted into a surplus by the end of 1960. Prices were stabilised and even went down in some cases; credit was severely restricted.[18] Deflation caused a fall in investment of 11 per cent and national income fell by 2·5 per cent. Certainly those at the lowest end of the pay scale were the hardest hit, especially by the curtailment of overtime and bonuses, causing reductions of up to 50 per cent of wages received prior to the Plan. Unemployment rose sharply but, happily for the Spanish government, this found an outlet in emigration to other countries in Western Europe. Between 1959 and 1961 half a million Spaniards went to live and work abroad. Sectors most affected in terms of production were coal-mining, engineering works, paper and textile factories. Whatever their standpoint, most observers agree that the stabilising measures were continued too long. This created uncertainty in Spanish business and a depression in long- and short-term capital markets, which lasted for more than a year. Towards the end of 1960 various reactivation measures were introduced. Investment by the public sector was increased and interest rates were lowered. By 1961 expansion was well under way.

INDUSTRIAL GROWTH AND THE 'MIRACLE'

This then was the background against which the 'Spanish Miracle' took place. At the beginning of the 1960s the Spanish economy and in particular Spanish industry presented a varied and uncertain picture. On the one hand was the legacy of 'autarky': small firms, under-capitalisation, inefficiency, antiquated machinery, low productivity and a mentality more often geared to obtaining the necessary licences and dealing with *tramites* (bureaucratic red-tape) than to forward-looking business planning. On the whole it had been necessary as well as helpful to be *enchufado* or 'plugged in' to the right man at the relevant ministry in order to secure your permits. On the other a great deal of cumbersome administrative machinery still existed from the previous decade. The World Bank Mission, presenting its Report in 1962, referred to the 1600 autonomous organisations 'each of which is at least nominally dependent upon a particular ministry'.[19] Greater integration with other economies was also bringing increased competition. The outlook was not only uncertain, for some it was bleak. Some Catalan textile manufacturers preferred to sell out.[20] 1961 was a year of expansion for some, but by no means for all and there was little indication of the scale of future growth.

In the pages that follow references to developments in the industrial sector may appear to give the impression that the pace of change was uniformly spread over the years in question. In fact this was far from the case. Since the beginning of the 1960s the economy has been characterised by cycles of varying duration of a stop-go character. In order, however, to present a picture of overall developments and government policies, it seemed less confusing broadly to ignore the impact of these cyclical variations, which are treated in more detail in Chapter 7.

Over the period 1960 to 1975 the average annual increase in Gross Domestic Product (GDP) was 6·9 per cent in real terms.[21] While growth in the agricultural sector was slow and the average annual increase was some 3 per cent, the service sector registered a 7 per cent annual increase, while industry and construction together averaged a yearly growth of 8·9 per cent. Since 1960 the construction and industrial sectors have provided employment for an additional 1 million people and the proportion of active population engaged in these sectors increased from 31 per cent in 1960 to 37 per cent in 1975.[22] Table 3.1 gives a percentage breakdown of GDP by sector in various years between 1964 and 1975 and shows how the share of agriculture has declined, while the service sector has maintained a fairly constant share of approximately 42 per cent and the share of industry has increased from 38 to 44 per cent.

TABLE 3.1 Sectoral breakdown of GDP at factor cost
(various years; 1964 prices)

|      | Agriculture | Industry | Services |
|------|-------------|----------|----------|
|      | *(percentages of GDP)* | | |
| 1964 | 18·2 | 38·3 | 43·5 |
| 1965 | 15·5 | 41·8 | 42·7 |
| 1972 | 13·6 | 44·3 | 42·1 |
| 1974 | 12·9 | 45·5 | 41·6 |
| 1975 | 13·0 | 44·3 | 42·7 |

Source: Bank of Bilbao, *Informe Economico 1975* (Bilbao).

While the industrial sector has expanded at a remarkable pace since 1960, developments have not been evenly spread between constituent sectors. Table 3.2 shows changes in production, employment and productivity per hour between 1962 and 1969. The trends of this period continued in the early 1970s. Production rose fastest in transport equipment followed by basic metals and chemicals. The expansion

TABLE 3.2 Indices of production, employment and productivity, 1969
(by sector; base 1962 = 100)

|  | Production | Employment | Productivity *(per hour)* |
|---|-----------|------------|--------------|
| Construction and Public Works | 183·2 | 141·2 | 129·4 |
| Public Utilities | 229·5 | 95·0 | 233·2 |
| Clothing and Footwear | 219·1 | 111·9 | 193·6 |
| Wool and Products | 166·3 | 96·5 | 179·0 |
| Food and Drink | 196·5 | 129·7 | 138·4 |
| Mining | 106·8 | 69·2 | 193·5 |
| Chemicals | 257·3 | 113·6 | 226·3 |
| Paper | 213·3 | 103·0 | 215·5 |
| Basic Metals | 271·3 | 105·0 | 258·9 |
| Building Materials | 219·7 | 117·8 | 193·4 |
| Other Metals | 247·7 | 124·2 | 200·0 |
| Transport Equipment | 315·6 | 162·7 | 189·7 |
| Textiles | 119·7 | 86·4 | 150·9 |

Source: AGECO, *Datos básicos sobre la evolución de la economía española 1960–1970* (Madrid, 1971), compiled from the National Accounts, Statistical Service of the Syndicates, Ministry of Industry and Bank of Bilbao.

of shipbuilding activity in the 1960s was extremely rapid and by 1972 Spain was seventh in the world league in building ships. Order books more than doubled between 1969 and 1973 and in terms of orders Spain ranked third in the international league. Car manufacturing also developed extremely rapidly in this period, as indeed did the domestic market for cars. In 1960 there were ten cars for every thousand inhabitants, while in 1969 there were fifty-eight and by 1975 there were one hundred and eleven. Steel production has also increased very rapidly although, in company with other branches of industry, from a very small base. In 1960 output reached nearly 2 million tons. By 1970 output totalled over 7 million and by 1975 combined steel production accounted for over 11 million tons. On the other hand, the output of most mining activities scarcely expanded at all and textile production increased only slightly.

In the period covered by Table 3.2 employment expanded most rapidly in the manufacturing of transport equipment and in the construction sector. This latter sector has, in absolute terms, produced the highest number of new jobs since the 1960s, although exact figures are hard to come by since many construction workers are casual labourers and therefore not shown in official employment registers. The construction sector has been the first port of call for a great many workers leaving the land. Productivity has increased little in this sector, which remains highly labour-intensive.

According to the figures given in Table 3.2, productivity per hour increased most in public utilities and the metal and chemical sectors between 1962 and 1969. Productivity per hour averaged over all sectors of industry doubled in the decade 1960 to 1970. It should however be borne in mind that the base for this growth was very low and currently productivity in Spanish industry is less than half the average for the Common Market countries. In steel, for instance, increases in output have been spectacular but productivity remains disturbingly low in comparison with European averages.[23] Overall, the sectors which have shown the greatest dynamism since 1960 have been the chemical, energy and machinery sectors. High capital investment has resulted in large increases in value added *per capita* in all three sectors and specialisation has taken place to a greater degree in these than in other sectors. These three sectors have also acted to some extent as catalysts for change in other parts of industry by virtue of their increasing importance as suppliers of intermediate goods to other sectors.[24] The fact that the most dynamic sectors have been those which are most highly capital-intensive may pose employment problems in the future.

The acceleration of industrial development in the 1960s resulted in an expansion of industrial activity in the traditional centres of Catalonia, the Basque country and Asturias. What was new in the period was the growth of Madrid as a focus of industrial activity. Between 1964 and 1973 the population of Madrid grew from 2·9 million to 4 million and the percentage of active population engaged in industry increased from 35 to almost 40 per cent.[25] Madrid has been transformed into an industrial centre, concentrating on light metal and engineering industries, chemicals, food and leather. The province of Madrid is second only to Barcelona both in numbers employed in the industrial sector and in value of industrial production. In Alava, Barcelona, Guipuzcoa and Vizcaya over 50 per cent of the active population was employed in the industrial sector in 1973 and more than 50 per cent of industrial production is concentrated in Catalonia, Madrid, the Basque country and Asturias. Generally speaking, metal-based industries remain in the northern provinces. Textiles are still mainly situated in the Catalan region, although Catalonia is far less dependent on textiles than previously and there has been diversification into chemicals, the food industry and light engineering. The continuing attraction of these industrial regions is demonstrated by the rapid rate of emigration from the agrarian areas which immediately surround them. In the north-east this has even caused the abandonment of fertile farm land. The area which has most recently become characterised by more intense industrial activity is the Valencia region, previously a centre of the food and leather industries. Light engineering and chemical works have grown up in the region and a large steel complex is under way at Sagunto. The Ford Company has built its new factory in Almusafes, also near Valencia. Seville has also become more industrialised. Despite the various development incentives for more balanced regional development, industry outside the few large centres continues to be scattered in almost haphazard fashion in the remaining areas of Spain.

THE KEY RÔLE OF IMPORTS

The rapid pace of industrial development prompts two related questions. First, what made such development possible in the 1960s, and second, to what extent did the government influence the course of events? A decisive factor in stimulating industrial activity at the beginning of the 1960s was the liberalisation of a large range of imports under the Stabilisation Plan measures. This allowed the import of the raw materials and capital goods which were indispensable for any substantial increases in output and changes in the structure of Spanish industry. The impulse given by such imports was particularly noticeable in the early 1960s in the chemical sector and in all parts of industry dealing with machinery of different kinds. It is difficult to conceive of any large-scale industrial development in Spain having occurred in the absence of this substantial liberalisation of imports. Initially, increased industrial activity used up the slack in the utilisation of productive capacity which was a widespread characteristic of much of industry in Spain in the 1950s. As the decade progressed the imports of different types of capital goods and machinery induced changes in the structure of Spanish output and allowed Spain to become far more competitive in world markets.

The demand for capital goods grew at a prodigious rate and between 1960 and 1970 output in the Spanish capital goods sector grew at twice the rate of overall industrial output. Nevertheless, the rise in demand for capital goods far exceeded the increase in domestic production and imports rose very substantially. The growth of some sectors, such as machine tools, was inhibited by the strength of foreign competition and the machine-tool industry has remained fragmented and inefficient.

SOURCES OF FINANCE

The lowering of trade barriers was not, however, the sole cause of industrial development. It was a necessary condition, not a sufficient one. Finance was required to make use of the opportunities opening up. Gross domestic fixed asset formation quadrupled to over Ptas 1000 billion between 1964 and 1974 and accounted for some 25 per cent of GNP in that period, although there have been slight variations from year to year.[26] Capital was therefore forthcoming to sustain this expansion. The level of self-financing is generally low in Spain, although it has risen slightly in recent years. Obviously the capacity for self-financing of activities varies according to the circumstances of individual firms and it is usually the larger firms which are self-financing to a higher degree. In 1973 even the top one hundred Spanish companies were less than 40 per cent self-financed.[27] As, moreover, the possibilities of raising capital on the stock market have remained limited to a few firms, the main sources of external finance have been the private banks, the savings banks and foreign capital. The State banks also lend money to the private sector but in relation to funds going to industry from other domestic sources the amount is small – some 7 per cent in 1974, including lending to State enterprises as well as to private-sector borrowers. The relation of the banks and the savings banks to the industrial sector and the rôle of the stock market are described in Chapter 6. Here it is merely worth noting that commercial bank lending to the private sector, which accounted for over one-half of all external financing from domestic sources in 1974, still consisted largely of short-term loans and bills of exchange. The insecurity and consequent lack of long-term planning which this entails is particularly damaging to small firms, which make up a large part of Spanish industry.

Foreign investment in Spain was important to the economy long before the 1960s. Foreign capital was largely instrumental in the last part of the nineteenth century in developing the basis of modern industry in Spain. Following the Civil War foreign investment was strictly regulated and, with the passing of the law on the Regulation and Defence of National Industry in 1939, foreign investment was limited to 25 per cent of any particular enterprise, although this could in theory be increased to 45 per cent by virtue of extremely complicated procedures.[28] Commercial enterprises could in principle be 100 per cent foreign-owned, and mining concerns up to 49 per cent, but this was a matter of administrative discretion case by case. All in all the inducement to invest in Spain was negligible and this, combined with the Second World War and its aftermath, resulted in a very low level of foreign investment. Although there are no official publications available on foreign investment between 1939 and 1960, such evidence as there is points strongly in this direction.

In 1959, in line with the other stabilisation measures, a new stance was adopted on foreign investment. Complete freedom was granted for such investment as long as foreign ownership of individual enterprises did not exceed 50 per cent. For investments involving over 50 per cent ownership applications had to be submitted to the Council of Ministers for approval. In 1963 eighteen special sectors were designated in which no limit was set to foreign ownership; these included steel, textiles, leather, shoes, machine tools, building and hotels. Defence industries and the media did not fall within the scope of the new law and these remained closed to foreign investment. Spain, from being a country of scarce interest to the foreign investor, within a very few years became one of great interest. Investors were attracted by political stability, the illegality of strikes, and relatively low labour costs. Between 1965 and 1975 foreign investment increased from Ptas 5 billion to Ptas 27 billion, although not at an even rate from year to year. Official figures published on foreign investment are unfortunately inadequate and do not give the full picture. One reason for this is that figures published by the office of the Presidencia refer only to investments which have been authorised, i.e. those which involve 50 per cent ownership or more, and therefore investments in the 'freed' eighteen sectors do not appear and it is precisely these sectors which have attracted large amounts of foreign investment. While the figures cover authorisations, they do not necessarily correspond (even time-lagged) to disbursements and, although breakdowns are given by country and by industrial sector, an individual country's participation within any specific sector is not obtainable.

Bearing these cautions in mind, the following figures show which countries have shown most interest in investing in Spain and which sectors have attracted foreign investment. Over the period 1960–75 the USA was the largest supplier of foreign funds, accounting for some 40 per cent of the total invested (and probably more if account is taken of investment by US subsidiaries in third countries such as Switzerland). Switzerland was the second biggest investor, supplying 16 per cent of foreign investment, although it should be borne in mind that funds which come through Switzerland do not necessarily originate there. The Federal Republic of Germany and the UK each accounted for a further 10 per cent and France followed with 5 per cent. By sector in this period, 31 per cent of all foreign investment in industry went towards the construction industry and the making of transport equipment, and 18 per cent into chemicals. Retail and wholesale distribution accounted for a further 8 per cent and electric machinery for 5 per cent. The degree of foreign ownership is difficult to determine but it is certainly high in chemicals, glass, food and printing. Between 1960 and 1969 total foreign private direct investment exceeded the total of investment in securities and in real estate from abroad.[29] In December 1973 the Minister of Commerce pointed out that one in five jobs were financed by foreign investment. This is not the sort of information which prompts gratitude and there has been a steady stream of criticism within Spain of the government for allowing the *renta de España por parcelas* – selling off Spain in plots. In particular there has been criticism of the mounting payments for royalties and technological assistance. In 1974 these amounted to some $210 million.[30] Between 1970 and 1974 payments increased by a yearly average of 18 per cent. In 1972, 2400 Spanish firms held foreign licences for production or received technical assistance. In a survey on American companies in Spain, however, it was noted that average technical fees per respondent company had declined and that there was an upward trend in local purchases.

Over the decade the Spanish government has gradually changed its views on the rôle of investment from overseas. In the years immediately following 1959 the government was primarily concerned with attracting new capital, creating new jobs and obtaining a wide spectrum of modern technology. By the 1970s, however, the government had adopted a more selective attitude. More emphasis was laid on the export potential of any firm setting up in Spain – this was very marked in the negotiations with the American Ford Company in 1972–3 over setting up a plant in Almusafes. The Second Development Plan (1968–71) specifically stated that the Spanish government wanted more research and development projects to be undertaken in Spain and since 1968 has offered incentives to encourage research programmes in industry. In line with promoting a greater Spanish participation in firms with a strong foreign bias is the emphasis laid on the greater use of local inputs, increased training for Spanish nationals and a reduced 'dependence' on foreign royalties and technical assistance. The government has also made it clear that it much prefers investment in manufacturing industry to investment in real estate.

On the other side of the picture, the outlook for the foreign company investing in Spain is not wholly rosy. Foreign interests in Spain find import restrictions and export procedures time-consuming and irksome, as is the limitation on local borrowing, while there are continual difficulties in transferring money in and out of Spain. A study produced by the Stanford Research Institute on American companies in Spain found that 'while the law may be good, there are too many variations in the interpretation and implementation'.[31] In the latter part of the 1960s, while foreign investment continued to pour into Spain, the same study noted that Spain was not such a golden goose as had once been assumed. It pointed out that on the whole American investments in other countries in Western Europe have been more profitable. Investment in Spain showed a higher return than in the EEC or in Western Europe as a whole only in three of twenty years. A feeling of uncertainty was generated among foreign investors by the restriction on the repatriation of dividends in force between 1967 and 1971 and this anxiety was not dispelled when in 1971 the restriction was only 'suspended'.

In a country like Spain which has experienced so much change with attendant disorientation in so short a time, foreign investment is an easy target for dissatisfaction. The government undoubtedly feels ambivalent. Since domestic savings are not sufficient to finance the scale of industrialisation required, foreign capital is necessary. On the other hand, there is a reluctance to see a growing proportion of Spanish industry under foreign 'domination'. In 1973 foreign investment and royalties were the subject of new regulations. The eighteen special sectors designated under the law of April 1963 no longer have special status and henceforward *all* foreign direct investments must be authorised by the government.[32] Since the end of 1974, however, investments involving foreign capital are no longer subject to authorisation as long as the company involved manufactures (in Spain) only capital goods which are included in the low customs annex of the customs tariff. In September 1973 the government set up a register in which all new technology contracts must be entered following their authorisation by the Ministry of Industry.[33] Registration is now a prerequisite for authorisation of royalty payments in foreign currencies. An attempt is being made to co-ordinate the handling of foreign investment and to regulate it more strictly. What remains to be seen is whether there will be a corresponding efficiency in the treatment of foreign investment which *is* allowed.[34]

TOURISM AND EXPORTS

The pace of industrialisation in the 1960s and early 1970s was also affected by the growth of foreign currency earnings, most directly of course by the rapid expansion of industrial exports with its stimulative effect on investment and less directly by the extraordinary rise in tourism over the period. The increase in industrial exports is discussed below. The growth in tourism is referred to more fully in Chapter 8. Here it is worth noting that the number of tourists increased from 6 million in 1960 to a peak of 34 million in 1973, after which there was a slight decline in numbers. In 1973 net tourist earnings brought some $2·8 billion into Spain. While lack of detailed information makes it impossible to estimate with any degree of accuracy what proportion of tourist receipts actually remain in Spain, let alone the extent of the impact upon a particular sector of the economy, the growth of tourism has had a marked effect on the industrial sector in two main ways. First, supplying even minimal tourist needs caused a boom in construction and infrastructure works and in a wide range of related industries. Second, wages paid to the associated service industries have over time stimulated domestic demand for consumer goods.

THE CONTRIBUTION OF GOVERNMENT POLICIES

Before attempting to determine to what extent the government has been responsible for determining the course of industrial development, it is necessary to examine the ways in which the government has intervened in the industrial sector over this period. Since 1959 State intervention can be divided into three categories. One method has been to intervene either in a sector or a region with the explicit intention of bringing about specific changes. This has characterised *acción concertada*, the joint-action plans, and also schemes aimed at encouraging mergers of firms as well as *industrias de interés preferente*.

The joint-action programmes were introduced in the First Development Plan and have been used in several industrial as well as agricultural sectors. Private firms within a sector agree on certain joint targets, such as increased production and productivity, improving the quality of goods and also increasing benefits to workers, through remuneration and professional training schemes. In return the State offers credit and tax benefits which vary according to sector. Official credit for up to 70 per cent of investment can be obtained with a five-year grace period. Tax benefits can include up to 95 per cent reduction on a range of taxes, including taxes on dividends. At the end of 1975 joint-action plans existed in the steel, coal mining, leather and footwear, pulp and paper, iron-ore mining, shipbuilding and vegetable-canning sectors, as can be seen in Table 3.3. The table shows that joint-action plans now cover 90 per cent of the coal mining sector, 85 per cent of shipbuilding and over 50 per cent of the steel sector.

TABLE 3.3    Joint-action plans, end of December 1975

|  | *No of factories affected* | *Percentage participation of factories in whole sector* | *Investment to be undertaken in joint-action plans*[a] |
|---|---|---|---|
| Steel | 17 | 56 | 61,296 |
| Coal mining | 16 | 90 | 6,300 |
| Leather and footwear | 158 | 42·5 | 2,000 |
| Vegetable canning | 66 | 22 | 2,447 |
| Pulp and paper | 26 | 28 | 7,900 |
| Iron-ore mining | 6 | 34·3 | 4,984 |
| Shipbuilding | 4 | 85 | 20,400 |

[a] In Ptas billion.
Source: Banco de Crédito Industrial.

In terms of quantity of investment envisaged the joint-action plans in steel and shipbuilding are by far the most important. Joint-action plans in the steel sector have been responsible to a large extent for bringing into a better state of equilibrium the acute imbalance of demand and supply in various stages of processing which characterised the sector in the 1960s. The joint-action plans in steel have not however brought about any fundamental restructuring of the sector and a wide variety of steel plants in terms of size and modernisation continue to exist side by side. Nor have retraining schemes been much in evidence. The steel sector itself complains that government grants obtainable through the joint-action plans are not particularly cheap, especially compared with State provision for steel in other European countries. The shipbuilding sector has certainly benefited from the credits conceded under the joint-action plans and the dynamism of this sector, at least until the collapse of the tanker market in 1973–4, was commented on earlier in the chapter. Leather and footwear continue to be one of the foremost exporting sectors in industry and here too the joint-action plans have been beneficial in producing improvements. While results have not been impressive in coal, the need for the joint-action plans has diminished with the increase in the participation of the Instituto Nacional de Industria in the sector through Empresa Nacional Hulleras del Norte SA (HUNOSA). Results in the remaining sectors have not been particularly encouraging. The joint-action plans have brought about demonstrable improvements in production totals and methods in the sectors where the plans cover a high proportion of production. Where the plans have failed is to bring about any fundamental restructuring of the different sectors, and this is essential for radical improvements in, for example, vegetable canning, as seen in Chapter 2.

To some extent the government has tried to tackle structural problems through policies designed to encourage the merger of different firms within a sector. One of the striking characteristics of Spanish industry is the great proliferation of small firms which is apparent in nearly every branch of industry and in particular in metal, wood, glass and ceramics, textiles, paper, leather, machine tools and many consumer goods. Large concentrations of small and medium-sized firms are to be found in Barcelona, Madrid, Alicante, Seville and Valencia. Over 80 per cent of Spanish industrial firms employ fewer than five workers. Based on a law passed in 1957,[35] *concentración de empresa* is a scheme which encourages mergers and groupings between firms in all sectors except real estate, insurance, banking and finance. This may be either on a permanent or a temporary basis. For up to five years firms which merge are granted tax rebates on a wide variety of activities ranging from registration taxes to customs duties. Between 1959 when the scheme first came into action and 1972, 1132 firms merged into 308. Jointly the capital of all these firms amounted to Ptas 149,183 million. By sector the largest mergers in value terms have taken place in the electrical, chemical and transport equipment sectors, accounting for 65 per cent of all mergers. By numbers of mergers the food and drink sector takes pride of place. The small numbers of firms affected in relation to the size of the problem reflects the inadequacies of government policy in this area. The same criteria are inflexibly applied to different sectors, whether the food or the textile industry, and no allowance is made for the complications caused by the presence of foreign capital. As with many official procedures in Spain, the time which the government takes first to approve a particular proposal and then to disburse the necessary credits is the cause of frequent complaints. This is also true of the joint-action plans.

Since 1963 some firms have been accorded preferential status, *industrias de interés preferente*, in return for willingness to establish industries in particular regions or in a particular area of activity. Tax and other benefits accrue to the preferential-status firms and this has been most widely used in the context of regional development planning and is referred to again in Chapter 4. Preferred sectors have included food-processing industries, certain steel plants, the production of sulphuric and phosphoric acids from Spanish pyrites and, since 1974, firms making motor vehicle components and electronics.

The second category of measures through which the government has intervened in industrial development has been of a more general character. These include export incentives, low interest rates and the whole gamut of incentives included in the development plans. Because development planning has occupied such an important rôle in the government's economic policies, discussion of the plans and their effects has been reserved for another chapter. Throughout the 1960s and early 1970s interest rates in the private sector as well as for official credit have been deliberately kept low by the government in order to encourage investment. This has undoubtedly been of great importance in stimulating industrial investment.

Export incentives have ranked high in the Spanish government's aids to industry. The two most important have been the *desgravación fiscal de la exportación*,[36] which is a tax rebate on exported goods, and official credit for exports. The *desgravación fiscal de la exportación* has risen from Ptas 1 billion in 1961 to Ptas 57 billion in 1975 and now accounts for 13 per cent of the value of all exports.

In the 1960s special rediscount lines were the main instrument of official credit. Set up in 1960 as part of the reactivation programme, the lines were intended to expand credit facilities of a longer-term nature. Terms and conditions of the Spanish lines to be rediscounted at the Bank of Spain were determined by the Treasury. Initially this type of credit was not channelled to any especial activity and it remained at a moderate level. After 1962 it was stipulated that the special rediscount lines had to be used for specific operations within particular sectors. The sectors which benefited most were capital goods, shipbuilding and exports. In each of these, the scale of operations covered by the special rediscount lines was continually expanded and revised. Machine tools and fruit-producing were added later in the 1960s but never attracted much of this type of credit.[37] From 1964 onwards credit obtained under the special rediscount lines expanded at a brisk pace and by 1970 credit disbursed in this way amounted to Ptas 63 billion, of which one-half went towards exports. Official credit for exports was also forthcoming from the Banco de Crédito Industrial which provided some Ptas 10 billion for exports in 1969. Following the Matesa scandal in 1969 official credit was reorganised, the special rediscount lines were abolished and since 1971 the banks and savings banks have been required to channel prescribed proportions of their deposits into export finance[38] and lending by the Banco Exterior de España in support of exports has substantially increased. Export credit from these sources in 1975 amounted to Ptas 98 billion,[39] of which approximately one-half was spread evenly between machinery and ship exports.

Sectors or industrial firms may be granted a certificate award, the *Carta de Exportador*, as a result of being good exporters over a period. Export credit insurance is also available. However the *desgravación fiscal de la exportación* and official credit from the banks' obligatory savings coefficient and the Banco Exterior de España remain the most important sources of export credit. The rise in industrial exports has been very rapid since the early 1960s. Exports of manufactured goods expanded at an annual average rate of 19·6 per cent and by 1968 had become more important than agricultural exports in value terms. While this was in part a natural consequence of industrialisation, government incentives to industrial exports certainly played a large part in enabling Spain to take full advantage of its competitive strength in terms of low labour costs.

Another way in which the government has intervened in the industrial sector is through the control of prices. While price control in the industrial as well as the agricultural sector has its roots in the period immediately following the Civil War, endemic inflation has meant that prices throughout the 1960s and early 1970s have been subjected to varying degrees of control. In 1967, for instance, a complete freeze on prices was declared for all goods and services. Prices for products of heavy industry have, on the whole, been most often subject to restrictions.

At the end of 1973, in conjunction with other anti-inflationary measures, action was taken to control the rise in prices. A list of eighty-two items was drawn up for which official authorisation for any increase in price was needed. A further forty-nine prices were placed under 'special vigilance'. Price increases in industrial goods and services were permitted to rise only if based on a wage increase or a rise in the price of raw materials. These regulations have remained in force with only slight modifications mostly of an institutional nature. In fact, increases in the cost of living index in 1974 and 1975 suggest that price control has been patchy in application and efficacy. It has, however, been sufficient to exacerbate financing problems in large numbers of firms and it is this that has constituted the biggest problem caused by price controls in the industrial sector since the early 1960s. Moreover, the failure to ease controls once the immediate crisis had passed, as for example after 1967, caused distortions in investment. Prices tended to rise, even although unauthorised, in light industry and it was here that investment was attracted. Heavy industry, understandably a target in terms of anti-inflationary measures (which could the more readily be implemented because of the relatively high degree of State ownership in this sector), tended to be left short of funds from private sources and consequently to increase its use of the 'privileged circuits' described in Chapter 6.

The third way in which the State intervenes in the industrial sector is the most direct, through owning industrial companies, and this is done through the Instituto Nacional de Industria (INI). INI, based on the IRI in Italy,[40] was created in 1941 in the immediate aftermath of the Civil War, and its specified objectives were to strengthen industries necessary for national defence and to provide the basis for an economy oriented towards economic self-sufficiency by supplementing the private sector where private business could not fulfil investment needs.[41] In order to do this the INI was given powers to take over existing businesses or create new ones if necessary. The INI was also supposed to militate against monopoly situations. The founding capital was Ptas 50 million and the Institute was a dependency of the Presidencia del Gobierno until 1968 when it came under the Ministry of Industry. The INI fulfilled few of its initial objectives. The Institute did not hold a strong position in industries connected with national defence and the armed forces are now largely reliant on the USA for modern equipment. As far as its obligations to fill up 'lacunae' in the economy, INI's efforts do not appear to have been very effective, for, in addition to creating new and frequently inefficient industries, the Institute's activities often actually inhibited the activities of private interests instead of complementing them. There is little evidence, either, of any serious effort on the INI's behalf to break monopoly situations. It could even be argued that in certain cases, for example the car-manufacturing sector until recently, the INI had actually created its own monopolies.

Until 1958 the INI received direct budgetary support and credits conceded by the Bank of Spain, which created serious inflationary pressures in the economy. At the beginning of the 1960s, the Institute's activities were difficult to categorise in relation to any overall strategy of government economic policy. The INI had become the State holding company and had interests in many fields through a mixture of wholly and part-owned or 'mixed' companies. On the whole INI companies enjoyed a favoured position from the point of view of obtaining resources and permits from the government.[42] Jobs at the top of INI companies were often a reward for political services rather than proven business acumen and the reputation of INI companies was one of inefficiency and complacency.

This picture remained virtually unchanged throughout most of the 1960s. At the end of that decade certain changes took place. Control of the Institute was transferred from the Presidencia del Gobierno to the Ministry of Industry, making it possible, in theory at least, to bring the INI more in line with the rest of the industrial sector. In

1970 a new president, Señor Claudio Boada, was appointed from the ranks of private industry and his appointment was heralded as a sign that the INI would be given a new look and its rôle in the Spanish economy subject to reappraisal.

Following Boada's appointment, innovations took place in the financial structure of the INI which indicated a more realistic approach to the financing of industrial companies. After 1958 when the INI ceased to receive budgetary support, the level of self-financing among INI companies had fallen dramatically from 83 per cent in 1957 to 18 per cent in 1970. Government subsidies are now allowable to meet deficits of certain INI companies which are deemed to run unavoidably at a loss. This stems from the precedent of a subsidy of some Ptas 3900 million granted in 1970 to the coal-mining company HUNOSA in order to meet losses incurred between 1967 and 1970. HUNOSA was set up by the INI in 1967 to reorganise the coal industry and has run at a very heavy loss.[43] An interesting facet of the provision of subsidies for some industries was that for the first time it was publicly admitted that some INI companies were not economically viable but were nevertheless being maintained at a loss for non-economic reasons. The new president also made it clear that companies which did not suffer from inherent structural difficulties were expected to become economically viable and INI companies were subjected to an overhaul on a company by company basis.[44]

The key word was *'rentabilidad'* – viability. This had become very necessary. In the period 1968–71, 72 per cent of INI investments were directed towards activities which were either economically unviable or practically so.[45] This was partly due to the subsidiary rôle to which the INI was relegated in the first two plans.[46] Far from acting as an instrument of industrial policy, the INI was expressly intended to play second fiddle to private interests. Nor was the Institute used, for instance, to promote government objectives in regional development.[47] In the First and Second Development Plans (1964–7 and 1968–71), the proposed sum of investments by INI companies was small, in both plans in the region of Ptas 56 billion. The Third Plan (1971–5) reflected the more aggressive approach of Señor Lopez de Letona, who became Minister of Industry in 1960, and Señor Boada, the new president of the INI. Forecast investment by INI companies almost doubled to Ptas 96 billion and emphasis was laid on the INI maintaining a strong position in basic industries, although in practice competition with private interests sometimes made this difficult. According to the Third Plan, INI was also to use its investments to restructure industrial sectors, to co-operate in the task of technological research and to follow the line of government policy in decentralising industry. This touched on a much criticised aspect of the INI, that research and industrial training have been given such low priority over the years. No indication was given, however, as to how these various objectives were to be achieved. Improvements in the financial structure of many companies, excluding INI firms connected with defence matters, placed the INI in a stronger position in the early 1970s. It did not, however, solve the underlying problem of what rôle the INI is supposed to play in the economy.

In 1974 the then president of the INI, Señor Fernández Ordóñez, indicated that the Institute was no longer to remain in the background of the industrial sector. Statements by the Minister of Industry as well as the president of the INI have since specified that the INI is to be the mainstay of basic industries, in particular mining, iron and steel and petrochemicals, and to take the lead in sectors of sophisticated technology such as electronics and aircraft engineering. The government has therefore made it clear that in the wake of the crisis caused by the rise in crude oil prices in 1973 the INI is to play a more dominant part in the industrial sector. At the end of 1974 production by INI companies in the refined petroleum sector amounted to 32 per cent of the national total. In cars, ships, aluminium and coal the INI is responsible for more than 50 per cent of total production and in steel and lignite for over 40 per cent. In the same year the INI participated directly in 60 companies of which 15 were wholly owned by the Institute. The INI holds a majority share-holding in a further 27 and a minority holding in 15. In the remaining 3, shares are divided 50/50 between the INI and private interests. These companies in their turn hold shares in others and in this way the INI's zone of influence extends to a further 185 companies. The group of firms which the INI controls directly constitute the largest industrial group in Spain. INI companies provide employment for 4 per cent of the active population and provide some 22 per cent of all industrial investment. They produce some 12 per cent of manufactured exports. Over one-half of all INI investment is in basic industries, e.g. petroleum, public utilities, steel, mining and chemicals, and a further 31 per cent goes towards transport equipment of various sorts.

The effect of the oil crisis on the Spanish economy has reactivated government interest in INI's activities. Hispanoil, which is 70 per cent owned by the INI, has been extremely active since 1974 in the search for oil deposits both in Spain and abroad. In 1974 the merger of three INI refining companies resulted in the creation of Enpetrol, which has the sixth largest refining capacity in Europe and is the biggest company in Spain in terms of sales.[48] In the next four years the INI plans to invest Ptas 500 billion, of which 50 per cent will go towards the energy sector. It may well be that the increased prominence given to INI activities in government calculations may go some way towards solving the vexed question of how the INI's activities are supposed to fit into the overall industrial context. At present problems still remain. The relationship between private and State interests within particular sectors has not been resolved either in theory or in practice. The 'mixed' companies pose this in an acute form. The financing mechanisms described in Chapter 6 are still geared in some respects to maintaining the privileged position which the INI enjoyed in the 1940s and 1950s. A fundamental difficulty in using the Institute's companies for 'restructuring sectors', or indeed in making long-term plans of any nature, is the vulnerability of highly-placed officials in the organisation to political changes. This is not unique to the INI; it is common to most government departments and other official bodies. However, a turnover of four presidents with accompanying changes of staff in eighteen months such as occurred between 1973 and 1975 is not conducive to effective reappraisals of the INI's rôle.

Any assessment of the government's influence on developments in the industrial sector would be incomplete without consideration of the development plans. This is deferred until the next chapter. Here it remains to identify the problems which have remained a constant feature of the industrial scene before and after the Stabilisation Plan.

THE CONTINUING LEGACY OF THE PAST

A salient characteristic of Spanish industry has remained the extreme fragmentation referred to earlier in this chapter. Allied with this is the very small number of large firms in Spain. In most sectors a few large firms exist side by side with a host of extremely small ones and in nearly all sectors the largest Spanish firm is considerably smaller than equivalents in the Common Market countries. There are exceptions, such as the building firm Dragados y Construcciones and the ship-building company Astilleros Españoles, but these are far from being the rule. Government programmes such as *concentración de empresas* have failed to make any significant impact on this problem and in the Third Plan a change of tactics was noticeable. The virtues of small firms were enumerated and they were held to be the 'key to regional development'. The evidence of the past decade and a half, however, does not bear witness to the advantages of small-scale industry in Spain. The most dynamic sectors have been those where the existence of larger firms has made widespread technological changes possible. Moreover, while in theory small firms may well be suitable for accelerating regional development, industrial development in Spain has remained concentrated in very limited areas.

Another related problem is the financing difficulties which face small companies. The extent of their self-financing facilities is very restricted and so are their opportunities for raising capital on the stock market. Most firms rely heavily on short-term credit and bills of exchange which, despite basic low rates of interest, has tended to inhibit expansion because it has induced a strong element of uncertainty about both the availability and the cost. Monetary policy in the 1960s relied heavily on expanding and contracting the amount of credit available through the banking system. The smaller firms with looser ties with the banks tended to be badly hit in the periods of credit restriction.

The small size of many firms and the problems of financing have undoubtedly had a harmful effect on research and development. In 1971 an OECD report found that the sums spent on research and development in Spain were 0·27 per cent of GNP, as compared with between 2 and 4 per cent in other member countries,[49] and since then this has dropped to 0·1 per cent. Spanish industry has often found it simpler to rely on foreign patents and this has been very noticeably the case in the production of cars, motor cycles, electric machinery, pharmaceutical products and electrical consumer goods. In 1961 the Comisión Asesora de Investigación Científica y Técnica was created under the auspices of the Presidencia del Gobierno. The results have, however, been meagre and there is a lack of co-ordination between programmes of research undertaken by the government and private enterprise. The Comisión Asesora will finance up to 50 per cent of any project approved by them but these have been very small in number and scale.[50] In the development plans the government seems to have accepted that the private sector would make only a very small contribution to research and development but it does not seem to have found it necessary to accelerate its own provisions for doing so.

Many levels of business transactions are still affected by *tramites* – bureaucratic red-tape. While this may seem more onerous to a foreign company operating in Spain than to a Spanish business which is accustomed to them, the quantity of *tramites* which are involved in comparatively simple operations, and above all the time involved, is irksome and wasteful. Moreover, 'the many small business interests are inadequately organised and lack ready access to ministerial departments',[51] which, given the very personal nature of relations between government departments and industrial firms, is often a substantial disadvantage to the numerous small firms which still make up a large part of Spanish industry.

Despite the rapid expansion of the industrial sector since 1959, large parts of industry remain inefficient and insulated from competition by the levels of protection referred to in Chapter 8. Increased efficiency may be brought about by closer economic integration with the Common Market.[52] A stimulus to further efficiency may also result from rising labour costs in Spain. Since the Stabilisation Plan Spain has enjoyed an abundance of cheap labour. While there is still no shortage of labour, Spanish workers are now in a far stronger position to press for higher wages. In order to retain a competitive edge in exports, Spanish industry may be forced to adopt more efficient procedures. It is of course incomplete to leave the industrial sector without considering the rôle of credit, labour relations and the trade unions in greater detail. Taxation policies and distribution networks are also relevant. For the sake of clarity, however, these topics have been left for later chapters. It is impossible to proceed further without considering the development plans.

# 4 Industry: Planning, Regional Policy, Wages, Unions

PLANNING

After the Civil War the Spanish economy was subject to an extensive network of government controls which were not, however, subject to any overriding economic plan.[1] Following the Stabilisation Plan and subsequent related measures greater reliance was to be placed on market forces. It was moreover decided that economic growth should be stimulated and guided by the publication of a government plan on economic development. The development plans, of which there have so far been three (1964–7, 1968–71,[2] 1972–5), have been the subject of intense debate within Spain throughout the decade, partly perhaps because economics was a field in which comparative freedom of debate was possible and political views and criticisms of the *status quo* were voiced in relation to planning in a way which would not have been possible in a more overtly political context.

The Spanish style of planning is indicative, meaning that, while its precepts are binding on the public sector, they are merely indicative as regards the private sector, and it is based very closely on the French system of planning both in nomenclature and in organisation. Thus, in formulating the plans, eight *ponencias* corresponding to the French 'horizontal' committees considered general topics such as commerce, finance, and labour problems, and twenty *comisiones* reflecting the French 'vertical' committees represented specific sectors, for example agriculture, steel and iron, textiles, education, etc.[3] In the initial stages of planning the *ponencias* and *comisiones* were supposed to formulate their ideas and base their programmes on the 'inputs' of projected growth rates and employment requirements which were laid down by the Planning Commissariat staff economists. The Commissariat would then in turn draw up an overall plan which, once approved by the ministerial committee for economic affairs and the government, would take on the force of law through ratification by the Cortes. One of the problems of Spanish planning has been the anomalous position of the Commissariat in the government system. While the Commissariat was established under Señor López Rodó within the Presidency, final formulation and implementation of the plans depended jointly upon the Commissariat and the economic committee of the government. As has been observed, 'the precise nature of the relationship remains obscure but the Commissariat has clearly tended to be a junior partner'.[4] Difficulties in co-ordination were compounded by the identification of the Opus Dei group with planning, as this provoked hostility in some quarters. In 1973 a separate Ministry of Development Planning was set up, but this was closed down at the end of 1975 and its work taken over by the Presidencia and the Ministry of Finance.

The First Plan emphasised that it was the private sector which should lead and the public sector which should fill in the 'gaps' which could not be covered by private industry. In the public sector an effort was made to make the autonomous organisations, i.e. the INI, RENFE, etc., which accounted for over one-half of the State's expenditure in the First Plan, fulfil their investment plans. Some, however, fell short of proposed expenditure by some 30 per cent and some pursued their own plans heedless of the national plan.[5] The INI's rôle, as we have seen in the previous chapter, remained ambiguous and not comparable to the rôle of similar French public bodies. Meanwhile, the private sector was given encouragement through various incentives such as the *acción concertada* and *concentración de empresas* referred to in the previous chapter. Following the French pattern, development poles were set up in various parts of the country. The First Plan was really a collection of projects put together to form a plan. Some, for instance the Plan General de Carreteras (1961) (Highways Plan) and the Plan Nacional de la Vivienda (1961) (Housing Plan), were simply incorporated wholesale into the First Plan despite discrepancies in growth rates and investment ratios. There is little information available on the implementation of the social aspects of the First Plan. What there is suggests that public investment (only 77 per cent of proposed investment was actually carried out) was most lacking in education, public health, welfare and professional training.[6] In certain sectors, such as tourism and construction, growth was underestimated. While there was a high rate of growth during the years of the First Plan, much of it appeared to happen independently of the Plan's prescriptions. The annual growth rate of GNP was forecast at 6 per cent and grew by 6·2 per cent during this First Plan. Prices and wages, however, also rose steeply. In 1965 Spain began to register a trade deficit and by 1967 was facing a crisis similar in nature to that of the late 1950s and the government again resorted to monetary and fiscal measures to 'stabilise' the economy.

The devalution of the peseta in November 1967 caused a profound revision of the Second Plan and delayed its start until February 1969. This time emphasis was placed on presenting a more selective list of projects. Agriculture and education were given priority, followed by the 'social' side of economic development, housing, town planning and health. 'Alarm signals' built into the Second Plan (based on the French *clignotants*) were supposed to spot harmful tendencies well in advance and therefore prevent a downswing of the economy similar to that at the end of the First Plan.[7] In spite of the 'alarm signals', however, inflationary pressures in 1969 led to a 'braking' in November of the same year and the cycle of stop-go proved to be unbroken by the Plan. Incentives to industries, such as *acción concertada*, were simply continued with little change. Four new development poles were added. Despite the emphasis on a more selective approach, it has been pointed out that 90 per cent of new investment in the Second Plan went to the same sectors as during the First Plan.[8] The sectors specifically picked out by the Second Plan as 'strategic' sectors, such as agriculture, were little affected by the Plan. The proposals on agrarian improvements, for example, were couched in vague well-sounding phrases, such as 'maximum profits', but the topics which had also been itemised in the First Plan, such as access of landless labourers to property, consolidation of land holdings and the creation of more co-operatives, received very little more concrete attention than in the First Plan.[9] Emphasis in both the agricultural and educational sectors was on the expansion of existing public sector activities, but it is striking that public investment in agriculture and in education expanded only minimally in both the First and the Second Plans.

The Third Plan was technically far more advanced, being based on an econometric growth model. Optimistically it assumed a growth rate of 7 per cent per annum, following a decade in which growth was more rapid in the first than the latter part.[10] Emphasis was laid on a better use of resources; forecasts were made to the *horizonte* of 1980. The private sector was to be left more to the mercy of market forces while at the same time more was expected of the public sector. 'The quality of life' was decreed important and it was stated that a higher degree of labour mobility should be achieved although no clear position was taken *vis-à-vis* the right of dismissal. The Third Plan was complex and long and it is not possible to examine it in any detail here.[11] An unrealistic feature was the projected rate of inflation, which was unaccountably low. The rate of growth in exports and imports was also underestimated.

REGIONAL POLICY

Although regional development became incorporated as part of the ethos of development planning at a fairly late stage in the formulation of the First Plan, it is the policy which has become most strongly identified with planning in Spain. Attempts at regional planning date from Primo de Rivera's Confederaciones Hidrogràficas which were intended to develop and exploit the resources of several river basins, but for a variety of reasons these did not develop into a significant national policy. After the Civil War various regional plans were considered, resulting in the Badajoz Plan (1953) and the Jaen Plan (1954), which were basically politically-motivated projects aimed at improving living standards in both provinces by a grand gesture. These plans were directed by interdepartmental committees under the auspices of the Presidencia. In practice, co-operation gave way to a competitive process between ministers which resulted in a tendency for plans to be 'a series of loosely related departmental projects each based on partial studies of local problems'.[12] The formulation of further plans dealing with the Hierro Islands and Fuerteventura led to the establishment of a secretariat in 1958. This did not, however, lead to any greater co-ordination and different plans tended to exist independently of one another.

With the publication of the First Development Plan the concept of regional development as part of a national strategy was promulgated for the first time. It was also the first occasion in which industry was made a focal point. Previously the emphasis had been on agricultural improvement schemes. In the First and Second Plans regional policy in so far as industrial development was concerned was predominantly a development pole policy, again following French methodology and experience. The choice of a pole policy seems in some ways to represent a compromise between the 'structuralist's' desire for a root and branch reform of economic 'structures' and the preference of the *sindicatos* for provincially based plans. The fundamental idea of the poles policy is that investment should be attracted to a suitable centre in a low-income area and that this in turn should generate further growth in the surrounding region. Of the two types of poles, the *polos de desarrollo industrial* were to be situated where there was already a certain degree of industrialisation and the *polos de promoción industrial* where there was very little industry but human and natural resources were available.

The original seven poles set up in 1964 were La Coruña, Seville, Valladolid, Vigo, Zaragoza, Burgos and Huelva. The first five were *polos de desarrollo* while the latter were designated *polos de promoción*.

La Coruña and Vigo were granted *polo* status for eight years and Zaragoza, Seville and Valladolid for seven, while Burgos and Huelva were allowed five years as industrial promotion poles and a further five years as poles of development. In 1969 four more poles were named, Córdoba, Granada, Logroñno and Oviedo, and in 1970, Villagarcia de Arosa. The latter five all have a life span of approximately ten years. Firms are offered the same inducements to invest in either type of pole, with the exception of the initial investment grant, which is 10 per cent in development poles and 20 per cent in the industrial promotion poles. Other advantages accruing to firms investing in the poles are certain fiscal exemptions, i.e. reduction of up to 95 per cent in transfer taxes and import duties on machinery and equipment not manufactured in Spain and free depreciation allowances during the first five years. Preference is also given in the allocation of official credit and this, in practice, has been the most influential instrument, representing over two-thirds of government expenditure on financial incentives to firms. In order to qualify for these benefits, firms have to commit themselves to minimum investment and employment figures depending on which type of pole they have in mind. Applications are presented at a rigorous *concurso* (competitive contest) which is held once a year, but the criteria by which certain firms are 'chosen' are not revealed.

Investment in the poles has on the whole been at a disappointing level in national terms, accounting for under 3 per cent of all investment. Table 4.1 gives figures for investment and numbers of factories and jobs created between 1964 and 1970. In the First Plan (1964–7) 25 per cent of all 'pole' investment went to Huelva, where investment was highly capital-intensive due to the high level of investment in the chemical and energy industries. A further 15 per cent went to Burgos. The creation of jobs has not been a striking feature of the poles policy, either. While the number of new jobs was highest in absolute terms in Burgos, Seville and Zaragoza, figures for jobs held at the end of 1970 in relation to population in the various poles show that the percentage of jobs available in relation to total population was lowest in Seville and La Coruña, while it was highest in Burgos and Vigo.[13] Estimates of jobs created by the poles vary from 2 per cent to 3·1 per cent of the total population of the poles, but even put at the latter figure this is equivalent to only some 0·4 per cent of the total labour force.[14] Employment opportunities in the poles have reached only 59 per cent of what was forecast in 1964. It is difficult to assess the total number of new jobs which have actually been *added* to the economy, since some jobs merely reflect a diversion of the labour force to a different location.

Table 4.1 shows the number of new firms installed in the various poles between 1964 and 1970. What is striking is the divergence between the number of eager applicants – over 1000 applications were

c

TABLE 4.1   Poles: forecasts and realisation (1964–1967–1970)[a]

| Poles | First round of applications (1964) | | | Number approved after 5 rounds of applications (at end of First Plan) | | | Position at 31 December 1970 | | |
|---|---|---|---|---|---|---|---|---|---|
| | No of factories | Investment | No of jobs | No of factories | Investment | No of jobs | No of factories | Investment | No of jobs |
| Burgos | 236 (100) | 13,104·6 (100) | 23,123 (100) | 321 (136·0) | 14,683·5 (112·1) | 29,774 (128·8) | 136 (57·6) | 11,523·2 (87·9) | 11,450 (49·5) |
| Huelva | 96 (100) | 10,429·8 (100) | 7,572 (100) | 171 (178·1) | 24,299·8 (232·3) | 23,791 (314·2) | 83 (86·5) | 20,327·9 (194·9) | 5,768 (76·2) |
| La Coruña | 81 (100) | 5,627·9 (100) | 4,988 (100) | 109 (134·6) | 7,860·4 (139·7) | 6,789 (136·1) | 47 (58·0) | 7,719·8 (137·2) | 2,553 (51·2) |
| Seville | 175 (100) | 11,789·9 (100) | 17,356 (100) | 204 (116·6) | 12,761·6 (108·2) | 19,315 (111·3) | 103 (58·9) | 9,855·4 (83·5) | 11,009 (63·4) |
| Valladolid | 85 (100) | 4,977·8 (100) | 9,838 (100) | 131 (154·1) | 9,946·4 (199·8) | 15,027 (152·7) | 72 (84·7) | 5,792·3 (116·4) | 8,375 (85·1) |
| Vigo | 113 (100) | 7,295·0 (100) | 15,727 (100) | 132 (116·8) | 10,690·9 (146·6) | 17,783 (113·1) | 68 (60·2) | 4,385·4 (60·1) | 9,810 (62·4) |
| Zaragoza | 217 (100) | 10,780·6 (100) | 21,261 (100) | 295 (135·9) | 16,676·7 (154·7) | 26,415 (124·2) | 136 (62·7) | 7,605·3 (70·5) | 10,156 (47·8) |
| Total | 1,003 (100) | 64,014·0 (100) | 99,865 (100) | 1,363 (136·0) | 96,849·4 (151·3) | 138,894 (139·1) | 645 (64·3) | 67,209·3 (105·0) | 59,121 (59·2) |

[a] Indices in brackets are based on 1964 = 100.
Source: Luis Gamir, *Política económica de España* (Madrid, 1972) p. 254. Table compiled from figures of the Comisaría del Plan.

put forward in 1964 alone – and the number of concerns, 645, actively under way or initiated by the end of 1970. The greatest discrepancy between initial aspirations and actual performance was in Burgos, La Coruña and Seville. The gap between expectations and realisation both in terms of firms actually set up and jobs created indicates that the deliberate building up of new factories in new places has been more difficult than was originally foreseen in the Plan. Overall, Valladolid has probably been the most successful pole, benefiting from its existing industrial base and its proximity to Madrid, although Valladolid's very success may have limited the growth potential of Burgos. A large proportion of firms applying for pole benefits were small-scale operations – 56 per cent applied for an investment of less than Ptas 50 million, and only 23 per cent for over Ptas 100 million in the 1960s.[15] There has been a high concentration of firms in the chemical and metal products sectors, which constituted approximately 50 per cent of overall investment. Foreign capital on the whole has not been much attracted to the poles, although this may well have been partly because of lack of information about the specific concessions available. By the time the Second Plan was under way, the State was in the position of providing assistance to the development poles and poles of promotion in addition to subsidising investment in the Plan Integral de Canarias, the Plan Tierra de Campos (in Castile), the Plan de Campo de Gibraltar with its overtly political *raison d'être*, and promoting development in the Sahara.[16]

In the Third Plan, emphasis was laid on the region rather than the pole itself. References were made to wider participation by local officials in the mechanism of planning and it was suggested that provinces, let alone poles, constituted too small a base for efficient regional development. There was mention of the poles being transformed into *ejes de desarrollo* – development axes. While the existing poles would be kept in operation until their designated demise, no new ones were planned. Instead, while for political reasons 'regions' were not specifically alluded to, presumably *espacios supraprovinciales* amounted to something very similar and this concept was taken to be the most efficacious in stimulating economic development. Regional and sectoral plans were to be linked by a series of policies and, while the 'axes' of development were not specifically referred to in the main body of the Plan, the line of thinking remained similar. Interest moved from the poles to decongestion of the large industrial zones and in encouraging large-scale investment in non-congested zones. How this was to be effected was not elaborated. The designation of two metropolitan areas of Galicia (Pontevedra-Vigo and La Coruña-Ferrol) and three development poles, Vigo, La Coruña and Villagarcia de Arosa as a *Gran Area de Expansión Industrial* (GAEI) based on the French idea of *industries motrices* is difficult to understand. This GAEI is expected in principle to produce industrial goods on a competitive basis, but the area referred to is remote, inaccessible and devoid of any basic infrastructure.

In addition to the poles, *polígonos industriales* and *polígonos de descongestión* were created in the First Plan. *Polígonos industriales* are zones in which official credit facilities are available but which do not enjoy the full benefits of the actual poles, while decongestion poles, of which there were initially five, were formed with the intention of lessening the increasing pressure on Madrid.[17] The *polígonos de descongestión* have not been very successful, partly because three were too far from Madrid,[18] and partly because Madrid remains infinitely more attractive in terms of amenities. Also transport is not particularly easy between the capital and the *polígonos*. In practice they have tended to act as poles of development in their own right, attracting rural emigrants rather than inducing the existing population of Madrid to move out.

The development poles have not produced the dramatic results which were hoped of them, and since they have become closely identified with regional planning in Spain and even the development plans themselves, it is worth taking a closer look at the ideas which lay behind them and the shortcomings which have been evident in practice. One factor which has inhibited the potential dynamic effect of the poles has been the short period for which support was to be provided to each pole. If the idea of the pole is that it should generate ecenomic development in the surrounding areas, then the time-limits granted have been insufficient for complementary growth of infrastructure and housing which are essential for any substantial growth. Another has been the degree to which government credit has been subject to the cyclical movements of the economy.[19] Due to the low level of self-financing in Spain, most firms are extremely susceptible to changes in credit policy and firms operating in development areas have not been immune from these difficulties. We have already mentioned the *concursos*, which are annual events and whose timing does not therefore provide a flexible approach. It has also been suggested that the capital-intensive bias of the incentives in view of the small scale of much of Spanish industry, the possible input distortions arising from tax exemptions sought on a short-term basis and the low investment subsidies all militate against the success of the poles.[20]

One unexplained feature of the poles is their location. Contrary to expectations the poles were not placed in the most backward parts of Spain. This may be due to some extent to the influence of the World Bank Mission which, while it did not actively promote a regional policy, recommended developing areas which already showed a certain degree of development.[21] Thus the original seven poles were set in the provinces which rated 13, 15, 18, 27, 34, 37 and 40 in *per capita* income terms and the more recent ones at 9, 20, 44 and 46[22] (out of a total of 52). In terms of regions not one pole has been situated in the poorest region of all, Extremadura. In *per capita* terms the actual gap between the richest and the poorest province in Spain is lessening. In 1955 the coefficient of variation was 4·4, whereas in 1970 it had fallen to 2·8. It is, however, migration to the traditional industrial centres and Madrid which has done much to bring about this convergence. The existence of the poles has not lessened the attraction of the two main metropolitan centres of Madrid and Barcelona and the largest proportion of new jobs is still to be found in the north, north-east and Madrid. The actual criteria by which the poles were located or indeed were supposed to have been located remain mysterious. It is probable that political pressures and individual pressure groups were decisive – at the least they were strongly influential.

One of the difficulties which has not been satisfactorily resolved is the relation of the pole to its surrounding zone. Initially the actual limits of the zones were usually confined to the municipal boundaries of the selected towns, although occasionally this was extended to the immediate surrounding region. Unfortunately, instead of benefits percolating through to the surrounding region, the pole itself has tended to keep any expansion within its walls, sometimes producing chaotic growth, as in Burgos, and, if anything, to enhance the gap between the surrounding region and the pole. As we have seen, the planners themselves found the development pole concept inadequate, and in the Third Plan announced their intentions of promoting regional development on a wider scale. While there is talk of improvement in regional infrastructure and of *ejes de desarrollo*, the practical implications are not yet clear. An example of this is that subsidies are no longer confined to the limits of the pole itself but have been extended to the surrounding area. However, in an effort to attract larger firms to invest in development regions, small investment projects no longer qualify for a subsidy, and since it would be reasonable to expect some smaller firms to be interested in and suited to the surrounding area, the combination of these two rulings may to some extent cancel each other out. One of the fundamental difficulties facing the promoters of regional development is that any regional scheme would more readily take root if it were grafted on to historic regions which exist in the popular consciousness if officially unacknowledged. However, since regionalism as opposed to the promotion of economic growth on a regional basis is anathema to the government, it is very difficult to see how this can be resolved until and unless political attitudes change.

Three other factors have undermined the effectiveness of planning both on a national and on a regional level. One has been the inability to decide what rôle the public sector should play in planning. Plans for the public sector have in principle been 'binding' but have not been enforced. The public sector was given a residual rôle in the first two plans and expenditure proved in reality to be little closer to the initial targets than were the results in the private sector. While the Third Plan stressed the importance of the public sector, it remained unclear what changes this would in fact entail.

Second is the low level of local participation in the formulation of the Plan. Neither the *ponencias* nor the *comisiones* are representative of local interests.[23] Moreover, neither in the choice of sites nor in the implementation of policies has there been more than a minimal consultation with local interests. This is in part due to the structure of local government in Spain. Throughout the twentieth century the State has shown an increasing tendency to remove the administration of its services from local control and to place them in the hands of the Administración Periférica – the central administration's field services.[24] At the extreme in Zaragoza, the local dignitaries, including the Civil Governor, the mayor and syndicates, were all strongly opposed to the choice of their city as a pole. Not even the physical boundaries of the zones seem to have been subject to local consultation. Initially a mayor was appointed in each pole and acted as a representative of the Planning Commission in each area. The Commission was constituted of the Civil Governor, the mayor and seven syndicate members. In theory the Commissions had a powerful rôle co-ordinating public services and channelling applications for grants, etc., to Madrid. In reality, however, their rôle was minimal and decisions were taken in Madrid. Lip service was paid to increasing local participation in the Second and again in the Third Plan but the effect up-to-date has been negligible. In some cases, for example in housing, specialised autonomous agencies dependent on the Ministry of Housing have been created which are under no local control in the zone in which they may be working. The centralised approach has not helped to endear the *polos* plans to local inhabitants, and the government's fear of granting greater local autonomy has created inevitable frictions.

The third factor has been the lack of co-ordination in the execution as well as the compilation of the plans, conspicuous examples of which remain the lack of proper provision for housing and education within the confines of regional planning, although this lack of co-ordination is by no means peculiar to the Plans. Rivalries between ministers and ministries as well as within ministries, either on political grounds or resulting from the competing aspirations of the numerous corps within the Civil Service, combine to produce a situation little short of chaotic.

A particularly striking example of this is in the central administration's field services. Not only does each ministry tend to have representatives in all the provinces, but so too do particular departments within ministries, most of which work without reference to one another. Thus representatives of different departments of, for example, the Ministry of Agriculture, may have no working knowledge of what policy their colleagues are pursuing even in the same provincial capital. The First Plan recognised the problem of the plethora of field services and in 1967, after severe resistance by the administrative corps within the Civil Service, a certain degree of reform was achieved, and it was decreed that all field services emanating from one department should be unified under a provincial *delegado*. Whether this will in fact bring about any real change remains to be seen. Certainly the number of services has not been reduced, although they may in future be better co-ordinated.

APPRAISAL OF INDUSTRIAL POLICIES

One of the puzzles of planning in Spain is to what extent it is a political rather than an economic exercise. Obviously any attempt to direct the economic forces of a country involves political decisions. In Spain, however, despite the economic language in which the plans are couched, it is arguable that political motivation constitutes the predominant force. The First Plan can be seen as a basis on which collaboration could be achieved between competing political forces, rather than a basis for allocating economic resources. Even in 1969, the Minister of Planning, Señor López Rodó, said of the first two plans that they served to provide continuity to the régime and that a development plan could be considered to have any real significance only in relation to politics. The Third Plan was far more sophisticated in the economic techniques employed. One is still left with the impression, however, that the primary purpose of planning has often been to provide a basis for agreement between rival groups. It has also provided a platform from which to make judicious statements on the social welfare of Spain. Despite increasing emphasis on social change and betterment, these have been more in evidence in words than deeds.[25] Whether or not planning influenced the evolution of the Spanish economy to any significant extent, it has served a useful political purpose.

A casualty of the recent economic recession has been the attention bestowed on development planning. As noted earlier, the Ministry of Development Planning was closed at the end of 1975. The Fourth Development Plan was supposed to come into force at the beginning of 1976 but it appears to have been postponed indefinitely. This points to a certain disillusionment with planning in government circles. No one can deny that the Spanish economy, and in particular the industrial sector, expanded vigorously in the 1960s and early 1970s despite cyclical fluctuations. What is open to doubt is how much the existence of the plans actually influenced developments in this period. This is not to discount specific factors which were due to planning. Thus, despite their relatively slight impact, the designation of certain towns as development poles *did* affect life in the poles themselves. New jobs were created and new factories built and the transformation wrought, for instance in Huelva by the chemical industry, is profound. So too, *acción concertada*, while cumbersome and erratic in execution, has brought about changes, particularly in the steel sector. However, it cannot be said that the plans have provided a strategy for development. Nor has planning lived up to Pierre Massé's view that the prime importance of an indicative plan is as the 'great reducer of uncertainty'. Overall, the impression remains that the Spanish economy has evolved along its distinctive path almost independently of the plans.

If, by and large, the various mechanisms introduced under the three development plans cannot be deemed to have provided sufficient impulse to account for the scale of industrial development after 1959, this does not mean that the government's rôle in the industrial sector has been negligible. On the contrary, government policies on export subsidies and interest rates have strongly influenced the way in which certain industries have developed. Government policies have affected the course of events but not as the result of a co-ordinated strategy. In some ways the situation is more confusing than in the era prior to the Stabilisation Plan. Before 1959 the extent of government intervention was more clearly defined and specified intentions broadly coincided with the facts. Since then the government has in theory adopted a more liberal approach to the industrial sector while in fact retaining many controls. Moreover, the policies which have been most specific in intention, such as the *concentración de empresas*, have usually been the least effective in practice. Government policies have had a profound influence on industrial developments but generally not through the most publicised projects.[26]

LABOUR, WAGES AND WORKING CONDITIONS

Any description of the evolution of Spanish industry remains one-dimensional unless the wider framework embracing conditions and prospects of work is also considered. The remainder of this chapter attempts to set out the changes in employment and wages during the 1960s and early 1970s, and the rôle played by the social services, as well as tracing the evolution of labour relations over the period. Some reference is made to developments in the agricultural and service sectors where the context enables developments in the industrial sector to be more clearly understood.

As seen in Chapter 1, the percentage of active population in relation to the total population dropped very slightly between 1960 and 1974. This was due to a variety of factors, including the scale of emigration abroad, the extension of higher education and the still low numbers of women in paid employment. In Barcelona, Madrid and the Basque country, the active population grew by more than 15 per cent between 1962 and 1967 and a moderate growth in active population was noticeable in the Balearic Islands, Valencia, the Catalan region (apart from Barcelona), Navarra and the Canary Islands. In parts of Spain, however, the level of active population remained more or less stationary, as in Aragon, Castile and the coastal areas of Galicia; while in some parts, such as Leon, Extremadura and the inland parts of Galicia the level has fallen substantially. Despite the claims of the *polos*, the largest numbers of new jobs have in fact continued to be in the traditional industrial centres of the country, in Barcelona, the Basque country and Madrid.

A change in the structure of employment has been the growth of salaried workers as a result of the exodus from the countryside and also of the decline in numbers of small shopkeepers and artisans. Another has been the increase in women working, although this increase has not been very large. According to a survey by the Instituto Nacional de Estadística undertaken in 1974, only 21 per cent of the female population were in active employment.[27] Such increases as there have been in women working have been mainly in the agricultural sector. While the agricultural population has diminished rapidly, the number of women in agriculture has, with the exception of 1967, increased steadily, both in absolute numbers and in relation to the active agrarian population. This is part of a trend in evidence from the 1940s. Between 1960 and 1970, in which latter year women engaged in agriculture numbered 784,700,[28] the percentage of women in relation to the active agrarian population rose from 12 per cent to 22 per cent. The active female agrarian population is characterised by the number of older women who work on the land, left as a result of the flight to the cities of the younger generation. In 1965, 42 per cent of women working in agriculture were over forty-five and by 1970 this had risen to 49 per cent. This is in striking contrast to the general youthfulness of the active working female population in towns in Spain. Both in 1965 and in 1970 only 32 per cent of the overall total were over forty-five years old.

Employment in the industrial sector rose substantially between 1960 and 1975, although figures for the rate of expansion vary considerably according to source.[29] What is clear is that employment opportunities in industry have not kept pace with the labour supply from the countryside. One of the limits to greater employment opportunities in industry has resulted from the laws affecting the *despedida* – the dismissal of personnel. Since it is difficult to get rid of labour in times of recession, employers often prefer if possible to use casual labour which is not covered by the same legal framework and can therefore be fired without difficulty if it becomes necessary. Casual labour is also attractive from the employer's point of view in that contributions towards social welfare, which fall heavily on the employer, are avoided. While there has been caution in expanding the workforce in many plants, so too there have been difficulties in obtaining workers with specialised technical skills. The vast majority of labourers leaving the land have very few or no qualifications and usually go directly into the building industry or into the service sector, if they do not emigrate. In the 1960s, there was little evidence of any large-scale efforts to provide training centres which would add to the productive capacity of these men.[30] As was seen earlier, despite the stated intention of the plans to provide substantial employment opportunities, many of the projects selected were in fact capital-intensive. Modernisation, which usually means mechanisation, has also limited the market for jobs in various sectors of industry. Despite the limitations noted here, the employment index in industry grew steadily throughout the 1960s, with the exception of the recession of 1967–8 when the index fell slightly.[31] The sectors in which employment opportunities were greatest were in transport equipment, followed by building and public works and in the food industry. Employment opportunities dwindled in public utilities and declined more severely in textiles and mining activities.

Although the increases in active population did not keep pace with the growth of population, this resulted until 1975 in large-scale emigration rather than widespread unemployment. Officially unemployment was below 2 per cent and frequently below 1·5 per cent of the active population in the 1960s and early 1970s. Statistics on unemployment are, however, notoriously unreliable. Figures coming from the same source do not necessarily concur and the discrepancy between figures from various 'official' sources is often bewildering.[32] Furthermore, information from other sources gives the impression that the figures may be considerably larger than at first appears. One of the difficulties lies in the methods by which figures for unemployment are calculated in Spain.[33] These are based on the numbers of unemployed registered at the Ministry of Labour's Oficinas de Colocación at which in any case those who are unemployed often fail to appear. The 1975 OECD survey on Spain pointed out that in the 1970 census 'the number of persons stating they were looking for employment was almost twice as high as those recorded in the monthly statistics'.[34] An example of the conflicting views obtainable from different sources is given in the OECD Development Study in Andalusia,[35] which, referring to the composition of the agricultural labour force, states that 'sources differ so fundamentally that it is impossible to perceive the reality'. It goes on to say that 'according to the censo agrario (1962), there were 256,725 daily hired workers in Andalucia, [while] registers of the Mutualidad de Previsión Agraria state 521,908 daily hired workers for 31 December 1962 which are twice as much as in the other source'. This also exemplifies a further difficulty in so far as agriculture is concerned – that of calculating the number of daily hired workers who still constitute a substantial although diminishing part of the agricultural working force, particularly in Andalucia. A particularly difficult problem is to assess the amount of hidden unemployment concealed in the figures for agricultural employment.

It has been suggested from surveys taken in Madrid that the unemployment figures in 1970 may for instance have been as high as 6 per cent. In the absence of more reliable statistics, however, it is useless to try and formulate any alternative to the official figures and impossible to reach any quantified conclusion as to the amount of hidden unemployment and underemployment. What is clear is that unemployment has been least serious in the service sector and that both in absolute and relative terms larger numbers are now out of work in industry than in agriculture. The rise in unemployment in the construction industry has also posed serious problems in periods of recession. In 1967 and 1968 large numbers of construction workers were unemployed and in 1976 it was estimated that over 10 per cent of workers in the building trade were without work. In absolute terms unemployment is greatest in the towns of Madrid, Barcelona and Zaragoza where high figures are due to high population totals. The worst affected provinces are Orense, Cadiz, Jaen, Zamora, Cordoba and Malaga,[36] and in agricultural areas in the south unemployment can still reach high proportions. In the fourth quarter of 1975 unemployment exceeded 10 per cent of the active population in Andalusia compared with a national average of 4·5 per cent.[37]

A distinctive feature of employment in Spain is the practice of holding more than one job at a time. A survey of multiple employment in Madrid in 1969 found that one-fifth of all employees, including white-collar workers, were in the position of having more than one job,[38] and that the number had increased since a similar survey undertaken in 1966.[39] The possession of more than one job at a time is not limited to any particular stratum of the population, but the proportion tends to rise in relation to the income status of the employee. Thus the proportion in Madrid in 1969 was 36 per cent for *empleados altos* or highly paid white-collar workers and 15 per cent for unqualified labourers.[40] It is not unusual for bankers or university teachers to hold down more than one job concurrently. In fact, not to do so is unusual. In the Civil Service multiple employment became prevalent in the 1930s.[41] One result of the system of holding down more than one job at a time is that the number of hours worked is frequently very long.[42] The legal maximum working week in Spain was until recently forty-eight hours, plus overtime. According to a survey on active population published by the National Institute of Statistics in 1969 approximately one-half of the population worked a normal working week of between forty to forty-eight hours, while 35 per cent worked for more than forty-nine hours a week, of which 14 per cent worked more than ten hours a day and sometimes up to fifteen and this did not include travelling time. In a survey of workers in Barcelona,[43] over 56 per cent worked more than eight hours a day and the survey of Madrid referred to above found that 45 per cent of manual labourers worked more than fifty hours a week as did 40 per cent of white-collar workers.[44] On top of this, it is common to work hours of *recuperativa* for time lost in *fiesta* days. The *días recuperables* are often a point of contention between management and workers since *fiestas* or public holidays, of which there are a considerable number in Spain, are not paid holidays and workers are expected to work extra time to make them up. Hours for the Spanish worker are long and the burden is the heavier if account is taken of the propensity to work at more than one job. Demands for a reduction in the legal working week have therefore played a large part in strikes throughout the twentieth century in Spain. But until workers feel that wages earned in their main job are sufficient, multiple job-holding and long hours will persist. Irrespective of the number of jobs held, a pension accrues only in respect of the principal job held. In April 1976 a labour relations Act was passed which reduced the working week to forty-four hours and limited overtime to not more than two hours a day, twenty hours per month or 120 hours per year. Annual paid holidays were increased to twenty-one days a year. Article 35 of the Act makes it extremely difficult for employers to dismiss personnel.

An integral part of working conditions in any modern industrialised society are the various kinds of insurance against sickness, unemployment and accidents. In 1908 the Instituto Nacional de Previsión (INP) was established to administer a voluntary social security scheme and from 1919 the INP administered a growing number of insurance schemes.[45] During the Civil War a Workers' Charter was published which sketched out provisions for more comprehensive social security policies. These were gradually elaborated by the INP and provided for compulsory insurance for sickness, maternity, unemployment, industrial accidents, and old age. The INP is an autonomous body, dependent on the Ministry of Labour. Funds for social security are collected and supervised by the INP but are disbursed locally by the Syndical Organisation. Unemployment benefit became law in 1959. However, while the Ley de Bases de la Seguridad Social was passed in 1963, it was not until 1966 that a unified social security system was set up. Prior to that a variety of bodies provided different types of insurance, including private insurance companies, some bodies attached to the syndical movement and also the *mutualidades laborales* (workers' mutual aid associations), although in many cases the services provided overlapped. Even after the law of 1966 various sections of society (such as the military, domestic servants and students) did not fall within the province of the new law, and not all administrative bodies were streamlined.[46] Agricultural workers were not fully included in general insurance schemes until 1974.

Expenditure on social services is still small in relation to GNP compared with other Euopean countries. It has, however, risen rapidly since the beginning of the 1960s and, while substantial changes in social security arrangements in 1967 make comparisons with earlier years difficult, it is possible to say that expenditure on social services nearly trebled in relation to GNP between 1960 and 1972. In this latter year expenditure represented some 9·7 per cent of GNP.

The principal sources of finance for the social security system are contributions from employers and from workers and the State. By far the largest proportion is provided by employers, amounting to over 80 per cent of the total. Workers directly contribute approximately 8 per cent, while the contribution of the State is small and has been in the region of 5 per cent for the last few years. The extent of the State's participation is very much below the average in West European countries.

Until 1972 calculations of social security contributions were based on a 'theoretical' wage which by 1971 was equal on average to approximately 50 per cent of actual wages. This system has produced many anomalies. The various categories in which employees are classified for the calculation of the theoretical wage possess a logic of their own which bears little relation to reality. Thus possession of a university degree means that both the newly appointed assistant and the professor of many years' standing may well be charged on the same theoretical base, despite large differences in actual earnings. In practice, the system has tended to militate against the less well-paid whose theoretical base is closer to the actual wage level. In 1972 the base on which social security contributions were calculated was changed, and contributions are now related to the actual wage. This change entailed an increase of costs for factories of 40 to 45 per cent. The new system was supposed to come into force in April 1974. Fears that this would add appreciably to the difficulties already faced by many enterprises and would increase inflationary pressures in the economy led to the postponement of the introduction of contributions based on wages actually received. Further postponements ensued and the new system has still not been introduced.

In the 1960s a feature of the Spanish social security system was the high level of surpluses registered each year, still accounting for 8 per cent of contributions in 1970. More than one-half of these surpluses were invested in INI bonds. It is not clear why in face of these surpluses the government continued to make transfers to social security. It may, however, have been due in part to the confusion caused by a diffusion of responsibility in managing different funds. A major reorganisation in 1967 attempted to integrate the various existing funds, to standardise benefits paid and to bring contributions more in line with payments. The scope and amount of benefits were expanded and contributions were also raised substantially. At the end of the 1960s surpluses declined appreciably and had practically disappeared by the mid-1970s.

Detailed information on social security disbursements are meagre. In broad terms it can be said that in 1974 nearly two-thirds of a total expenditure of Ptas 422 billion went towards sickness benefit, unemployment benefit and family allowances and pensions. The rest went towards health insurance and nearly half of this was spent on pharmaceutical products. A breakdown of social service expenditure between 1971 and 1975 revealed that 31 per cent was spent on health benefits, 14 per cent on family allowances, 36 per cent on pensions and 2·5 per cent on unemployment benefit. Provision of health care by the social security system is discussed in the next chapter. While social security provisions have become increasingly comprehensive since the early 1960s and the coverage of benefits has increased, there is still room for considerable improvement, especially as it is frequently the less well-off and particularly those in rural areas who suffer from the deficiencies in the existing system. Disability and old age pensions have until recently been minimal and are not automatically granted in practice.[47] The low level of disability benefits is disturbing given the high rate of industrial accidents in Spain. In 1975 there were over 1 million accidents and, with over six fatal accidents a day, Spain has the worst record in this respect in Western Europe. Unemployment benefits are far from adequate. Benefit is available to the unemployed for six months for total unemployment and one year for partial unemployment. In 1973 the average monthly benefit for both categories was well below the minimum wage, which in turn is well below average earnings. This has a bearing on unemployment figures. The latter are

often lower on paper than in reality because unemployment benefit
is no longer being provided. This does not mean that the erstwhile
recipient has necessarily found another job. Moreover, implementation
of procedures in providing various kinds of benefit is frequently haphazard. As often in Spain, theory and reality are separated by the
existence of overlapping organisations, bureaucratic *tramites* (red-tape)
and administrative difficulties in the implementation of such policies
at local level. It is noteworthy in this context that in 1973 out of a
total of some 180,400 estimated unemployed, a monthly average of
only 61,900 were receiving unemployment benefit.[48]

Looking at Spanish industry during the 1960s and early 1970s, it
is essential to look at the structure of wages in this period. Unfortunately, in this as in other areas of investigation in Spain, considerable
problems are caused by the lack of reliable statistics. The normal
difficulties exist of conflicting data from different sources. For example,
figures from the National Institute of Statistics and from the
*mutualidades laborales* differ considerably, in addition to other
anomalies such as figures produced by the Mutualismo Laboral showing
a *decrease* in average wages in current pesetas in a large number of
sectors over the period 1963–6.[49] Quite apart from this is the problem
contributed by the veil of secrecy surrounding actual wage levels which
has been summed up as follows:[50]

> It is no secret, in fact quite the opposite, that in Spain one doesn't
> only conceal what one earns from the tax inspector, the labour
> authorities, the trade unions [*sindicatos*] or any other official body,
> but also from one's own friends. And in this there seems to be a
> tacit agreement between workers and employers.

Until 1958 Spanish wages were based on *reglamentaciones* of the
Ministry of Labour.[51] These set minimum levels of wages for each
industry and aimed at keeping wages under severe restraint in order
to keep prices down. In fact, however, while wages remained heavily
controlled, prices rose undeterred. Between 1940 and 1955 agricultural
and industrial wages increased by 100 per cent, while the cost of living
rose by 240 per cent.[52] In 1956 and 1957 it became clear that this
situation could not continue. The wave of strikes and the change in
government heralded the introduction of *convenios colectivos* – collective
bargaining – and it is under this formula that negotiations over wages
have developed throughout the 1960s. The effects and workings of
these *convenios colectivos* is examined later in the chapter in the context of labour relations and the rôle of the *sindicatos*. One aspect of
the policy of depressing wage levels was the compensating growth of
fringe benefits, i.e. protection against being laid off, security bonuses

and allowances. The continued existence of many of these 'perks', which are often difficult to quantify or indeed fully to discover, compound the problem of examining the level of real wages. In the 1960s fringe benefits increased at a greater rate than 'agreed' wage rates, although the latter continued to be the most important constituent of wages actually received. One study estimates that the 'agreed' wage was equal to approximately 80 per cent of total wages at the beginning of 1960 and only 60 per cent by the end of the decade.[53] It is within these and the above-mentioned limitations that the evolution of wages in the 1960s and early 1970s must be considered.[54]

In 1964, 61 per cent of the active population were wage-earners. By 1973 this had risen to 69 per cent. The distribution, however, varies between different sectors and in industry the percentage of wage-earners is predictably highest, accounting for some 89 per cent of all those employed in the industrial sector in 1973. In the service sector wage-earners accounted for 73 per cent and only 34 per cent in agriculture.[55] In 1960 wages represented 49 per cent of national income. The share of wages increased only slowly over the 1960s and in 1973 wages, including social security contributions, amounted to 55·8 per cent of national income, which was still low compared with other European countries.[56] In the following two years the share of wages increased appreciably faster than previously, representing 57 per cent in 1974 and 60 per cent in 1975.[57]

Table 4.2 shows wage increases per hour over the years 1966 to 1974. The small rise in 1968 was caused by a wage freeze while the relatively small increase in 1971 was caused mainly by the sharp rise in prices that year. In 1974, while wages increased at an unprecedented rate

TABLE 4.2   Annual indices of wages/hours

| Years | Current pesetas | | Current pesetas[a] | |
|---|---|---|---|---|
| | Index | Percentage increase | Index | Percentage increase |
| 1966 | 135·73 | 17·00 | 114·44 | 10·06 |
| 1967 | 156·97 | 15·65 | 125·08 | 9·30 |
| 1968 | 171·24 | 9·09 | 129·58 | 3·60 |
| 1969 | 191·24 | 11·70 | 140·44 | 8·38 |
| 1970 | 218·34 | 14·15 | 150·27 | 7·00 |
| 1971 | 249·10 | 14·09 | 158·81 | 5·68 |
| 1972 | 291·63 | 17·07 | 171·46 | 7·97 |
| 1973 | 349·13 | 19·70 | 183·61 | 7·08 |
| 1974 | 442·49 | 26·74 | 198·54 | 8·13 |

[a] Deflated by cost-of-living index.

Source: INE, *La renta nacional y su distribución* (Madrid, 1975).

of 26 per cent, the rise in the price level reduced this to an increase of 8 per cent in real terms. In 1975 wages rose by 30 per cent in money terms and 11 per cent in real hourly earnings. Since 1960 wages in industry and the service sector have grown at a faster rate than those in the agricultural sector. Within the industrial sector wages increased by 8 per cent as an annual average in real terms in public utilities, mining and construction, by over 7 per cent in investment goods, by over 6 per cent in commercial activities and by more than 5 per cent in consumer goods and banking between 1963 and 1974.[58] In 1963 average earnings per hour were highest in banking, followed by insurance companies, coal-mining and public utilities. In 1974 the order had changed slightly and banking was directly followed by coal-mining and then public utilities. Earnings in the construction sector improved gradually over the decade although these are still below the average wage in the industrial sector as a whole. Those working in the leather and wood related industries remain the most poorly paid.

Overall the rapid pace of industrialisation seems to have had little effect on pay differentials between the different sectors. Within sectors differentials have tended to widen in graphic arts, chemicals, iron and steel, textiles, banking and transport and diminished in food, construction and leatherwork, where the level of pay has been low throughout. Since 1970 there has been a certain levelling of the gap between the lowest and the highest paid, largely due to the distribution of wage increases in 1970 and 1971. Prior to this the gap had tended to widen, not diminish. In some professions the gap is still very wide. In the Civil Service, for instance, it has been estimated that the highest-paid officials earn forty times more than the lowest-paid.[59] Wage differentials between men and women have lessened slightly since the beginning of the 1960s.

In 1956 minimum daily wages were fixed according to three zones at different levels of 36, 33 and 31 pesetas. These different levels created anomalies between one region and another, as well as being very low. In 1963 a minimum 'interprofessional' wage was set up on a national basis at Ptas 60, a figure which met with severe criticism even from quarters not directly affected. The level of the daily minimum has been a matter for dispute ever since and certainly in the middle of the 1960s the increases were derisory. By 1 October 1967 the basic minimum was only Ptas 96 a day. In 1966 the government provided for an annual revision but this did not always happen in practice, as in 1968 when, although a revision of Ptas 6 increase a day was published in September, the ruling did not come into effect until the beginning of 1969. In April 1976 the minimum wage paid was raised from Ptas 225 to Ptas 345 a day.

Increases in the minimum wage did not always keep pace with the rise in the cost of living and in 1966 this was officially recognised and provision was made for increases in wages through collective negotiations to be linked to the cost-of-living index. The effects of this have, however, frequently been nullified by subsequent wage freezes, which are examined in more detail later in this chapter. A further anomaly arises from the fact that despite the legal existence of a minimum daily wage, some wages have actually appeared to be *below* the minimum. Thus in 1964 when the minimum monthly salary was Ptas 1800, a lawyer (*abogado del Estado*) began with a salary of Ptas 1520, a director of an Institute with Ptas 1790 and a doctor in the State corps of pediatricians with Ptas 1540. In all these cases the total sum earned would exceed the salaries stated through other emoluments not the subject of prescribed rates. In the case of State employees, as we have already seen, the size of a civil servant's salary depends very largely on the strength of the corps to which he belongs. In 1965 a law was passed to reform the official pay structure, complementary to the law a year earlier which was intended to overhaul the structure and workings of the Civil Service. Both reforms, however, ran into severe difficulties, partly because the reforms were associated with the Opus Dei group and this aroused hostility in some quarters, and also because many of the corps subject to reform had a vested interest in the survival of the old ways. The law on pay provided a basic minimum salary for all civil servants subject to annual increases by regular increments. Complicated calculations to assess the latter were to reflect the individual's status and also the prestige of his corps. The reforms, however, have not led to substantial changes in procedure and pay still seems to depend largely on the bargaining strength of the independent corps.

Nor has the basic minimum wage in the Civil Service developed in line with the minimum interprofessional wage, as presumably it was intended to. In 1965 the base of Ptas 2400 a month was chosen to coincide with the figure it was thought would be chosen for the interprofessional salary. In 1969 a slight divergence was apparent, the basic minimum for civil servants being fixed at Ptas 3000, while the 'national' minimum was Ptas 3060. The Ptas 3000 was not, however, brought into effect until 1971, by which time the minimum interprofessional salary had reached Ptas 4080. In fact the basic wage is now usually about one-quarter or one-fifth of the total salary received. It is, however, the base on which pensions are calculated. Obviously such a situation encourages multiple job-holding and the expansion of fringe benefits, which in turn reinforces the survival of the corps which secure them.

The introduction of a national minimum salary has diminished regional differences in pay at the lower end of the scale. It has not, however, brought about greater harmonisation of pay levels in the higher levels even between areas of roughly comparable states of development. In the middle of the 1960s it was found that for a particular job within the same industry and in the same geographical area some factories were paying wages up to three times as high as others.[60] In the Civil Service, too, men of comparable age and standing are often paid very different rates according to the size and influence of the corps to which they belong. The differentials in pay and prospects which exist for employees doing approximately similar jobs in comparable branches of industry, even within the same region, highlight the inflexibility of the Spanish labour market and the lack of mobility. This is institutionalised by the laws protecting workers from being fired[61] and by the bonuses paid for seniority in a firm and, as a counterpart, there is very little knowledge of employment opportunities even within the same locality. As mentioned earlier, there is often ignorance of what others may be earning in other grades among fellow workers. Wage levels seem to have played as minimal a rôle in the distribution of manpower in Spain at the beginning of the 1970s as in the early 1960s. Despite the emphasis in the Third Plan on introducing a higher degree of mobility into the labour market, there are no concrete suggestions for dealing with a fundamental cause of rigidity, that of the *despedida*. On the contrary, in the Labour Relations Act of 1976, Article 35 made it virtually impossible to dismiss personnel.

The years since the Stabilisation Plan have been punctuated by wage controls. After the initial freeze which accompanied the Stabilisation Plan had been relaxed, it became evident that inflation was still not under control. Consequently, among other anti-inflationary measures, a maximum limit of 8 per cent increases was imposed on wages at the end of 1965. Following the devaluation in November 1967, wages were again frozen in what was optimistically described as an incomes policy. At the same time monetary restrictions were introduced, public consumption cut back and prices of goods and services were subjected to severe controls. This affected the supposedly automatic revision of wages built into wage agreements already in existence covering some half a million workers.[62] In August 1968 wages were allowed to rise once again but a limit of 5·9 per cent was imposed for the duration of 1969. Despite the limitation, wages rose by slightly more than 8 per cent in the course of 1969. In December 1969 it was announced that collective wage negotiations could sanction wage increases of 8 per cent, if the agreement was scheduled to last for more than two years, but only of 6·5 per cent for wage agreements of shorter duration. At the end of 1973 a further round of wage restrictions was introduced and it was announced that no collective wage agreement would be accepted in 1974 which would allow an increase in wages higher than the rise in the official cost of living index and that no collective wage agreement would be accepted if its impact on prices was higher than 5 per cent.

By 1975 wage controls had been eased, only to be reinstituted in April of that year. Wages might only rise by as much as the cost of living plus 2 per cent. This limitation has remained in force with the proviso in the Labour Relations Act of 1976 that the minimum wage should be revised every six months if the cost-of-living index should rise by more than 5 per cent in the period. Pegging wages to the cost-of-living index has proved increasingly difficult to enforce, not least because of the general disbelief in the official cost of living figures. Inflationary tendencies have been reinforced in the mid-1970s by the increasing tendency to demand flat-rate rather than percentage increases.

In both 1967 and 1973 there was talk of an incomes rather than just a wages policy. This in both years led to attempts to control dividends by relating benefits to levels achieved in previous years. These measures have not had much impact, however, partly because there is a considerable lack of information on income of this nature and also because firms often get round the restrictions by making 'bonus' issues to shareholders. It would be fair to say that incomes policies in Spain have up to now been primarily and almost exclusively concerned with wages. The limitation on negotiating freedom which government intervention of this kind inevitably entails is discussed more fully in the next section of this chapter dealing with collective wage agreements.

The question of wages cannot be considered outside the more general context of the development of labour relations in Spain. This is a complex topic and particularly so because entities such as the trade union organisations (the *sindicatos*) and the works councils (*jurados de empresa*) are so constituted that, despite their apparent nominal similarity to bodies in other European countries, this is in fact frequently misleading. Before examining the machinery of collective bargaining and the pattern of labour relations, it is necessary first to consider the make-up and the rôle of the *sindicatos*.

The roots of the *sindicatos* lie in the *fuero de trabajo* (labour charter) of 1938 and the Trade Union Unity Act of 1940.[63] The *sindicatos* were to be based on unity, totality and graduated authority (*jeraquía*) and were to assist the State in its economic policies including 'intervening in the conditions of labour', if necessary. The *sindicatos* were and are 'vertical' – that is to say, employers and employees were combined together in the same *sindicato*, which would represent one aspect of economic activity. In 1941, twenty-four different *sindicatos* were created to cover the gamut of economic life. The fundamental premise of the syndical organisation was that the State would look after the worker and that in return the worker had to offer 'fidelity' and 'subordination' to his employer. The employer in his turn was to be responsible to the State for the running of his business. The syndical organisation is both the only official framework for the representation of organised labour and a stronghold of the Movimiento.[64] The Delegado Nacional of the *sindicatos* is also the Secretary-General of the Movement and the post is a political appointment. In the years after the Civil War until 1958, wages were fixed by the *reglamentaciones* of the Ministry of Labour, as were the conditions of labour by the *reglamentos del regimen interior* of the same ministry. To strike was illegal and considered *lese-patria*. During this period the rôle of the *sindicatos*, while all-pervasive, was not subject to any severe trials. The main function of the industrial *sindicatos* originally was to 'know the problems of production' and to act as pressure groups *vis-à-vis* other government bodies. At a provincial level, syndical officials were expected primarily to maintain 'social discipline'.

Changes, or more accurately changes in expectations, began with the introduction of collective bargaining in 1958 and the alteration of the penal code so that strikes which were held to be of an economic nature were no longer considered subversive. Before examining the extent of change actually brought about in the 1960s, it is worth making a brief survey of various bodies involved in exercising power officially and unofficially in labour relations in this period.

In 1947 the concept of the *jurado de empresa* – 'factory jury' or 'works council' – was established by law. The regulations necessary for the actual establishment of the *jurados* were not however introduced until 1953. The *jurado* is compulsory for any factory which employs more than fifty employees. The *jurado* gives the impression of a body inherently endowed with contradictions, because it is supposed by its constitution to represent workers equally to the management of a particular factory, to the syndical organisation and to the State. It is designated as a 'legal instrument of participation' but the limitations to participation are such that this is virtually meaningless. The rules regulating the *jurado* prevent it from being a body in any way genuinely representative of the workers. Subordinated to the syndical organisation and subject to the disciplinary powers of the government, the *jurado* is expected to act as a consultative body. The *vocales* (members) of the *jurado* are chosen from management, technicians and workers in elections held by the syndical organisation. The president is always a representative of the management side and is also appointed by them.

It is difficult to see what purpose the *jurado* was meant to serve in labour relations, given the restrictions on action and the contradictions between the composition of the body and the rôle it is supposed to play. An examination of the *jurados* as originally set up gives the impression of a gesture towards participation, yet within the all-embracing system of the *sindicatos*, which in effect would neutralise any effort to make the *jurados* represent the workers *against* the management. In fact, however, the *jurados* developed during the decade of the 1960s in a slightly different manner than was originally foreseen.

Central to the official view of the *sindicatos* is that they are 'representative', which is taken as axiomatic since 'all Spaniards engaged in production' are included in the organisation. As Señor García Ramal when National Delegate put it, 'Everything is representative in the syndical organisation from top to bottom. Or am I myself not considered a representative?'[65] Since in a vertical syndicate it is inherently impossible to allow for the possibility of conflicting interests between employers and employed, it may have been hoped in the early stages of the syndical organisation that this would actually be the case. Between 1939 and 1958 Spanish labour was at its weakest. This is not to imply that there were not evident signs of tension and even strikes, illegal though they were. Rather, at that stage, it was possible to maintain the illusion of harmonious relations between employers and employed more successfully than during the 1960s and later.

By making a very broad generalisation, it is possible to say that tension in labour relations focused on four main issues, although these of course were interrelated and related in turn to other issues : namely, the question of representation within the *sindicatos*, the closely connected issue of separate trade unions, the right to negotiate freely in collective bargaining and over the right to strike.

As originally set up, the *sindicatos* had bases at local, provincial and national levels, each of which were controlled by appointed officials. In 1943 elective posts were created at all levels of the organisation by indirect elections, but the office of Delegado Nacional remained a direct appointment of Franco and delegates at provincial level were also appointed, not elected. In 1947 the *jurados de empresa* were first introduced but did not become a reality until six years later. Even then their rôle merely as a consultative body was severely limited, often because of lack of information, and was in no way genuinely geared to representing any one body to another – certainly not the workers to the management. Further moves towards greater participation were made in the early 1960s. In 1961 a Syndical Congress was organised which was intended to increase communication between appointed and elected delegates. The Congress was to be held at regular intervals. In 1964 the third Syndical Congress created the *consejos de trabajadores y empresarios*, councils of workers and councils of employers, which were to exist at both national and provincial levels. These councils, while mainly constituted of elected representatives, also included appointed posts which to a considerable degree negated the original idea of creating more 'democratic' units. Neither of these creations could be said to have radically altered the structure of the syndical organisation. In 1962 a law was passed enabling representation of workers on the boards of directors, but since this law was applicable only to firms employing more than 500 regular employees and the board could veto candidates put forward, this has had very little impact.

A lesser-known feature of the *sindicatos* are the associated agencies which cover professional training schemes, housing, health, education, welfare and legal staff. These are financed by compulsory contributions from employers and workers, the former paying 1·5 per cent of the total payroll of the business and the latter 0·003 per cent of their basic salary.[66] In 1965 these activities accounted for two-fifths of the syndical budget but control of the funds is not held by elected representatives within the syndicates and this has often been a ground for complaint.

During the 1960s and early 1970s, despite the innovations mentioned above, the basic structure of the syndicates was left virtually unchanged. Any move towards greater participation was carefully hedged in by limitations which in effect neutralised the possible changes. What did alter, however, was the conception of many workers as to how they could use the existing structure of the syndicates to their own advantage. The fact that they were able to do so for a period in the 1960s was due to a combination of economic and political factors propitious for new forms of activity. The 'liberalisation' period was short-lived on all fronts, however, and by 1969, with the declaration of a state of exception, it could be said unequivocally to have come to an end. Prior to this, an attempt was made by workers in many parts of Spain to use the syndical apparatus to elect members of the unofficial labour organisations, the *comisiones obreras* (workers' commissions), to official positions within the syndicates and in this way to make their needs felt.

The *comisiones obreras* were never a coherent national force and they gathered strength from *ad hoc* committees which sprang up in relation to the organisation of specific strikes. The *comisiones* developed in different ways in different parts of the country. Since any kind of association of more than five people was forbidden in Spain at that time, the amount of organisation achieved during the middle years of the decade while the *comisiones* were flourishing is remarkable. Since the key to obtaining a position of influence in negotiating collective agreements and thereby improving standards of pay and work on a company basis lay in being a member of the *jurado de empresa*,[67] the workers' commissions concentrated very largely on getting candidates elected on to the *jurado de empresa*. This generally started in a single factory and gradually extended to other firms in the same branch of industry in a particular area. Thus in Madrid the Federación Siderometalúrgica was powerful, and in Seville the Federación de Construcción, while the textile federation flourished in Catalan towns.[68] The workers' commissions grew from the 'grass roots'.

A study by Amando de Miguel and Juan Linz found that it was businessmen in the less highly industrialised areas of Spain who depended most heavily on the syndicates.[69] The large, modern firms in Madrid, Barcelona and the Basque country tend to be less interested in the syndicates, although they have to contribute funds. Since employers' views on the syndicates are not unanimously favourable, some managements, although by no means all, appeared to come to terms with the existence of the workers' commissions inside their factories. Some found it a definite help to feel that, after the syndical elections of 1963 and 1966 when many of the 'candidates' of the workers' commissions were elected to the *jurado*, they were dealing with genuine representatives of the workforce. There has been frequent evidence of a desire on the part of employers as well as employees for a more representative structure in the syndicates. An example of management dealing with a *jurado* which was not considered as representative by the workforce was the strike at ITT Standard Electric (Madrid) in January 1974 when a wage agreement accepted by the *jurado* was immediately repudiated by the rest of the workforce, with ensuing strikes and lockouts. The fact that the *jurado* in this case was not the one which the electing workers wanted, because of dismissals among the members of the *jurado*, highlights the dilemma in which both management and workers find themselves when those negotiating on behalf of the workers are not in fact chosen by them, or rather not allowed to retain their positions if, once chosen, they prove troublesome to the management. While the process of negotiation may be smoother with picked candidates in the *jurado*, the end result may well be one of greater tension in labour relations, leaving both sides dissatisfied.

The workers' commissions found themselves in trouble after they had achieved some degree of strength on the *jurados*. Once a member of the *jurado*, there was no guarantee they would stay so. Trouble-makers were often sacked and in the years 1964–6 1800 elected syndical officials were dismissed.[70] Not all firms were anxious to come to terms with the workers' commissions and as recession took hold in 1966 and 1967 and unemployment grew, so too did struggles over collective bargaining. The subsequent wage freeze ran counter to the success of the workers' commissions. As militants on the workers' side became more vociferous, so they were more rapidly dismissed and in some areas arrested. By 1969, when there was a political clamp-down, the workers' commissions had been effectively disbanded and many of the leaders were in gaol.

The fact that the workers' commissions failed to revolutionise the syndical apparatus and make it more democratic or to form recognised trade unions of their own does not mean that the position of labour at the beginning of the 1970s was the same as a decade earlier. On paper, certainly, the syndicates themselves had changed little, despite the eagerly awaited syndical law of 1971. The new law did not change the process of indirect elections nor were employers and employees separated into different syndicates and nor indeed was there any reference made to the right to strike.[71] There had been no changes of substance. The fact that the syndicates were for a short period more truly 'representative' was due to the fact that unofficial and official labour groups merged briefly. But the workers' commissions left their mark. Over the decade, as labour realised more of its potential strength, so too power shifted from the syndicates to the factory level, mainly because of the way collective bargaining has evolved, although the syndicates still exercise considerable powers over the actual process of collective bargaining. At the same time the potential of the *jurado de empresa* as a body representative of the workforce was realised. The fact that in the 1970s the position and composition of the *jurado* has frequently been a matter of conflict is evidence that the workers' commissions' use of the *jurado* to press forward demands has had lasting effects. In more general terms it is interesting to note that despite the virtual destruction of the original workers' commissions in 1969–70 militancy in industrial relations did not diminish. Whether the *sindicatos*, as long as they retain their original 'vertical' structure, can accommodate themselves to the demands of labour in Spain is very doubtful.

The 1958 law of Collective Contracts supplanted the previous system of wage decrees and also the *reglamentos del régimen interior* which regulated working conditions in individual factories, both of which were laid down by the Ministry of Labour.[72] Four types of contract are possible. First, contracts can relate to all factories in a particular sector at local, provincial or inter-provincial levels, and second, to a specific group of factories at either local, provincial or inter-provincial levels. Third, they can apply simply to a specific factory, or fourth, to a group of workers within a particular factory.[73] In bargaining carried out on a local, provincial or inter-provincial level, negotiations are carried out by elected members of the social and economic section of the syndical organisation. When negotiation relates to a firm or a group within a company, negotiations are carried out by representatives of labour and management within the firm, although (see below for further detail) the syndicates still exert a certain amount of influence in this type of bargaining. If no agreement can be reached, the negotiations are referred to the Ministry of Labour which gives a Norma de Obligación Cumplida (NOC), an arbitration award.

The three characteristics which emerged over the 1960s in relation to the development of collective bargaining were the preference for negotiation on a company basis (rather than a provincial one) within the different kinds of collective bargaining available, the increase in one-year agreements, and the growing preference of workers to get in the position of being awarded a Norma de Obligación Cumplida. This statement needs further elaboration. First it should be remembered that only firms employing more than fifty workers can request the opening of collective bargaining. Moreover the changeover to collective bargaining did not take place with great speed. Between 1958 and 1961 (inclusive) only 829 contracts were concluded, affecting 1,711,963 of the labour force. Part of the lack of enthusiasm was due to the slow adjustment to a new system and part to the extreme delays of the Ministry of Labour in giving final approbation. The slow growth of *convenios colectivos* – collective agreements – was also due to the wage freeze and unemployment instigated by the Stabilisation Plan. Following the strikes of 1962 the process of dealing with *convenios colectivos* was speeded up. Between 1962 and 1967 roughly 1000 *convenios* were concluded every year. In 1968 the number, due to the wage freeze, fell to 165 and swelled in compensation to 1578 in 1969. Between 1969 and 1974 numbers oscillated between approximately 1100 and 1600. At the beginning of the 1970s over 40 per cent of the Spanish labour force were covered by *convenios*. Not surprisingly the majority of *convenios* relate to industry. In 1969 the percentage of the labour force *not* affected was as follows : agriculture, 47·2 per cent; industry, 10·5 per cent; services, 35·1 per cent.[74]

On the whole it has been the larger firms who have preferred to make use of negotiations on a plant basis. While both the number of *convenios* and the number of men affected by contracts on a plant basis is much smaller than those affected by *convenios* on a provincial basis in absolute terms, the number of plant-based contracts has been increasing at the expense of provincial ones and in 1973 totalled 743 as against 629 provincial contracts. The other noticeable feature has been the growing use of the Norma de Obligación Cumplida. This has been especially striking in factories and sectors as well as areas where there is a tradition of labour unrest. Guipuzcoa and Vizcaya, despite the difficulty in obtaining accurate information, appear to have the highest number of arbitration awards for each industry. One advantage from the workers' point of view in eschewing traditional bargaining techniques is that, while individual awards are not necessarily always at a higher level than those achieved by bargaining, over a period of years this has undoubtedly been the case. Another is that wage awards are usually settled with far less delay than is caused by waiting for the Ministry of Labour's approval on a collective agreement, which sometimes has taken longer than the actual negotiations (which may themselves have lasted months). A certain disillusion with developments within the *jurados* may have increased the propensity of workers to by-pass the collective bargaining mechanisms and try their luck with a direct decree from the Ministry of Labour. Although on the increase, the percentage of contracts and workers covered by Normas de Obligación Cumplida is still quite small. In 1972 arbitration awards accounted for 13·1 per cent of total wage agreements and 13·9 per cent of the working population were covered by negotiations that year.

In the following paragraphs the amount of freedom of manœuvre which is possible in this type of collective bargaining is considered. The 1958 law represented a definite and deliberate break with the past practice of wage decrees. Unless other arrangements are made, collective agreements are valid for two years. They are renewable from year to year by tacit consent until revision is requested. In the 1960s increasing preference was shown for annual instead of biennal *convenios*, despite the official syndical line manifested in the 1973 law on *convenios colectivos sindicales* which strongly favoured two-year agreements. The growth of one-year agreements has helped to raise wage levels and is a sign of the increasing strength of Spanish labour. However, freedom of action has often been curtailed through various constraints, including the powers of intervention by the *sindicatos* which are greater than they at first appear. While the syndical organisation is responsible for carrying out negotiations for agreements at provincial level, plant-based agreements are also subject to syndical influence. To begin with, permission must be requested of syndical officials either by the *jurado de empresa* or by the management for negotiations to begin. Since the president of the *jurado* is a member of the management who is usually part of the negotiating management team, he must vacate the presidency during negotiations and his place be taken by someone nominated by the syndical provincial delegate and who, amongst other necessary qualifications, has undergone syndical training, so that in practice the president of the commission is usually a professional official of the syndical organisation. The syndical organisation normally provides 'independent' assessors and a secretary as further neutral elements to aid negotiations.[75]

It can therefore be seen that the influence of the syndicates within negotiations is strong. While it is greater in local or provincial agreements where representatives of management and labour are chosen by indirect election in relation to the industry as a whole and negotiations actually take place in the local syndical headquarters, negotiations on a plant basis cannot be held without the assistance of the syndicates.

Not only does the relevant syndicate have the power to decide whether or not to accede to the request to *open* negotiations, and to supervise the procedure through the presidency of the negotiating commission, but it also has power through the president to suspend or close negotiations if he so decides and to send the agreement to the Ministry of Labour for final acceptance or for arbitration if deadlock has been reached. It is not within the power of the individual negotiating parties to close negotiations if they so wish.

If a collective agreement is brought to a successful conclusion, it is then referred to the Ministry of Labour, which is supposed to give its assent within fifteen days. In practice the average delay is usually months rather than days. As we have seen above, the Ministry of Labour is also the arbitrator in negotiations which have reached deadlock. A collective agreement once reached is enforceable at law. Should the firm fail to meet its obligations, it can be tried by a labour court which is part of the Ministry of Labour. A worker, on the other hand, who is similarly considered not to have complied with the contract is 'disciplined' by his employer. The Ministry of Labour and the syndical organisation share the responsibility of mediating in interpretation of contracts.

Another limitation on the freedom of negotiation has come from the wage controls referred to earlier in the chapter. It is this in particular which until recently has caused the freedom to negotiate collective wage agreements to appear illusory; ironically, since 1974, the growing militancy of the labour force has in turn made wage controls look increasingly irrelevant. The power of the State applied through both the Ministry of Labour and the syndicates, and the growing feeling in the late 1960s that the *jurado de empresa* could not be turned into a representative body of the workforce to negotiate with management, caused disillusion and frustration with the processes of collective bargaining. More especially since it was evident that the intervention of the State was not limited to the use of these official institutions. For example, in a strike in 1962 in Asturias, the government finally by-passed the syndicates to settle the strike. Sometimes intervention has been of a violent nature, as in Granada in 1971 when three workers were shot by the police during demonstrations arising from bargaining disputes in the building industry. An incident of a similar nature took place in the Bazán factory in El Ferrol in 1972 and again in Vitoria in 1976. Striking is not an activity which is officially recognised in Spain and when some reference is unavoidable, it is usually to 'collective conflicts' which may mean either strikes or other expressions of dissatisfaction, such as boycotting of factories and demonstrations. In September 1962 modification of Article 222 of the Penal Code allowed stoppage for 'non-political ends'. This, however, allowed a wide range of interpretations as to what might be considered political and in December 1967 the Supreme Tribunal ruled on a test case that strikes for 'social ends' were illegal. While this ruling did not stop strikes, it made it easier for management to get rid of troublemakers.

To strike, therefore, in Spain has remained a serious step to take, even though the risks are generally considerably lower than in the 1950s. Because the government viewed any disturbance as potentially politically disruptive, it has felt free to make use of the various branches of the police to break strikes, and indeed demonstrations, and this has frequently led to arrests, and occasionally deaths. Nevertheless strikes have continued to be a feature of Spanish industrial life, although causes and motivation have altered over the decade. Accurate figures on collective conflicts are virtually impossible to come by, but days lost in strikes are on the increase. In the first two months of 1976, more days were lost in strikes than in the whole of 1975. The focus of conflict, sectors most affected and motivation have varied from year to year and also according to the different areas of Spain. As would be expected the centres most given to labour unrest are Madrid, Vizcaya, Barcelona and Asturias, although this by no means implies that there have not been bitter disputes in other towns and areas, such as Seville, Granada, Zaragoza, as well as others. In sectoral terms, iron and steel and metalworking have been centres of conflict in Madrid, as has transport. Iron and steel has been the focus of extreme tension especially in Vizcaya and to a lesser extent in Barcelona, Asturias and Seville. The chemical sector has also been involved in disputes in Madrid, Seville, Vizcaya and Zaragoza. A feature of most disputes is, not surprisingly, that they have taken place in the larger factories and therefore the sectors which include a fair proportion of big factories.

What has emerged clearly from the 1960s is the growing power of the labour force in Spain. Compared with other West European countries, however, Spanish labour is still in a disadvantaged position. Trade unions which do not include employers are illegal and any kind of association for discussion of working conditions is still fraught with difficulties and sometimes dangerous. Nevertheless, despite constraints on their bargaining position and despite the small defence which Spanish workers have against arbitrary dismissal of troublemakers, there is every indication that labour unrest has not abated and is unlikely to do so. The lack of the right to strike, and police intervention in disputes, have not stemmed determination to express dissatisfaction. The waning power of the *sindicatos* is much in evidence. This does not necessarily mean that their formal demise is imminent. Abolition of the *sindicatos* would have strong political overtones. It would also entail finding employment for the 25,000 currently employed full time in the syndical apparatus, a matter of especial sensitivity in a time of high unemployment. The influence of the *sindicatos* will, however, continue to decline. Opposition labour groups have proliferated in the mid-1970s and come increasingly into the open. The strength of such groups is demonstrated in the size of recent wage increases, which are far above officially permitted levels.

# 5 Social Conditions and Government Policies

It is indisputable that increases in *per capita* income have been considerable since the mid-1960s, although figures for individual years vary according to source.[1] Until 1963 Spain could be described as a developing country in terms of the United Nations' classification of *per capita* income levels. In 1963 *per capita* income at market prices crossed the $500 line,[2] and by 1971 had doubled to over $1000. In 1975 income per head at market prices was $2574. In order to see this rapid rise in relation to the expansion of other countries, Table 5.1 gives some comparisons of GDP *per capita* in various countries in 1961, 1970 and 1973.

Seen in relation to increases in GDP *per capita* in other European countries, Spain's achievement is impressive but not exceptionally so, except in comparison with Turkey. While it is easy to see that the level of national income has increased rapidly, it is more difficult to

TABLE 5.1  GDP *per capita* at market prices in
various countries, 1961, 1970, 1973
(in $ US)

|  | 1961 | 1970 | 1973 |
|---|---|---|---|
| USA | 2862 | 4879 | 6267 |
| Common Market Countries (average) | 1269 | 2488 | 4117 |
| Japan | 566 | 1902 | 3755 |
| Australia | 1543 | 2777 | 4965 |
| France | 1440 | 2863 | 4904 |
| United Kingdom | 1441 | 2185 | 3096 |
| Italy | 766 | 1728 | 2511 |
| Ireland | 687 | 1335 | 2132 |
| Spain | 407 | 990 | 1842 |
| Greece | 469 | 1091 | 1788 |
| Portugal | 299 | 713 | 1247 |
| Turkey | 196 | 360 | 539 |

Source: Monthly bulletin of Eurostat.

assess the effects of this and how, for instance, as a result, living conditions have changed in different regions and to what extent increases have been evenly distributed over the population. Overall the rise in living standards and expectations has been enormous since the early 1960s, but some sections of the community still live in conditions of considerable poverty. The effects of the dramatic rise in *per capita* income can be seen in the rise in purchases of consumer durables and in the change in spending habits on food, clothing and housing. In 1961 there were 60 telephones, 9 television sets and 12 cars for every 1000 inhabitants. By 1975 this had risen to 195 telephones, 260 television sets and 111 cars,[3] which indicates substantial increases in disposable income, although these later figures are still well below the European average.[4] Similarly, in 1960 only 4 per cent of Spanish households owned a refrigerator and 19 per cent a washing machine. In 1971 66 per cent of households possessed a refrigerator and 52 per cent a washing machine. With rising incomes, a smaller proportion of total expenditure goes towards food. This trend has been very much in evidence in Spain. In 1958 over 55 per cent of all expenditure was on food. By 1964 this had dropped to 48 per cent and by 1973–4 to 38 per cent. Despite the decreasing percentage of expenditure on food, the proportion of the family budget spent on food in 1970 was still higher than comparable figures for Greece and Italy and well above figures for Britain, France and Denmark.[5] Table 5.2 sets out the changing proportions of expenditure on different categories of goods in various years between 1958 and 1973–4 and shows that expenditure on clothing and shoes also fell in proportion to total expenditure, whereas spending on housing more than doubled. Expenditure on household goods increased slightly while spending on other goods and services including holidays, which accounted for only 17 per cent of consumption in 1958, represented 31 per cent by 1973–4. In 1970

TABLE 5.2   Percentage average annual consumption *per capita* in relation to total consumption (various years)

|  | 1958 | 1964 | 1968 | 1973–4 |
|---|---|---|---|---|
| Food | 55·3 | 48·6 | 44·4 | 38·0 |
| Clothing and shoes | 13·6 | 14·9 | 13·5 | 7·7 |
| Housing | 5·0 | 7·4 | 10·3 | 11·6 |
| Household expenditure | 8·3 | 9·2 | 8·1 | 11·1 |
| Other expenditure including holidays | 17·8 | 19·9 | 23·7 | 31·6 |
| Total consumption | 100·0 | 100·0 | 100·0 | 100·0 |

Source: INE, *Encuesta de Presupuestos Familiares, July 1973–June 1974* (Madrid: May 1975).

expenditure on consumer durables in Spain accounted for approximately the same proportion of family consumption as it did in other European countries, exceptions being Denmark, where expenditure was proportionally much higher (18 per cent of the family budget), and Greece, where at 4 per cent the figure was much lower than the average.[6]

In Chapter 2 reference was made to changing dietary habits in Spain and in particular to the increase in the consumption of meat and dairy products. Over the 1960s there was a distinct shift in overall dietary composition. The calorie level remained relatively stable at a daily average of approximately 2700 calories per head but the proportion of calories derived from cereals and potatoes dropped from 50 per cent in 1961 to 43 per cent in 1970. Consumption of proteins rose overall by almost 10 per cent and of animal proteins from 29 per cent in 1961 to 44 per cent in 1970.[7] In a breakdown of expenditure on various categories of food the most striking changes have been the smaller proportion now spent on bread and cereals (18 per cent of all expenditure on food in 1958 and 10 per cent in 1973–4) and the far larger percentage expended on meat products (17 per cent in 1958 and 29 per cent in 1973–4).[8]

We have seen that national income rose substantially in the 1960s and early 1970s and that this produced different spending patterns which constituted evidence of a higher standard of living being generally enjoyed. At the same time, it is worth taking a closer look at the disparities which are sometimes obscured by the general upward trend. One of the most obvious of these is to be found in the *per capita* income levels of different provinces. In 1973 Vizcaya, Madrid, Barcelona, Alava and Guipuzcoa all enjoyed a *per capita* income of over Ptas 130,000. The national average income per head in 1973 was Ptas 99,000 and at the bottom of the list the poorest provinces were Orense, Granada, Badajoz, Caceres and Lugo, with *per capita* incomes varying between Ptas 62,000 and Ptas 57,000.[9] The five provinces with the highest *per capita* incomes contain some 29 per cent of the total population. In 1973 thirty-five provinces, containing 53 per cent of the population, came below the national *per capita* income average. The fifteen provinces which enjoy a *per capita* income above the national average geographically lie in the north and north-east along the axis of the River Ebro and also along the Mediterranean coast to Valencia. The only exceptions to this geographical pattern are Madrid, Valladolid and the Balearic Islands. The most densely populated provinces, Barcelona, Madrid and Vizcaya, have the highest income *per capita* levels. Since the beginning of the 1960s population, production and income have increasingly been concentrated in a small number of provinces. Over the period, however, there has been convergence rather than a widening of *per capita* income levels in different

D

provinces, due in large part to the scale of migration flows from the provinces low in the *per capita* 'league'.

While a breakdown of the regional distribution of income is useful in giving a general idea of the geographical location of richer and poorer areas, it gives little idea of actual living conditions in the poorer rural areas, nor does it take into account the substantial pockets of poverty which have developed in the big cities as a result of migration.

Despite the inflow of migrants to the towns from the countryside, those left behind have often continued to live in conditions little touched by overall improvements in economic conditions in Spain. Various books written during the 1960s testify to the continued existence of poverty and restricted horizons in different regions,[10] for instance in the north-east and eastern parts of Castile, in particular Las Hurdes, and also in Andalusian villages which have remained little touched by the tourist boom on the coasts.[11] Impressionistic evidence gained while travelling in the more remote areas of these regions confirms what is indicated by these various studies. Incomes per head in the agricultural sector, even allowing for statistical inconsistencies,[12] is far less than in the industrial or service sectors. In 1972 the average annual wage in the agricultural sector was Ptas 80,278, whereas in the industrial sector it was Ptas 121,502 and in services Ptas 161,161.[13] While it can be argued justifiably that life is generally less expensive outside towns, this is little consolation if basic amenities and services taken for granted in urban life are almost totally lacking in rural areas.

In 1968 the National Institute of Statistics undertook a survey of 'family equipment and cultural level' by province. At national level 34 per cent of households did not have running water. In Orense 80 per cent of households were without running water. In Cuenca and Soria three-quarters of the population were without running water, in Badajoz, Lugo and Pontevedra over 60 per cent, and in twenty-one provinces over half the households had none. In some provinces in the regions of Galicia, Extremadura, Andalusia and Castile a high level of illiteracy was still to be found amounting to one-fifth of family 'heads' in some provinces.[14] In a similar survey undertaken in 1975 the situation had improved, but in rural areas a large proportion of households were still without running water. Despite the prescriptions of the Third Development Plan, about 1 million Spaniards in rural areas were still without electric light in 1974. The Foessa report of 1970 comments on the low standard of living in municipalities of less than 2000 people which in 1965 contained some 4 million inhabitants and in 1970 still some 3·7 million.[15] These small towns, in addition to bad housing, lack educational and recreational facilities and transport. The villages which suffer most are naturally the most isolated and are situated mainly in Old Castile and eastern Andalusia.

The Foessa report also points out that in 1965, when the average *per capita* income was Ptas 35,000, over 1 million people were living in villages where the average income was under Ptas 5000 a year. In small villages where municipal budgets are tiny, it is impossible to bring about any real changes without substantial government assistance. While the government pays lip service to improving life in the country-side, there has been no evidence of any real intention to do so.[16] The depressing sight of deserted or semi-abandoned villages is not an un-common one and provides no incentive for the younger generation to stay on the land. Life in the small and often isolated villages is made harder by the fact that social services are often practically non-existent. Hospital beds provided by the Dirección General de Sanidad tend to be located only in provincial capitals, as are most medical services. Pensions are not always claimed, either through ignorance on the part of the pensioner or through lack of a suitable administrative framework, and unemployment pay is often equally deficient. As the OECD study on the Regional Development of Andalusia put it :[17]

There is an impressive variety of welfare measures in Spain nowa-days, but many of them are endowed with too small amounts of money. The subsidies are likewise small and difficult to obtain, because they depend on the existence of various pre-conditions and furthermore a lot of information is needed to know where and how subsidies can be claimed.

In addition to the continuance of traditional rural property, a new source of poverty has grown up with the *chabolismo* in the cities. Shanty towns have sprung up, especially in Madrid and Barcelona,[18] peopled by migrants who may aspire initially to move on to better conditions but who usually fail to do so. The extent of these shanty towns is difficult to estimate as there are no reliable figures, but it is a problem which is growing rather than diminishing, and presumably will continue to do so as long as the rural exodus continues. Scarcely any of the huts have running water. In a study undertaken in the late 1960s by Foessa 67 per cent of those interviewed had access to water in the same district but 23 per cent had to bring it from outside the immediate district and 5 per cent were forced to buy it. The huts have no water since they fall outside the municipality's sphere of operations, nor do they benefit from other public services. They do, however, mostly enjoy the benefit of electric light, which is provided by private companies. While the inhabitants of the shanty towns possess a fairly high quantum of consumer goods, such as radio or television, furnishings in general are extremely limited and the limited space very overcrowded. In a report made by Doctors Ortega, Rubio and Villanueva on the Bilbao zone in Madrid, the following 'unfavour-able' items were included : piles of garbage, lack of hygiene, con-taminated water, lack of sewerage facilities, rats and bugs, quite apart from the damp and the cold.[19] In addition to the cramped and un-hygienic conditions the shanty towns suffer from their isolation from public services and also from amenities such as transport and markets.

The standard of living in the shanty towns of the big cities and in the small villages bears witness to the continuance of poverty for a sizable number. While life has become easier for many, the prevalence of multiple job-holding and the long hours worked even amongst the better-off members of the community indicate that the standard of living has not reached the heights which are sometimes assumed. A survey undertaken by the INE in 1965 found that approximately 80 per cent of Spanish families were living on monthly incomings which were below the national monthly average of Ptas 9446.[20] Table 5.3 shows the structure of earnings in 1969 according to the National Institute of Statistics. Consideration of this table in the light of various estimates of minimal family budgetary requirements in 1969 meant that for a family of more than three, wages earned would be insufficient for the 77 per cent who earned Ptas 9000 or less, unless two or more of the family were wage-earners.[21] The Foessa survey of 1970 estimated that in 1969 some 10 per cent of the population lived against a 'back-ground of poverty', which was defined as monthly earnings of Ptas 2500 per household. Table 5.4 gives the structure of wages in 1973. As would be expected the number of workers and the share of total earn-ings in the lowest levels had fallen sharply following high wage increases. Whereas in 1969 60 per cent of all wage-earners were paid Ptas 7000 or less, four years later the same proportion were paid Ptas 12,000 or less. In both cases, however, 60 per cent of wage-earners accounted for approximately 36 per cent of total wages.

Table 5.5 shows the distribution of yearly disposable family income in 1974. Clearly large differences in levels of disposable income persist and disposable family income at the highest level of Ptas 700,000 and more, while representing only 4 per cent of households, still accounts for nearly 30 per cent of total income. At the bottom end of the scale some 3 per cent of households with annual disposable incomes of up to Ptas 60,000 account for 0·33 per cent of total income. Between 1960 and 1970 there was practically no change in the distribution of dispos-able income.[22] If anything, disparities widened and, while the numbers of very poor households diminished, those with high levels of income tended to increase. Only since 1970 has there been evidence of a slight levelling in income distribution, due mainly to high wage increases and a change in the distribution of these increases. In 1974 some 32 per cent of households received less than one-half of the national

TABLE 5·3   Wage structure in 1969

| | | | Cumulative | |
| Monthly average wage | Workers (percentage) | Earnings (percentage) | Workers (percentage) | Earnings (percentage) |
|---|---|---|---|---|
| Less than Ptas 3000 | 9·4 | 2·7 | 9·4 | 2·7 |
| Ptas 3000–5000 | 27·9 | 15·7 | 37·3 | 18·4 |
| Ptas 5001–7000 | 23·5 | 19·5 | 60·8 | 37·9 |
| Ptas 7001–9000 | 16·9 | 17·7 | 77·7 | 55·6 |
| More than Ptas 9000 | 23·3 | 44·4 | 100·0 | 100·0 |

Source: INE, *Informe sobre las rentas* (Madrid: 1970).

TABLE 5.4   Wage structure in 1973

| | | | Cumulative | |
| Monthly average wage | Workers (percentage) | Earnings (percentage) | Workers (percentage) | Earnings (percentage) |
|---|---|---|---|---|
| Less than Ptas 3000 | 3·0 | 0·5 | 3·0 | 0·5 |
| Ptas 3000–5000 | 8·2 | 2·7 | 11·2 | 3·2 |
| Ptas 5001–7000 | 14·6 | 7·0 | 25·8 | 10·2 |
| Ptas 7001–9000 | 15·8 | 10·2 | 41·6 | 20·4 |
| Ptas 9001–11,000 | 12·9 | 10·4 | 54·5 | 30·8 |
| Ptas 11,001–12,000 | 5·7 | 5·3 | 60·2 | 36·1 |
| More than Ptas 12,000 | 39·8 | 63·9 | 100·0 | 100·0 |

Source: INE, *La Renta Nacional en 1974 y su distribución* (Madrid).

TABLE 5.5   Distribution of annual disposable family income, 1974

| | Percentage of households | Percentage of total income |
|---|---|---|
| Less than Ptas 60,000 | 3·26 | 0·33 |
| Ptas 60,000–84,000 | 2·96 | 0·53 |
| Ptas 84,001–120,000 | 6·02 | 1·57 |
| Ptas 120,001–180,000 | 13·04 | 4·75 |
| Ptas 180,001–240,000 | 18·00 | 9·45 |
| Ptas 240,001–480,000 | 39·47 | 35·54 |
| Ptas 480,001–700,000 | 13·11 | 18·95 |
| More than Ptas 700,000 | 4·14 | 29·88 |

Source: Calculations by Angel and Julio Alcaide based on INE, *Encuesta de Presupuestos Familiares, July 1973–June 1974* (May 1975) and estimates of National Income and Disposable Family Income for 1974.

average income, which represented a smaller proportion than in 1970. Moreover, the number of households receiving double the national income average had also diminished and in 1974 accounted for less than 4 per cent of all households. Given the extremes of poverty and wealth which existed in Spain prior to the period under consideration, it is by no means surprising ·that there are still wide disparities in income levels and standards of living in different areas. In the development plans the government has, however, frequently emphasised its commitment to policies designed to improve living conditions and in the remaining part of the chapter health, housing and educational policies are considered in order to determine what effect such policies have had.

Expectations of life span have risen remarkably during this century. In 1900 life expectancy for women, traditionally the hardier sex, was thirty-six years. By 1960 it had doubled to seventy-two. By this most obvious yardstick conditions of sanitation and health had improved enormously. As we saw earlier in the chapter, however, there are still widespread pockets of poverty and insanitary living conditions both in rural areas and in the new shanty towns in the large cities. Both urban and rural poor areas suffer from the same basic defects. Actual living conditions are bad; for example, the frequent lack of running and often of pure water and the lack of sewerage. Moreover, both categories fall outside the networks of private and State organisations which are designed to cater for the health needs of Spaniards.

Medical care is available from a series of unco-ordinated networks which fall under different government auspices. The division is not simply between State and private institutions. Ministerial departments with responsibilities for hospitals include the Presidencia del Gobierno, the Ministerio de Trabajo, Ministerio de Educación y Ciencia, Ministerio de Justicia and the defence ministries. In addition to these there are other official bodies dependent on the Ministerio de la Gobernación which run certain services and centres.[23] Provincial and municipal services exist side-by-side with central ones. The Church and private clinics provide the greater part of private medical care. In 1972 the civilian and military ministries provided 37,959 out of a total of 177,385 hospital beds; local authorities were responsible for 52,657 beds and private organisations accounted for 53,793.[24] Beds provided under the aegis of the social security system represented some 30 per cent of the total. In 1968 the ratio of beds to inhabitants in Spain was 4·3 for every 1000 inhabitants, one of the lowest in Europe.[25] Since that date, despite declarations of intent, the number of hospital beds has not increased appreciably and, while there has been some growth in population, the ratio of beds to people remains practically unchanged.

The number of hospital beds is not the be all and end all of medical care in a country. However, the number of beds available and the conditions attached to their use are indicative to some extent of the state of medical care. As described above, hospitals are under the jurisdiction of a large number of organisations and departments, which makes any enforcement of standards or co-ordination of policy virtually impossible in practical terms. When the Ministry of the Interior, which has a general responsibility for health matters, attempted to introduce a law which would have resulted in co-ordination of all hospital services, the final result was so watered down as to be effectively inoperative.[26] Lip service has been paid in the Second and Third Development Plans to the ideal of greater co-ordination but hospital services remain largely independent of one another. Private clinics are for the use of those who can afford to pay the high prices necessary and are therefore not accessible to more than a small proportion of the population. Military hospitals also cater for a minority. These two categories of hospitals account for approximately one-fifth of all hospital beds available.[27] The remainder are divided between hospitals used by social security contributors, those of a 'charitable' status coming under the loose heading of *beneficiencia* and hospitals run by the State and local authorities, the Church, the Red Cross and others.

The main change since the early 1960s has been the number of people covered by national social security schemes, which rose from 38 per cent of the population in 1960 to 56 per cent in 1967 and 83 per cent in 1972. A dramatic increase in numbers took place with the incorporation of agricultural workers into the social security network, albeit under a special scheme. Under the social security system, hospitals in towns are usually well equipped but elsewhere are often of poor quality or indeed non-existent. Services to rural districts are often lacking altogether. Under social security provisions a patient cannot expect to stay in hospital for non-surgical reasons.[28] Medical care under the scheme does not extend to dentistry or, for instance, to providing spectacles. Nor are all kinds of medicines covered by sickness insurance. Moreover the number of beds per person covered by the social security sickness insurance in 1968 was 1·05 beds per 1000 inhabitants and subsequent increases in social security coverage have not been matched by a corresponding growth in hospital accommodation.

This minimal figure would be less important if there were more co-ordination between the charitable hospitals and those under the social security scheme. The charitable hospitals and those run by the social security together provide about 3·9 beds per 1000 people. As it is, most beneficent institutions have taken the line that those who qualify for sickness insurance under social security schemes are not sufficiently poor to enable them to be admitted to a charitable hospital.

Those who are insured under the social security scheme, and by virtue of its limitations are unable to gain access to the social security hospitals on account of the nature of their illness, are therefore effectively barred access to any medical source, unless they can afford to pay a private clinic.[29]

The ratio of doctors to population in Spain was one to every 808 inhabitants in 1971, which is not dissimilar to ratios in other European countries. The national figures both for hospital beds and doctors cover wide regional discrepancies, however, and in Andalusia, Extremadura, New Castile, Galicia and Murcia the ratios are often very low.[30]

Since the beginning of the 1960s there has been no radical change in health services in Spain. Medical care has not been the subject of especial governmental interest and hospitals continue to run in most cases independently of one another. The greatest change has been the enlargement of the scope of social sickness insurance under social security schemes. A factor which has curbed the expansion of facilities available under the social security system has been the rapid increase in expenditure on pharmaceutical products. In 1973 these amounted to 44 per cent of all health benefits. Much hospital equipment outside private clinics is antiquated and the general attitude of the charitable hospitals is towards saving on expenditure rather than costly modernisation. Some improvement, however, could surely be gained from co-ordination of existing networks. Until this is undertaken Spanish medical care will continue to reflect the haphazard nature of its organisation.[31]

Housing in Spain has been subject to State intervention since 1917 when legislation was passed to promote cheap housing. Rent control was imposed in 1920 in large urban areas.[32] Before the Civil War, however, construction of housing by the State was negligible. Faced with the shortage of houses after the Civil War, the State was stimulated into more positive action and sponsored subsidised housing programmes through the Instituto Nacional de la Vivienda (created in 1939) and the Comisaria del Paro. A national housing plan was undertaken for the period 1956–60 and in 1957 a Ministry of Housing was set up. Under this plan an annual target of 110,000 houses was announced. While subsidised housing did not meet this annual quota, figures showed that substantially more houses were being built under the various schemes of official aid by the end of the plan than had been earlier in the 1950s.[33]

In 1961 an ambitious sixteen-year plan, divided into four-year periods, was announced. Initially the programme undertook to build nearly 4 million houses between 1961 and 1976. It soon became clear that the initial forecasts were not realistic. While the plan had slightly overestimated the overall growth in population, it had underestimated the growth in internal migration, which over the course of the 1960s was some seven times greater than had been anticipated. The unrealistic basis of some of the figures was clearly shown when in 1963 target migration figures for 1967 had already been superseded. In 1965, in conjunction with other deflationary measures, housing was subjected to severe restrictions. In 1966 the plan was revised and emerged with new investment targets in relation to the GNP and gross fixed capital formation. It is not possible to enter into exhaustive detail of the annual progress of the various parts of the housing plan. Looking at the period as a whole, however, it is possible to draw some general conclusions about housing and housing policy in Spain.

The increase in construction rates is shown in the figures available for new houses finished in various years.[34] In 1960, 144,000 new houses were built; by 1973, this had risen to 348,000. Over the 1960s the number of houses per 1000 inhabitants rose from 257 in 1960 to 280 in 1970.[35] While it is true, therefore, to say that the housing situation in Spain greatly improved in national terms, it would be wrong to assume that this was uniformly the case. Between 1960 and 1970 the housing situation[36] in many provinces in the regions of Andalusia, Extremadura and the Canaries in no way improved. In Barcelona and Madrid, both of which have been subjected to immense housing pressure as a result of migration, increases in housing have simply not kept pace with the growth in population, although the situation has been better in Madrid than Barcelona in this respect. Proof of the inadequacies of the housing situation in these two towns is the continued existence of the *chabolas* or *barracas*, the shanty towns. Moreover there is evidence that these shanty towns are growing rather than being absorbed into the life of the host towns. In Spain as a whole the housing situation was worse in 1967 than at the beginning of the decade in the following provinces : Alava, the Balearic Islands, Barcelona, Gerona, Pontevedra and Tarragona, and in a further ten provinces the situation was similar in 1967 to that of 1960.[37]

At the beginning of the 1960s the State acknowledged a responsibility to make various kinds of accommodation, whether rented or owned, accessible to the poorer members of society. State assistance is available in two ways : either loans and subsidies are made available to a 'promoter' (or property developer), or assistance is given to the private sector through the medium of various official bodies such as the Instituto Nacional de la Vivienda and the Banco de Crédito a la Construcción. The proportion of house-building totally financed by the State has always been very small in comparison with that which benefited partially from State assistance. As the 1960s progressed, there was a perceptible shift within public expenditure on social activities away from housing towards other activities such as education and transfers to social security. The OECD says :[38]

> In this last area [i.e. housing] the stimulus provided by the public sector grew progressively weaker, declining from 1·4 per cent of GNP in 1962 to 0·6 per cent in 1972, with the result that in spite of the decrease in the share of housing construction in gross fixed asset formation, central government expenditure covered only 21·3 per cent of this item in 1971 compared with 25·8 per cent in 1962.

The report goes on to say that 'the central government's withdrawal in this area was only partly offset by private initiative . . .' .

While the decline in government interest in housing has not been wholly compensated by the private sector, the growth in house-building financed by private interests has developed in spectacular fashion over the decade. At the beginning of the 1960s housing provided by the private sector accounted for less than 15 per cent of total new housing. By 1968–70 this proportion had risen to 42 per cent, although the Second Development Plan forecast only 12 per cent of new housing being provided by the private sector.[39] The government seems almost unintentionally to have restricted its ability to provide more houses, as a result of the continued application of the restrictive measures of 1965, when quotas were imposed on the number of government-sponsored houses to be built and various types of official financial aids, such as assistance from the Cajas de Ahorros, severely limited. Since 1965 this restrictive policy has been followed virtually unchanged up to the present day. It is therefore not surprising that the private sector should once more have played a prominent part in supplying new houses.

One of the difficulties in considering housing policies in Spain is the lack of detailed information. It is quite possible for instance, for the number of houses built to increase rapidly and yet impossible for considerable numbers, even increasing numbers, of families to find accommodation they can afford. Another problem is that mere overall figures give little clue to the standard of accommodation provided.

There is evidence, and especially in the cities, of luxury houses or flats being built and remaining empty for considerable periods while at the other end of the market there is a pressing need for flats and houses.[40] This is not, of course, a problem unique to Spain. What is perhaps unusual in the Spanish context is the way in which State-sponsored programmes, apparently designed to produce cheap housing, made it perfectly feasible for the 'promoter' of the scheme to receive financial aids without having in fact to provide cheap housing in return. This situation has arisen from the fact that despite measures introduced in 1972 to reverse the position the basis of assistance under State auspices is almost entirely geared to the needs of the 'promoter' and not to the ultimate buyer and that in practice there has been little pressure on the recipient of these benefits to adhere at all rigorously to producing accommodation at low prices. In so far as rented accommodation is concerned, the lack of control stems from half-hearted enforcement rather than deliberate policy.[41] This has resulted in a severe shortage of low-cost accommodation.

According to estimates based on the Encuesta de Presupuestos Familiares and on the assumption that not more than 20 per cent of family earnings are spent on housing in Madrid, well over half the population is inadequately housed in terms of amount of accommodation.[42] According to Santillana's estimates, Madrid and Andalusia are the worst off regions in Spain from the point of view of housing. Of course different assumptions will result in different estimates. But there seems little doubt that in Madrid and Barcelona much of the new accommodation is of poor quality. In order to cope with the flow of migrants from the countryside, high-rise buildings with little thought for planning, green spaces, or indeed adequate internal accommodation, have shot up in both cities. While appreciably better than in the shanty towns, conditions are cramped and amenities and attempts to create any communal nucleus are few and far between. Between 1958 and 1965 the average size of new housing units fell from 75·8 square metres to 63·9 square metres. The European average was 73·2 square metres in 1965.[43]

A factor which has militated against the easy provision of low-cost housing has been the very fast rise in the cost of land. In large cities the price of land doubled in the latter part of the 1960s. In the Second Plan mention is made of putting a halt to land speculation and in the Third Plan this is again brought up in conjunction with measures to make loans and subsidies available directly to the buyer rather than an intermediary. So far none of these declarations have resulted in action and indeed the 1956 law on land still remains to be implemented.[44] The rise in land prices and the sharp rise in the costs of construction have made house-building an expensive proposition, and also in the boom years of the economic cycle a profitable one. An adequate amount of low-cost housing is increasingly needed and has not been forthcoming from either the public or the private sector.

The general lack of long-term credit makes the acquisition of a house difficult. Moreover a very large initial down-payment is required as the first step towards acquisition of a house or an apartment. This has meant that those who do not possess sufficient capital to pay the initial payment cannot proceed with the purchase, even though their means may well be sufficient to cope with subsequent payments. This has in practice been a substantial barrier to a sizable proportion of potential purchasers and its effects are not restricted to the poorest sections of society. Banks play a fairly small rôle in the acquisition of a house : about 25 per cent of house ownership is made possible through bank loans. Official bodies in various guises provide the backing for approximately 30 per cent of house-purchasing loans and the Cajas de Ahorros a further 28 per cent. Factories provide another 11 per cent and the rest is financed by family and co-operative ventures. The Cajas de Ahorros are obliged by law to invest a certain proportion of their deposits in housing loans and over the 1960s the Cajas de Ahorros became progressively more important as a source of finance for buying a house.

Housing policy in Spain appears to have become a less pressing problem in the eyes of the government than it was in the early 1960s. In overall terms no doubt this is justified, but various factors make complacency look premature. The fact that the construction industry is, in Spain as in other countries, especially vulnerable to the upswings and downturns of economic cycles makes it an easy target for policies which may sometimes be at variance with designated objectives in housing policy. The reliance by the government on financing an intermediary rather than the ultimate buyer has led to a shortage of low-cost housing which is acutely needed in certain areas. Speculation in the 1960s also led, in the absence of enforceable standards, to a good deal of poor-quality housing, especially in the larger cities. The fact that the Housing Plan was thought of as parallel to the development plans rather than an integral part of them has meant that housing has been divorced from the overall considerations of the development plans. A noticeable gap in this respect is the lack of any special provision for housing in the development poles. Of the seven original poles, only in Valladolid and Zaragoza were houses built in the 1960s at a rate comparable to the growth in population and even there this appears to have been by chance rather than design. If one of the functions of the poles was to attract labour from the surrounding countryside, it seems an important oversight to have failed to provide accommodation and particularly accommodation at feasible prices.

The government may have decided that it is unwilling to transfer resources from other activities to housing. Even if this is so, it should be possible to ensure that more of the current government spending on low-cost housing is in fact used to that end. While the rate of house construction has risen rapidly, this has been at the cost of squeezing the poorer end of the market both in quality and quantity. It is misleading to take the improvement in overall figures as implying an improvement in housing at all levels.

While government expenditure on housing has declined in relative terms in the last decade, expenditure on education has risen. In 1962 expenditure on education was 1·2 per cent of GNP whereas ten years later, in 1972, it accounted for 2·2 per cent.[45] Education expenditure has also risen substantially in relation to the total of budget spending, rising from 9 per cent in 1962 to 19 per cent of total budget expenditure in 1976.

The overall state of education in Spain prior to the 1960s was un-impressive and a brief survey in the World Bank Mission Report on Spain shows clearly that education at all levels, from primary schools to university and professional training courses, left considerable scope for improvement.[46] At primary school level attendance was low and in some areas this was aggravated by the lack of school buildings as well as of teachers. Secondary education was not geared to the needs of an expanding modern economy calling for a diversity of skills. Higher education showed similar lacunae, in particular in the paucity of scientific facilities and the almost total absence of adult training schemes.[47] The strong bias towards centralism made it practically impossible before 1957 to obtain any higher technical training outside Madrid. The emphasis in the immediate post-war period was to spend money on the more esoteric branches of education rather than the mundane. The 1945–60 credits granted to the Consejo Superior de Investigaciones Científicas (CSIC), a body set up in 1939 to develop and organise research in Spain, were six times greater than expenditure on the building of primary schools.[48] Despite Spain being one of the first countries to establish compulsory primary education, in 1950 attendance at primary schools was just above 58 per cent, while at secondary school level it was probably only 8 per cent.[49]

Over the decade of the 1960s State expenditure not only increased in absolute terms but also rose in relation to private expenditure on education. In 1960 private expenditure accounted for 43 per cent of total expenditure on education, and only 29 per cent in 1968. The rise in public expenditure was accounted for mainly by central government expenditure as during this period local government expenditure declined. Spain was committed to the OEEC Mediterranean Regional Project and a conscious effort was made by the government to improve educational opportunities.[50] Increased expenditure resulted in tangible improvements. Attendance at secondary schools rose substantially (although admittedly from a very low base) and illiteracy dropped from over 11 per cent in 1960 to below 8 per cent of the population in 1970. In 1969, a white paper, the *Libro Blanco*, was published, which aimed at a thorough re-examination of the state of education in Spain and in 1970 a new education law was passed.

Despite increased expenditure, developments in the 1960s have not solved educational problems in Spain. At present the State runs approximately 70 per cent of primary schools at which attendance is in theory obligatory from six to thirteen. Despite a crash building programme started at the end of the 1950s, there are still no places for some ½ million children of this age group. This is in part due to the flow of internal migration to the large cities and the inability of the government to cope with increased numbers. At the beginning of the school year it is not unusual in the poorer parts of Madrid to see notices stating that the schools are full and can take no more pupils. In primary schools the classes are often very large; sometimes as many as seventy children are all taught together. Despite the chronic shortage of teachers and school buildings at primary level, the proportion of the Ministry of Education's budget devoted to primary education actually fell between 1961 and 1969. Currently it accounts for approximately one-half of the ministry's annual expenditure.

Secondary education has always been predominantly in private hands, especially those of the Church, although in the last few years the State has expanded its activities in this area. State facilities have traditionally been meagre,[51] and in 1960 over one-half of secondary schools were run by the Church and 90 per cent of secondary education was in private hands. This is not particularly surprising given that compulsory school attendance was only raised to thirteen years in 1965. Since the mid-1960s the State has claimed a larger proportion of secondary education and in 1972 accounted for 30 per cent of education at that level. Since 1960 there has been a massive increase in secondary education. In 1961 pupils totalled 474,057, but by 1971–2 the number had swelled to 1,323,060. As with other amenities in Spain, the question of where you live has a strong bearing on what facilities are available. Both primary and secondary education tend to be better in terms of quantity and quality in the north of Spain (with the exception of Galicia).[52] As far as secondary education is concerned, in 1967–8 in thirteen provinces less than 20 per cent of the population received any secondary education.[53] Despite the increased numbers in secondary education, the small proportion of those who actually complete the *bachillerato* is comparable to figures available for Portugal and Turkey and below, for example, Italy and Yugoslavia. In both primary and secondary education teachers have not increased in proportion to the child population. In universities, too, the ratio of teachers to pupils is poor.

Another feature of the Spanish education system is its lack of flexibility and the lack of opportunity until very recently for those who start in State primary schools, i.e. the majority, to acquire much secondary education or anything further.[54] Despite talk of scholarships, in practice there are very few. The 1966 Report on the Mediterranean

Regional Project commenting on the level of instruction of the active population stated that under 2 per cent completed higher studies; 3 per cent reached the middle level and 90 per cent *no conoce sino las cosas más elementales* – know only the most elementary facts.

The first two plans listed a number of targets, but without laying down any system of priorities except to say that situations 'of urgency' and projects related to development should be given precedence. The place of education in the Third Plan was to some extent overshadowed by the 1970 law on education and the Third Plan therefore placed less emphasis on the subject. The *Libro Blanco* of 1969 makes good reading. If its precepts were followed, then there would be a far greater range of opportunities available to many more children and indeed adults as well, as the *Libro Blanco* recognises the scanty provision for professional training.[55] Universities would be subject to wholesale reorganisation. However, both the *Libro Blanco* and the subsequent law on education in 1970[56] fail to provide any realistic approach to the problem of how the fundamental reform envisaged, the provision of eight years of compulsory but non-fee-paying education, is to be made financially viable. In the immediate aftermath of the 1970 law there was no noticeable upswing in budget expenditure on education and it is unlikely that any radical reform of the educational system will now precede a more general social change. The tendency to resist fundamental change is likely to grow in direct relation to uncertainty concerning Spain's political future.

Up to now reference has been made mainly to primary and secondary education. The likelihood of any root-and-branch reforms being applied to higher education, despite the strictures of the *Libro Blanco*, is equally remote. The universities, which are nearly all State-run, suffer from severe overcrowding, staff shortages and often sheer administrative confusion. This is due in large part to the very large expansion in number of university students since the end of the 1950s. In 1960 these numbered some 77,000. By 1972 there were 240,892 students and the number of university pupils per 100,000 inhabitants had risen from 253 to 708.[57] Wastage, which the World Bank Report pinpointed in 1963,[58] still continues and the overcrowding and inflexibility of teaching methods have meant that the universities have repeatedly been a focal point of unrest. University lecturers are without any job security for a number of years and at the same time so poorly paid that most are forced to take other jobs at the same time. The larger universities such as Madrid and Barcelona have been particularly prone to the demoralising effects of periodic riots and closures of faculties. This has led to an increase in private *colegios* which for a substantial fee teach the material necessary for the examinations set by the university, which in turn has had a further lowering effect on teaching morale within the universities as lecturers tend to find teaching in the *colegios* more lucrative than straight university teaching.

Until recently a serious gap in the Spanish educational system was the lack of facilities available for the training of scientists and engineers. Prior to 1957 the few existing centres for higher technical education were almost all in Madrid. With the setting up of institutions outside Madrid and the easing of entry conditions, this gap has to some extent been filled, if belatedly. In 1960–1 13,071 scientists enrolled in university and higher technical education courses. By 1969–70 this number had risen to over 30,000.[59] In 1966, however, the percentage of scientists and engineers as a proportion of total manpower was only 0·3, a figure considerably below France, Italy and Britain.[60] Figures for teachers in higher education were equally low. A field which has suffered particular neglect is the application of modern scientific and technical measures to agricultural conditions in Spain. This is clearly illustrated by the minimal growth experienced in the number of agricultural centres and in pupils per centre during the 1960s and early 1970s.

The lack of emphasis placed on training scientists and highly qualified technicians has resulted in a very low ratio of research and development in Spain in the 1960s, under 0·2 per cent of GNP, which is less than is spent in Malta, Turkey and Italy, let alone other West European countries.[61] While there has been a shortage of qualified personnel, other obstacles have arisen from the paucity of government funds available and the fragmented state of most of Spanish industry, which does not favour the creation of research and development units.[62]

While university and higher technical training establishments expanded very rapidly in the 1960s, the same cannot be said of the training institutes for less qualified workers and retraining schemes. A variety of organisations are involved in this type of work. Labour institutes and labour universities (which are dependent on the Ministry of Labour and financed by 'mutual labour' funds) exist side-by-side, often with duplication of costs and effort. The *sindicatos* provide the motive force for the bulk of this type of professional education, ranging from apprenticeship to retraining schemes. The main programmes are the Formación Profesional Industrial (FPI), Formación Profesional Acelerada (FPA) and Promoción Profesional Obrera (PPO). In 1971–2 the FPI had 159,005 pupils. The limiting factor on the FPI's programmes seems to be shortage of pupils rather than lack of funds. In 1964–5 one-third of the places available were not taken up.[63]

While the FPI provides a basic training, the other two syndical programmes are intensive and designed to produce quick results. It is possible to criticise these programmes for attempting to force too much in too short a time. Part of the difficulty, however, lies with the Spanish business world, which does little to co-operate. Workers are expected to go in their spare time, which is in any case minimal, and no effort seems to be made to encourage attendance at intensive programmes. In 1970 the law on education brought togther the institutes dependent on the Ministry of Labour and the *sindicatos* within the orbit of the Ministry of Education and Science. However, while this represents a step towards greater co-ordination, a total synthesis has not yet been achieved, since the bodies connected with the Ministries of Commerce and Information and Tourism have not been placed under the Ministry of Education. This type of training has become especially important in Spain following the waves of migrants to the cities and the large numbers of barely qualified workers who have been in need of a basic training to be productively employed in Spanish industry. While it is not surprising that the construction industry is usually the first resort of those fresh from the land, it is disturbing that it often remains the only outlet.

In this chapter it has been possible to look only in the most perfunctory manner at some aspects of living conditions in Spain in the 1960s and early 1970s. It may be felt that the overall tone is unnecessarily critical. After all, given the very low living standards of the majority of Spaniards in the 1940s and 1950s, improvements in conditions have been enormous. A point that is sometimes overlooked, however, is that, while there have been many changes and an overall marked improvement both in actual living standards and in opportunities available, which would have been inconceivable even twenty years ago, the Spanish 'miracle' has not brought about a wholesale transformation.

Certainly it would be naïve to expect that a country undergoing so many economic and social stresses could at the same time react positively on all issues. The flight from the countryside has, in particular, created grave problems in the big cities. Nevertheless, it should be remembered that the general rise in the standard of living still covers considerable areas of poverty both rural and urban. Despite the government's emphasis on regional developments, parts of Old Castile, Andalusia and Galicia are still living in traditional poverty. Moreover, while housing, education and health policies have all been given unprecedented attention since the end of the 1950s, the lack of flexibility in approach and especially the lack of effective priorities in planning have meant that changes have failed to keep pace with needs. While opportunities are greater than in previous decades and more money can be earned by more people in an urban context, which in itself ensures a certain variety of employment, the present structure of education does little to facilitate the transformation from unskilled to skilled labour. Moreover, the prevalence of moonlighting at all levels of society indicates that economic pressures are still strong. Life is still hard for many Spaniards.

# 6 Banking and Credit

Banking in Spain is an emotive topic. The very close links which exist between industry and the banks have given the banks a powerful position in the economy and one which has not always attracted favourable comment.[1]

The earliest precursors to banks in Spain can be found in the fifteenth century with the establishment of the Taula de Canvi in Barcelona in 1401 and the Taula de Canvis o Dipòsits de la Ciutat de València in 1407. In 1782 the Banco de San Carlos was founded and eventually, through various transformations, became the Bank of Spain. In 1844 the first modern commercial Spanish bank was founded in Barcelona. This was followed by the Banco de Bilbao (1857), the Banco Hispano-Colonial (1876) and Crédito y Docks (1883). The colonial wars temporarily brought expansion of banking business to a halt. This was followed, however, by a new outburst of activity in part due to the repatriation of capital around the turn of the century, which brought about the establishment of new banks including the Banco Hispano Americano and the Banco de Vizcaya in 1901; the Banco Español de Crédito followed in 1902. The fall in the flow of foreign investment to Spain caused by the outbreak of the First World War resulted in a strengthening of the position of Spanish banks. In 1922 there were ninety-three banks compared with thirty-two at the beginning of the century.[2] Given the minimal rôle of the Spanish stock market, such savings as there were went mainly to bank and savings bank accounts and banks began to invest heavily in industry, either directly by buying shares in companies or through lending operations. This led to a position in which a lending bank would be inextricably bound up with a whole range of companies, the latter often heavily dependent on the banks. Ties were cemented not only by financial obligations and the holding of shares but also by bank directors having seats on many of their client companies' boards. As the law on Credit and Banking of 1962 pointed out, the way in which commercial banking in Spain had developed meant that not only did commercial banks constitute the chief means of financing, but they were rapidly becoming the sole source, virtually superseding the capital market. Between 1920–35 commercial banks provided about 30 per cent of the financing of the private sector; in 1940–59 they provided 60 per cent. A law on Ordenación Bancaria passed in 1921 was, despite its name, more concerned with fiduciary circulation and the relations of the commercial banking sector with the Bank of Spain than in laying down any general guidelines for banking operations. The law made it compulsory to enter any new bank in the newly created Comisaria y Consejo Superior Bancario and also created banking zones.

After the Civil War, in 1940, it was decreed that banks could not issue a cash dividend of more than 6 per cent. This is still operative, although ways and means of contravening the spirit of the prohibition have evolved over the period; in particular shareholders expect regular rights issues at par (in practice, well below market value). In 1946 a further law on Ordenación Bancaria affirmed the government's rôle in controlling commercial banking activity. Maximum and minimum rates of interest were fixed, and control was extended over the scale of lending operations. Quantitative and qualitative controls were exercised under the joint supervision of the Bank of Spain and the Consejo Superior Bancario in accordance with instructions from the Treasury. After 1936 it was practically impossible to obtain permission to open a new bank and this led to a substantial expansion of activity by existing banks. Between 1946 and 1957 the capital and reserves of the six largest banks (Banesto, Bilbao, Central, Hispano, Urquijo and Vizcaya) increased from Ptas 1998 million to Ptas 7046 million. During the same period deposits increased from Ptas 22,295 million to Ptas 109,011 million.[3] This expansion was greatly facilitated by long-term debt issued by the government in the form of long-term securities which could be automatically discounted with the Bank of Spain, and of which a very large part was held by the commercial banking sector. At the end of 1960 Ptas 90 billion of the public debt was outstanding and the greater part was held by the commercial banks.[4] This constituted a serious inflationary element in the economy.

REFORM AND THE COMMERCIAL AND INDUSTRIAL BANKS

In 1962 a comprehensive law, or *Ley de Bases*, on credit and banking set the tone for developments in banking and credit facilities in the 1960s.[5] Despite some initial scepticism it was generally thought in the first instance to reflect the new 'liberalisation' ethos of the Stabilisation Plan of 1959. As the 1960s progressed, however, many of the changes wrought by the 1962 law seemed more of form than substance and in many areas liberalisation could only be interpreted as a strengthening of government intervention, at least until the Matesa scandal prompted new legislation.

Under the 1962 law the Bank of Spain was nationalised, although this made little difference to the day-to-day activities of the bank. Control of financial policy was centred in three bodies : the Bank of Spain which supervised the commercial banks, the Instituto de Crédito de las Cajas de Ahorros (ICCA) to control the savings banks, and the Instituto de Crédito a Medio y Largo Plazo (ICMLP), which was to co-ordinate and control the affairs and operations of the official credit institutions. These bodies were united in the person of the Governor of the Bank of Spain who was president of all three. It was made clear, however, that 'authority' in monetary and credit matters lay with the government. The Bank of Spain was expected to follow the directives of the Treasury. The ICMLP operated practically as part of the Treasury, while the ICCA had little independent control over developments in the Cajas de Ahorros.

The official credit banks were also nationalised and were made directly dependent upon Treasury disbursements, which constituted the main source of finance. An annual ceiling on amounts of credit available for any particular sector was decided at ministerial level and this was subsequently implemented with modifications by the Treasury.

Apart from the creation of the ICCA, which had little direct effect on the development of the Cajas de Ahorros, the savings banks were encouraged to invest in certain activities which combined social and economic objectives, for example the construction of low-cost 'protected' housing, and percentages were laid down specifying the distribution of resources. In 1964 the Cajas were required by the government to invest 50 per cent of their resources in 'public funds',[6] i.e. either public sector debt or the debt of firms from time to time especially designated – see description below of 'privileged circuits'. The 1962 law also made reference to the capital market. The expected ruling (*Reglamento*) did not follow until 1967,[7] but the law made possible the creation of new types of financial bodies such as unit trusts which flourished in Spain in the late 1960s.

It was the commercial banking sector, however, which appeared to be most directly affected by the 1962 law. In particular, two aspects of the law had an immediate impact. First, the banks were forced to split into two groups : commercial banks and industrial banks. The former were to limit themselves to everyday payments and transactions and could provide credit only up to eighteen months; the industrial banks were expected to promote new industrial concerns (for which they obtained substantial fiscal benefits) and to finance medium- and long-term investment. Only industrial banks might accept time deposits of more than two years. Second, the banking *status quo* was modified and in theory at least the banking world was made more accessible to newcomers. The 1962 reform also enabled the authorities to prescribe various banking coefficients, which are referred to later in the chapter.[8]

The evolution of the banking sector in the 1960s does not suggest that the liberalising intent behind the 1962 law was in practice very influential. The conditions which had to be fulfilled in order to open a new bank proved to be so exacting that the number of new banks to appear was very small. Even when plans for the opening of a new bank satisfied the regulatory requirements, final authority on the decision rested with the Treasury. A new bank was permitted to open new branches only after a certain time had elapsed and plans had to pass through a complicated mechanism consisting of three stages designed to favour small banks. In reality the balance between banks has altered very little and the large banks continue to gain at the expense of the smaller. In some cases the larger banks have found it easier to acquire smaller competitors than to contend with the restrictions.[9] While few new banks opened in the 1960s, the number of outlets rose in a spectacular way, especially after 1963. Between 1950 and 1960 branches and agencies rose from 2228 to 2699 and by 1970 had risen to 4294. In August 1974 legislation on opening new branches was relaxed and in 1975, 1965 new branches were opened, bringing the total to over 7000. The new legislation of 1962 seems to have had little effect in altering the pattern of evolution of Spanish banking. The limited opportunities available to new banks has merely reinforced the dominant position of the 'Big Seven'.

Another feature of Spanish banking in the 1960s which developed in a spirit contrary to the 1962 legislation was the increasing lack of convincing differentiation between the commercial and industrial banks. In 1962 when existing banks were faced with the choice of opting for one or other category, only one chose industrial bank status.[10] The remaining fifteen industrial banks which came into existence during the 1960s were all new entities although ten had powerful connections with existing commercial banks. The stipulated objectives of the new industrial banks were to promote new companies and to provide medium- and long-term credit. On the whole the industrial banks have shown more interest in the latter activity. Nevertheless, the percentage of loans of over three years' duration accounted for only 43 per cent of total loans by industrial banks in 1969. Moreover the distribution of loans shows a wide spread over many small companies, which is not what was intended by the 1962 law. The distinction between the two types of bank was further whittled away by the decision of the government in 1973 to allow commercial banks to accept deposits of more than two years' duration and to pay interest on them. Moreover, in

August 1974, commercial and deposit banks were allowed to issue deposit certificates, a concession previously limited to the industrial banks. The distinction between the two types of bank was formally abolished in August 1974. By the end of 1974 the capital and reserves of the eighteen industrial banks represented 22 per cent of the total and deposits accounted for 13 per cent of total bank deposits.

Table 6.1 shows the relative sizes of the different types of bank in 1974. This table shows the overwhelming dominance of the national over local banks and also the very small number of foreign banks allowed to do business in Spain. In 1975 the Banco Arabe-Español

TABLE 6.1   Distribution of capital and reserves and deposits between various types of bank, 1974

| Banks | No of banks | No of branches | Deposits (Ptas billion) | Capital and reserves (Ptas billion) |
|---|---|---|---|---|
| National | 18 | 4163 | 1776 | 126 |
| Regional | 12 | 672 | 117 | 15 |
| Local | 56 | 472 | 157 | 16 |
| Foreign | 4 | 23 | 19 | 0·9 |
| Industrial | 18 | 108 | 324 | 44·7 |

Source: Economist Intelligence Unit, *Quarterly Economic Review*, No 4 (London: 1974).

was the first foreign bank to be allowed to set up in Spain since the Civil War and was permitted to do so by special ministerial decree. Since Spanish banks are now expanding business and branches abroad, there is increasing pressure from foreign banks to be allowed to operate in Spain. This could at present, in view of existing legislation, only be permitted by special dispensation. The largest seven commercial banks have controlled some 70 per cent of total assets in the commercial banking sector since the early 1960s. The position of the 'Big Seven' has altered little, although the proportion of loans provided by the largest banks has increased. Since the mid-1960s bank deposits have grown rapidly. In 1964 bank deposits amounted to Ptas 468 billion; by 1974 they totalled Ptas 2393 billion. Sight deposits dropped from 48 per cent of total deposits in 1964 to 39 per cent in 1974. In the 1960s the percentage of total deposits invested in public funds (36 per cent in 1956) fell from 26 per cent to 19 per cent. This disguises a sharp decline in the early 1960s following the end of automatic discount facilities which the banks had hitherto enjoyed with the Bank of Spain and a subsequent increase in public funds held by the banks, both in absolute and relative terms, following pressure on the banks to increase their holdings of such funds. (The pattern of lending in the early 1970s is shown in Table 6.2.)

TABLE 6.2    Credit institutions; distribution of funds to the private and public sector, 1972–5
(Ptas billion)

|  | 1972 | 1973 | 1974 | 1975 |
|---|---|---|---|---|
| Bank of Spain | 56·8 | 118·0 | 60·9 | 112·6 |
| Central reserves | 93·1 | 77·8 | −42·6 | −8·1 |
| Public sector (credit) | −22·0 | 23·8 | 78·9 | 96·3 |
| Other accounts | −14·3 | 16·4 | 24·6 | 24·4 |
|  |  |  |  |  |
| Commercial Banks | 345·5 | 458·1 | 551·3 | 636·4 |
| Public sector | 29·2 | 11·3 | 28·8 | 47·2 |
| Private sector | 312·1 | 412·0 | 495·4 | 548·7 |
| Other banks | 4·2 | 34·8 | 27·1 | 40·5 |
|  |  |  |  |  |
| Industrial Banks | 75·8 | 123·6 | 106·9 | 124·0 |
| Public sector | 1·0 | 1·6 | — | 7·1 |
| Private sector | 66·5 | 117·2 | 107·3 | 111·6 |
| Other banks | 8·3 | 4·8 | −0·4 | 5·3 |
|  |  |  |  |  |
| Savings Banks | 142·7 | 186·6 | 193·1 | 247·9 |
| Public sector | 27·7 | 18·9 | −9·8 | 8·8 |
| Private sector | 115·0 | 167·7 | 202·9 | 239·1 |
|  |  |  |  |  |
| Official Credit Institutions | 19·5 | 26·0 | 52·3 | 77·6 |
| Public sector | 8·9 | 9·4 | 14·2 | 19·1 |
| Private sector | −0·9 | 16·2 | 37·4 | 59·3 |
| Other | 11·5 | 0·4 | 0·7 | −0·8 |
| Total | 640·3 | 912·3 | 964·5 | 1,198·5 |

Source: Bank of Spain, *Informe Anual 1975* (Madrid) p. 217.

THE SAVINGS BANKS

While the restrictions on entry into the banking world have strengthened the position of existing banks, the growth of the Cajas de Ahorros (savings banks) in recent years has demonstrated that the position of the banks, while privileged, is not inviolate and the growth of the savings banks has begun to cause the banks some unease. The earliest antecedents of the savings banks date from the Middle Ages but the beginnings of the savings banks in their present guise are to be found in the nineteenth century. The origins of the savings banks as charitable institutions of the Church designed to provide money for the needy at low interest rates has influenced the development of these banks which still have a bias towards promoting activities on grounds of social benefit rather than on strictly economic criteria. While savings banks at the end of the nineteenth century and the beginning of the twentieth century developed often along individualistic lines, decrees passed in the 1920s and 1930s went far towards producing a unified pattern of development.[11] In particular the law of 1933 which approved the statutes of the Instituto de Crédito de las Cajas Generales de Ahorro Popular.

The banking law of 1962, while it concentrated primarily on commercial banking and official credit institutions, also affected the development of the savings banks in two main ways. First, the Instituto de Crédito de las Cajas Generales de Ahorro Popular was given more authority over the individual savings banks. At the same time the Institute was more closely tied to central financial policy by making the Governor of the Bank of Spain *ex officio* president of the Institute.[12] In 1971 the Institute was relieved of its responsibilities and its duties were taken over by the Bank of Spain.[13] Second, the field of operations open to the savings banks was expanded, specifically towards loans with 'social objectives' (*fines sociales*) for small-scale farmers and artisans and more generally towards the agricultural sector. These objectives were made more explicit in 1964. First the percentage of deposits which savings banks were compelled to invest in 'public funds' was lowered to 50 per cent. (In 1967 this was lowered further to 45 per cent and in 1973 to 40 per cent.) Loans towards the building of 'protected' housing were to represent 7 per cent of deposits, and loans of a 'social benefit' nature to small-scale farmers, craftsmen, fishermen and for co-operative ventures 17 per cent. Six per cent of deposits were to be used to enable small savers to acquire possession of their houses. In 1967 it was laid down that of the 17 percentage points allocated to 'social benefit' loans, 10 were to be directed towards agriculture.

The savings banks operate under a severely regulated régime. Forty per cent of their deposits must be invested in public funds, 13 per cent goes towards loans of a non-economic nature to agricultural entrepreneurs, 9 per cent of similar loans to small industrial and fishing concerns, 7 per cent towards financing cheap housing and 6 per cent to individuals, particularly farmers who wish to own their own land or become self-employed, which in total means that over 70 per cent of the savings banks' resources are deployed according to government regulations. As a further 10 per cent has to remain liquid, under 20 per cent is effectively free for use at the discretion of the savings banks themselves.

Despite this high degree of government control, the evolution of the savings banks in the 1960s was not as closely allied to the stipulated objectives as might be assumed. Some specified obligations were met. For instance, one-half of the annual surplus of the savings banks was set aside for welfare work such as facilities for handicapped children, homes for old age pensioners and professional training.[14] On the other hand, loans to agricultural projects, which enjoy a preferential position in the official sectoral allocation of loans, rose by under 2 per cent between 1965 and 1969, accounting for nearly 21 per cent in 1969, while loans to industry increased from 12 per cent to 23 per cent over the same period.[15] During the second part of the 1960s housing loans continued to represent a very substantial part of all loans although the percentage fell from 53 per cent in 1965 to 44 per cent in 1969. One result of the regulation of investments has been the channelling of savings banks funds in considerable quantities to industrial concerns. Originally the 'public funds' coefficient was amply covered by INI issues. These, however, became insufficient and the savings banks were authorised to count purchases of bond issues of certain private companies towards meeting the 'public funds' coefficient and one-half to two-thirds of bond issues are now taken up annually by the Cajas de Ahorros. This means not only that the savings banks are necessarily lending an increasing amount to industry but also to the larger firms which are in a position to issue bonds. This goes against the stated philosophy of channelling funds primarily towards small and medium-sized firms. The savings banks are now in a position of providing finance for the largest firms, through buying up bond issues, and also for the smallest, which can make use of loans with a 'social' content. Credit forthcoming for small-scale enterprises is, however, limited by the meagre amounts available overall and this is further restricted by the low maximum limit of a loan which can be made to industry.[16]

While the savings banks may not have developed in the way that was envisaged by the 1962 law, their activities have expanded considerably since the beginning of the 1960s. In the 1960s, deposits of the savings banks were equal to 2·68 per cent of national income. By the end of 1972 they equalled 5·86 per cent. In 1962 deposits in the Cajas de Ahorros represented 27 per cent of total deposits in banks and savings banks and 31 per cent in 1974. Despite low rates of interest on deposit accounts, consequent on the fact that most savings bank loans are made at interest rates fixed by the government and below commercial bank rates, small savers continue to be attracted to the savings banks. It is noteworthy that this has taken place over a period of continued inflation. Part of the attraction lies in the 'welfare benefits', for example, obtaining a loan for low-cost housing, which is not available from commercial banks, and other fringe benefits derived from the annual surplus mentioned above. To some there is also the psychological attraction of putting one's money in a non-profit-making organisation. Much of the growth, however, may be put down to the fact that until 1975 the savings banks had many more local branches than the commercial banks. In 1973, the eighty-seven savings banks were represented by over 6000 branch offices (compared with 4924 commercial bank offices). With the relaxation of restrictions on opening new bank branches in 1974, this situation has for the time being been reversed. Unlike the banks, the savings banks have been subject to few government restrictions on expansion and they were therefore able to make the most of the growing number of small savers in the 1960s. Related to the smaller number of bank branches has been a corresponding dearth of information on the comparative terms obtainable from different financial institutions. To many small savers the banks are not even considered as a financial alternative. A savings bank is the 'natural' place to go.

The savings banks have also benefited by being to some extent exempt from the periodic restrictions on lending which have hampered the banks' activities. If the savings banks continue to expand at a comparable rate, they will probably face heavier restrictions in line with the banks.[17] On the other hand, the savings banks are not able to compete with the commercial banks in discounting customers' bills of exchange. Nor until 1971 were the savings banks able to extend credit for exports.

The savings banks represent a curious amalgam of interests and intentions. In theory their chief aim is to finance small entrepreneurs and objectives which are deemed socially desirable. In practice, while this has to some extent been realised, the savings banks have become increasingly important as buyers of industrial bonds, so much so in fact that there is evidence that the price of bonds is in some cases determined by the savings banks. Deposits in savings banks come mainly from the less well-off members of the rural community. A very substantial part of these funds is lent at rates well below the market rate to certain industrial companies which form part of the so-called 'privileged circuits' and whose bonds count in effect as 'public funds'. An irony of this situation is that such companies are often owned by the savings banks' chief competitors, the commercial banks.[18] A further anomaly is that, while the percentages of deposits to be deployed for particular purposes are laid down presumably to fulfil government aims in these fields, these have been applied indiscriminately in all regions of Spain. They have not necessarily produced investment where it is most needed. It also tends to mean that funds are redistributed to the richer industrialised regions, rather than the poorer ones.

OFFICIAL CREDIT INSTITUTIONS

The official credit institutions have been the other important source of external finance for firms. Before the 1958 law,[19] there was no connection between the different official credit agencies. With the creation of the Instituto de Crédito a Medio y Largo Plazo in 1962, the official credit banks, namely, the Banco de Crédito Agrícola, Banco de Crédito Industrial, Banco de Crédito Local, Banco de Crédito a la Construcción and the Banco Hipotecario de España, were nationalised[20] and 99 per cent of their resources between 1959 and 1969 were supplied by the Treasury, which raised the money by *cédulas de inversión*. These investment bonds are bought either voluntarily by industry or by obligatory subscription from commercial banks and the savings banks. Most of the funds thus raised from the private sector (by way of the Treasury and the Institute of Official Credit)[21] are used by the official credit institutions to finance the private sector (some 76 per cent of funds in 1975). Only the Banco de Crédito Local and the Banco de Crédito a la Construcción deal regularly (the latter almost exclusively) with public sector activities. The function of official credit was explicitly referred to in the First Plan, where it was specified that official credit was to be used to service the private sector 'in default of other sources of finance'. Beyond this, however, there was no clarification of how this was to be achieved and, while official credit grew by leaps and bounds during the 1960s, it is difficult to discern the criteria by which it was allocated. A wide range of sectors and projects was assisted, some of which were viable and others not. Some projects financed were new, while others were simply existing ones taken over by the official institutions from the commercial banks.

An area which experienced especial growth was export credit, which absorbed 0·7 per cent of total credit provided by the official credit institutions in 1964, 8 per cent in 1970 and 20 per cent in 1975. By 1968 approximately one-half of all export credit came from the official credit institutions. Credit to industry represented 13·7 per cent of all official credit in 1964 and 22 per cent in 1970, falling to 19 per cent in 1975.[22] Industrial projects which were particularly favoured were those included in *acción concertada* and the development poles. Official credit to agriculture remained relatively stable at 13 per cent of total official credit provided in 1964, 16 per cent in 1970 and 15 per cent in 1975. In relative terms loans to housing and shipbuilding, which constituted the most important sectors in 1964, later both lost ground.[23] Loans authorised by all official credit bodies increased from Ptas 45,263 billion in 1964 to Ptas 99,869 billion in 1975. In the 1960s the Banco de Crédito Industrial and the Banco de Crédito a la Construcción experienced the greatest expansion.

The rapid increase in the level of official credit disbursements in the 1960s brought to light the ambivalent rôle played by the official credit bodies in the overall provision of credit, especially in relation to authorisations for the private sector. This stemmed from two causes. First, the lack of any substantive guidelines as to what criteria were to be used in assessing projects for the allocation of official credit and, second, the attractive terms of public credit brought in projects which could well have been dealt with by the private sector. Interest rates and conditions compared very favourably with private-sector terms and there was a considerable variety in terms offered by the various official banks.[24] Thus official funds were often diverted from those more in need of beneficial terms, and the original purpose of supplying *supplementary* finance to the private sector tended to be forgotten. These problems were compounded by the fact that official credit activities were not limited to long- and medium-term activities which would have provided some differentiation from the commercial banks at least until 1969.

The official credit institutions during the 1960s were subject to detailed supervision from the government in so far as terms and conditions of loans were concerned. All operations were minutely scrutinised by the authorities and this led to notorious slowness in dealing with applications. The bureaucratic insistence on detail did not however add up to effective control over the use of funds, and the Matesa scandal in 1969, in which it emerged that funds of the Banco de Crédito Industrial had been misappropriated on a large scale, led to a new law on official credit in 1971.[25] Under the new law the ICMLP was disbanded and its dealings with commercial banks and credit institutions (*entidades crediticias*) were taken over by the Bank of Spain, while the Treasury took over the ICLMP's former activities in the stock market and long-term capital market. An Instituto de Crédito Official was established to deal with matters directly affecting the official credit banks. The official banks themselves were made into limited companies entirely financed by public funds. Henceforward each application was to be considered individually on its own merits (rather than as before when projects were often accepted by virtue of belonging to a particular category of activity, if not sometimes more simply for reasons of *enchufe*, or knowing the right person). Projects were now expected to be economically viable except in cases expressly specified by the government. While the official bodies were to show a little more independence in assessing individual projects, the mechanism of financing public credit and allocation of credit between sectors continued to lie with the government, as did the fixing of interest rates which were kept at levels well below the market rate.[26] Under the new law special rediscount lines were brought to an end and official export credit was placed entirely under the control of the Banco Exterior.

The law of 1971 tightened up the *ambiente* in which official credit is made available, but it has not resolved the question of what the rôle of official credit is supposed to be in relation to credit from private sources. The 1971 law states that official credit is to be 'complementary' in rôle to other financial institutions. Unless clear criteria emerge by which projects are to be judged, or particular sectors are deemed especially in need of official credit, it is difficult to see how the situation is substantially different from that of the 1960s.[27]

Since the early 1960s, the Spanish government has been eager for investment opportunities to be met. To this end a policy of 'privileged circuits' and cheap interest rates has been maintained. Part of the mechanism of the privileged circuits has been referred to above in relation to the savings banks. The savings banks are required to put a high proportion of their deposits (50 per cent in the early 1960s, 40 per cent since 1973) in government securities or in bonds of companies which are considered of 'fundamental importance'. Since government bond issues have not been sufficient to meet the 40 per cent requirement, the savings banks have become increasingly important as buyers of new bond issues, in certain years taking up some three-quarters of all new private bond issues. The commercial and industrial banks are also required to invest a fixed proportion of their deposits in public debt and various forms of medium-term credit. The destination and type of credit will vary according to shifts in government priorities. An investment coefficient for the banks was set up in 1971 and replaced the public funds coefficient established in the 1962 *Ley de Bases* and also the special rediscount lines (referred to in Chapter 3). The investment coefficient was placed at 22 per cent in 1971, of which 15 per cent was destined for investment in public debt. In February 1975, the investment coefficient was raised to 23 per cent and in March 1976 to 25 per cent.[28] Of this 13 per cent is made up of credit to the Treasury and the remainder of special credits which go mainly towards shipbuilding, the purchase of capital goods and exports. The coefficient for the industrial banks is somewhat smaller.[29] Funds for the privileged circuits are also provided by the stock market and contractual savings organisations.

Those who have access to these funds are 'privileged' on two counts.

They can borrow at rates considerably below the market rate and often on a longer-term basis. Moreover, those within the circuit know that they will not be short of funds.

There are four main ways in which the circuit works. First, the savings banks buy private bonds to make up their 40 per cent investment quota. Second, bonds issued by the Instituto Nacional de Industria (INI) are automatically taken up by the savings banks. Third, through the obligatory sectoral allocations, for example in housing, which are laid down for investment by the savings banks. Fourth, since 1969, government issues of certificates of deposit are bought by the banks and the proceeds are then passed on to the official credit institutions.

The most direct way into the circuit for borrowers is to obtain credit from one of the six official credit institutions. Rates of interest charged on loans from these bodies are far lower than market rates available in the private sector. In order for a private company to obtain entry into the circuit through bond issues, the proposed issue must qualify as 'privileged' in the eyes of the General Directorate of Financial Policy. In the event of an application being refused, a company will probably have considerable difficulty in placing an issue, since private buyers are few in number and up to 90 per cent of new bond issues may be placed through the privileged circuit. In practice, it is usually the smaller companies whose issues fail to qualify for 'privileged' status. The automatic subscription to INI bonds by the savings banks seems increasingly difficult to justify, since INI activities are no longer confined, even in theory, to projects not considered viable by the private sector. It has been estimated that between 1966 and 1969 some 45 per cent of total borrowing by the non-financial sector from the various financial institutions was accounted for by the use of the privileged circuit.[30] While this diminished slightly in the early 1970s,[31] there are signs that the privileged circuits will gain in importance in the latter years of the 1970s.

INTEREST RATES AND THE AVAILABILITY OF CREDIT

The availability and terms of credit are of especial importance in Spain given the extremely low level of self-financing in most companies – under 40 per cent among the top 100 Spanish companies in 1973. Although reliable statistics are few and far between, calculations suggest that figures are considerably lower in the majority of companies. In 1975 share and bond issues accounted for just under 20 per cent of capital raised from external sources for the private sector. The banks constituted the most important source of external funds, supplying some 58 per cent, while the savings banks contributed nearly 14 per cent. While the privileged circuits were characterised by especially low rates of interest, interest rates in general were kept low until the end of the 1960s. Interest rates were not regarded as short-term monetary policy instruments but as a device to encourage investment. All interest rates were fixed and strictly regulated by the government. The rules governing rates on different types of operation were both comprehensive and complicated. In 1969 interest rates were linked to the Bank of Spain's rediscount rate by fixed differentials (with the exception of sight deposits). Some activities of minor importance were completely freed from official intervention. Commercial banks were allowed greater freedom in fixing rates for long-term loans and industrial banks greater flexibility in paying interest on deposits of over two years. Short-term lending rates were fixed by a 'ceiling' rate instead of the earlier minimum rate.[32] In principle the interest rate structure was simplified and made more flexible. The immediate effect was to raise interest rates.

Another characteristic of financing in the 1960s was the heavy dependence of industry on short-term loans and bills of exchange; approximately one-quarter of all borrowing was of this nature. This of course covers wide discrepancies and the construction industry, for example, has at times been financed by up to 90 per cent in short-term loans. As the official credit institutions and the savings banks are primarily concerned with long-term loans, short-term borrowing is mostly provided by the banks, whose lending practices have continued to be short-term and have seemingly been uninfluenced by the tendency for the term of deposits to lengthen.

These three factors, i.e. the 'privileged circuits', low interest rates and the predominance of short-term loans characterised borrowing by the private sector in the greater part of the 1960s. All were modified to some extent at the end of the decade. Revision of the structure of interest rates in 1969 and the reform of the official credit system led to a reduction in the differential in interest rates between 'normal' and 'privileged' borrowing.

In practice conditions of lending in the early 1970s were not markedly different from the 1960s. Despite a temporary reduction of 'privileged circuit' lending, a large proportion of credit to the private sector is still provided in this way. Similarly, despite the reforms in interest rate structure, interest rates still fail by and large to reflect market forces, as they are not changed with sufficient frequency. Interest rates are still kept low on any international comparison. Moreover, there is less flexibility than might have been expected in individual rates, since 'ceiling rates' have usually been adopted as *the* rate. To compensate for the lack of elasticity, a black market in money has evolved with the banks themselves paying and charging 'illegally' high rates for deposits and loans. This pushes up the cost of borrowing and small borrowers in particular tend to be adversely affected. The banks, however, are not necessarily in favour of a complete relaxation of controls on interest rates, since profit margins arising from lending and borrowing rates would be severely diminished.

The combination of these factors means that currently, as in the 1960s, the lack of adequate supplies of long-term credit remains the chief deficiency in the financial structure. Another constant feature is the disadvantageous position of the small and medium-sized firm. The smaller firms are unlikely to have access to the 'privileged circuits' either by issuing bonds which are deemed 'acceptable', or by having ready access to borrowing from the credit institutions. This latter problem is accentuated by the small number of local representatives of official credit institutions. The medium-sized and small firms are thus placed in an especially poor position to obtain medium- and long-term finance and this has two consequences. First, they are forced to rely almost entirely on short-term loans, which makes the smaller customers particularly vulnerable when squeezes on credit occur. Those who depend on short-term loans are the first to suffer from being required to pay 'black market' rates of interest.[33] While in any country it is the larger firms which are most likely to obtain long-term finance and on favourable terms, the problems faced by the smaller firms are often more acute in Spain because of the overall deficiency in long-term funds.

The mechanics of borrowing by small provincial firms are also complicated by the constant absorption of local banks by the national ones which tend to be geared in outlook and location to the needs of the larger firms. Second, the dependence on short-term borrowing has forged a sometimes burdensome link between the banks and many of the smaller companies. In order to survive through periods of tight credit when sources of short-term finance may, after becoming more expensive, actually dry up, small businesses have often given a seat on the board to a bank as well as share participation in the company, which effectively often means that, in order to ensure a flow of credit, the bank concerned must be allowed a free hand in the company's affairs. While no director of a commercial bank is now supposed to hold directorships in more than eight private companies, this is not strictly adhered to.

The extent to which so many firms depend upon the banks and are obliged to allow themselves to be in the last resort under their control in matters not only strictly related to finance is perhaps the feature which is mainly responsible for the widespread belief that it is the banks which control the course of economic and certainly industrial development in

Spain. It also colours popular reaction to the growing concentration of power within a few very large banks and the corresponding disappearance of small local banks geared to local conditions. While it is impossible to determine the extent of the banks' influence on the industrial sector with any precision, it is generally believed that through a variety of ways, ranging from majority ownership downwards, the banks own in the region of 40–50 per cent of industry. Some firms prefer to remain outside the aegis of the banks, but unless they are large this usually means that their growth depends entirely on self-generated funds. As seen in Chapter 3, the number of small and medium-sized firms is very great. In the Third Plan the government appears to have decided that it would be wise to make a virtue of necessity and emphasise their importance to the economy.[34] However, unless some practical solution is found to the problems which affect this kind of firm, governmental exhortations will have little effect and a large section of Spanish industry will continue to be unable to fulfil its potential due to lack of the necessary funds.

Foreign companies operating in Spain are discouraged from placing too much pressure on Spanish sources of credit. The law of 1959 allowed domestic lending to companies with foreign participation on the same basis as to wholly Spanish-owned companies, only if the percentage of foreign ownership was less than 25 per cent. Once this limit was exceeded, the firm could use long- and medium-term domestic credit only up to 50 per cent of its capital. Further uses of domestic credit sources above this limit were subject to the approval of the Ministries of Finance and Commerce. Generally, foreign companies applying for amounts in excess of the 50 per cent limit have been expected to match the additional sum by raising capital from non-Spanish sources. In 1965, when credit was tight, the Instituto Español de Moneda Extranjera (IEME) enforced a law of 1939 stating that Spanish banks could grant loans guaranteed from abroad only with the approval of the Institute.[35] Evidence suggests that foreign companies do not generally experience difficulties in borrowing within the permitted limits, although dealing with Spanish banks can be a time-consuming process and the foreign business community would welcome a relaxation of the present ban on foreign banks.

The special problems relating to agricultural credit are discussed in Chapter 2. Here it is merely worth noting the very small proportion of banks' funds which are used for agricultural purposes. In the latter part of the 1960s the proportion was less than 5 per cent. In common with procedures in allocating credit to the agricultural sector, loans for industrial projects are more often granted on the basis of the collateral offered than on the merits of the specific project.

While the 1971 law on official credit and the reform of the interest

E

rate structure two years earlier did improve the framework and terms of borrowing, many limitations remain. The insufficiency of long-term funds and the lack of adequate finance for small firms continue. Nor have the industrial banks provided an important source of pre-financing or a genuinely specialised package of services. The rôle of official credit has not been clearly delineated despite the emphasis since 1971 on the desired economic viability for projects. The continued existence of the privileged circuits leads sometimes to idiosyncrasies in the pattern of lending. At the root of many apparent contradictions between stated intent and reality (for example, the greater flexibility allegedly intended in the banking sector and the very limited amount of any real change) lies a more fundamental dilemma for the government : namely, that of creating a system more responsive to market forces while at the same time maintaining comprehensive control and supervision over financing facilities and the minutiae of banking activities.

### THE STOCK MARKET AS A SOURCE OF FUNDS FOR INDUSTRY

Earlier in the chapter reference was made to the fact that share and bond issues accounted for nearly 20 per cent of capital raised from external sources in 1975.[36] Since the early 1960s the stock market has expanded rapidly but nevertheless remains structurally a weak institution and the experience of a bear market in 1970 shook confidence considerably. Between 1964 and 1975 the number of quoted companies rose from 78 to 547.[37] Total capitalisation of the market is still low compared with figures for France, the Federal Republic of Germany and the UK,[38] but higher than in the Netherlands, Belgium and Italy. The Madrid exchange accounts for some 60 per cent of business turnover. The other two exchanges are Barcelona and Bilbao. While the number of quoted companies has expanded fast, the market is in fact far narrower than might at first appear. In Madrid approximately only one-fifth of listed stocks are traded regularly. Trading hours are restricted and each sector is allotted only a few minutes on each of the four trading days in a week. Prices movements are also limited and trading may end with buyers and sellers unmatched.[39] Trading amounted to only 4·7 per cent of total market capitalisation in 1974. The Spanish stock market is still to some extent characterised by lack of supply as well as of demand. The lack of supply is due to the reluctance of many companies to expose their activities sufficiently to make new issues. This is rooted in the widespread practice of tax evasion and might change if stricter action were taken to enforce taxation policies. The costs involved are also a disincentive to smaller companies entering the stock market. The lack of demand is associated to some degree with the lack of information available on many companies, which is again related to tax evasion. The small investor has difficulty in gaining access to relevant information particularly as neither brokers nor the banks see it as incumbent upon them to provide analysis or advice.

These conditions to some extent explain the rapid growth of the unit trusts which were first started in Spain in 1966. Investment fund managers have increasingly had access to 'inside' knowledge and have made the stock market a more attractive proposition to the small investor. In 1974 there were nineteen unit trusts with total assets amounting to more than Ptas 39,300 million, predominantly controlled by the commercial and industrial banks. Assets in 1969 represented some 3 per cent of the total market value of listed shares. In 1970, however, after a period of intense speculation, share prices fell sharply and, due both to the restricted workings of the stock exchange and the regulations controlling the unit trusts, the latter were unable to meet the sudden run on funds. The Bank of Spain bought up large quantities of industrial securities from the unit trusts and a tighter control was set up. The unit trusts were allowed to invest only 70 per cent of funds in securities instead of the original 90 per cent, leaving a larger margin to deal with sudden demands, and no trust may hold more than 5 per cent in any one company. The 1970 law also obliged the trusts to distribute all income acquired from investment and liquid assets to shareholders within one year of the purchase of the security. Confidence in the trusts seems to have been restored but the events of 1970 were useful in bringing to light the narrow base of the stock market and the lack of manoeuvre possible within current regulations. In 1973 bank shares comprised some 40 per cent of share turnover, utilities 33 per cent, industrials 24 per cent and unit trusts 3 per cent.

A feature of the stock market is the tendency of many Spanish companies to supplement (or substitute for) dividends with a rights issue at par, when the market price is several times above that level. This is a common practice of banks, which are by law limited to an annual 6 per cent dividend. The widespread practice of rights issues by the banks and some public utilities constitutes strong competition for smaller manufacturing companies whose shares do not offer such immediately attractive gains. As earnings are usually substantially underestimated, price-earnings ratios in Spain are high. The debenture market has not shown the same rate of expansion as shares have, chiefly because interest rates have not compared favourably with rates of inflation. The activities of the unit trusts widened the base for stock market transactions but the market is still a narrow one and is likely to remain so until more information is readily accessible on the real state of companies' affairs. In the absence of such developments, the stock market is unlikely to become an important source of long-term capital.

# 7 Public Expenditure; Fiscal and Monetary Policy

An adjunct of economic growth has been the growing share of the public sector in the economy. Between 1960 and 1972 public expenditure increased from 19 per cent of GNP to 25 per cent,[1] although the latter figure is still low compared with public expenditure in most European countries. Between 1962 and 1972 government expenditure for social purposes, in particular on education, in relation to GNP rose. Expenditure on economic activities, i.e. transport and agriculture, remained fairly constant at about 4 per cent of GNP. Spending on defence fell in relation to GNP from 2·6 per cent to 1·8 per cent in 1972. While public expenditure on housing declined in relation to overall spending, spending on infrastructure rose rapidly and increased from 2·2 per cent of GNP in 1960 to 5·5 per cent in 1967 and 5 per cent in 1969 and 1970.[2] Looking at categories of expenditure in relation to total budget expenditure, spending on defence fell from 19 per cent in 1962 to 13 per cent in 1976, while expenditure on social activities rose from 24 per cent to 40 per cent of the total and expenditure on education from 9 per cent to 19 per cent. Investment expenditure overall grew at approximately the same rate as GNP, lagging in health, education and agriculture, where there were delays in carrying out projects and towards the end of the 1960s a growing tendency to offset increases in current expenditure by cuts in investment expenditure.

Central government budget expenditure, however, is only one part of total expenditure by the public sector, the remainder being accounted for by local authorities, autonomous agencies, official credit institutions and social security funds. In 1976, proposed budget expenditure, at Ptas 782 billion, accounted for approximately 44 per cent of total public expenditure.

The autonomous agencies are each dependent upon a 'supervisory' ministry but have a separate legal existence. They also enjoy a considerable degree of financial independence and, in practice, effective financial control has been difficult to exercise. Despite the supervisory function of the relevant ministry, autonomous agencies have determined their own policies to a considerable extent.[3] While their independence was curtailed in the 1960s, it is still considerable and agencies are in some cases costly to maintain and in nearly all cases difficult to keep strictly in line with overall government objectives.[4] Despite a law passed in 1958 which made the creation of new agencies more difficult, there were still as many as 1600 at the end of the 1960s which qualified for inclusion in the consolidated budget.[5] Since 1967 the Treasury has published an annual consolidated account of public sector accounts, but these, while providing more information, are still lacking in detail. For budgetary purposes the autonomous agencies are divided into two categories : those which are of a purely administrative character and those which have a commercial basis such as RENFE. Only those in the first category are included within the consolidated budget and these represented some 8 per cent of total revenue and expenditure in 1972. Typically, these autonomous agencies deal in welfare, educational or research activities. While some bodies earn substantial income from the sale of services and fees, overall revenue accounts for some two-thirds of current expenditure and the remainder is obtained by transfer from central government. The other autonomous agencies, which include INI, RENFE, FORPPA, CAT etc., are not classified as part of the overall budget, although their estimated individual budgets are now added as an 'informative annex' to the budget.

In 1974 the estimated total of the combined expenditure of the autonomous agencies was Ptas 234,307 billion.[6] During the 1960s by far the biggest recipient of government aid was RENFE, which accounted in 1966 for approximately one-half of all current account subsidies and one-half of capital transfers. The Servicio Nacional de Cereales and CAT also qualified for large subsidies due to heavy losses. Overall, these agencies are not self-sufficient and they rely on subsidies from the central administration to provide about 5 per cent of current revenue and to finance about one-third of investment programmes. The remaining capital requirements are financed about equally by borrowing and by suppliers' credits. The fact that the autonomous agencies (taking both categories together) total an estimated expenditure equivalent to over one-third of central government spending illustrates the importance of the autonomous agencies in public expenditure. Since many still maintain a high degree of independence while at the same time claiming government subsidies, it also explains why it is difficult for the Spanish government to maintain effective control over a wide area of public expenditure and why the autonomous agencies remain a costly apparatus.

Local authorities in Spain have become increasingly dependent upon the central administration. Current spending of local authorities in relation to GNP rose slightly from 1·5 per cent in 1962 to 1·8 per cent in 1971.[7] Investment expenditure rose only from 0·6 per cent of GNP in 1962 to 0·7 per cent in 1971. But, while in 1962 indirect and direct taxation levied by local authorities accounted for 96·7 per cent of their current spending, in 1972 such revenue represented only 42·5 per cent of current expenditure, the rest being almost entirely supplied by transfers from the central administration.[8] The financial position of local government authorities in relation to the central administration reflects political reality. The political apparatus of Spain is based on a highly centralised system which in no way encourages local initiative either at the municipal, provincial or regional level. It is thus not at all uncommon for projects of local interest to be planned and carried out by State bodies. The experience of the development poles underlines the subordinate part played by local interests in local and regional matters. Local annual budgets are subject to the control of the Finance Ministry, which often extends to modifying and changing items within the budget to suit the Ministry's national policies. This control is intensified by the fact that most capital expenditure has had to be financed by 'extraordinary' budgets which involve the sanction of the Finance Ministry.[9] Moreover, tax reforms relating to local government finance in 1962 and 1966 which aimed at simplifying the existing structure of taxes have not resulted in any substantial increase of tax revenues generated from local sources. Further reforms introduced under the Ley de Bases de Régimen Local of November 1975 are intended to increase revenue from local sources, largely through more effective use of existing taxation channels.

An innovation under the law is the ending of the dual system of ordinary and extraordinary budgets. Since the 1975 law offers few changes of substance, however, it is unlikely to reverse the trend of the last few years : that taxes of a local nature are increasingly being replaced by taxes collected by the State on behalf of the local authorities. While the overall amount of revenue available from local sources increased in absolute terms, it declined in relation to GDP from 1·7 per cent in 1961 to 0·8 per cent in 1969. The tendency for central government to finance an increasing part of local government expenditure is acceptable to the central administration for political reasons and local authorities are not in a position to assert themselves even should they wish to do so. This is partly because they have so little effective control over their own budgets and in part because this in turn breeds an apathetic attitude which is not conducive to demanding a greater participation in local affairs.[10]

A feature of public expenditure at national level which merits attention is the growth in expenditure on subsidies and transfers. Such expenditure grew at a faster rate than any other category of public expenditure in the 1960s. Expenditure on subsidies alone grew at an accumulated rate of 22·6 per cent between 1960 and 1970. Until the end of the 1950s budgetary assistance to industry was directed almost entirely to public-sector enterprises. In the 1960s this situation changed. This was due mainly to the ending of the automatic right of public sector companies to such assistance. By 1969 private enterprise received just under 50 per cent of all such assistance to industry compared with 17 per cent in 1962.[11] Total assistance to public and private concerns remained at between 2·5 per cent and 3 per cent of GNP over the 1960s.[12] Capital aid and tax relief for exports constituted the bulk of governmental assistance to the private sector. Tax relief represents a fast-growing area and equalled approximately 11 per cent of the total value of goods exported in 1969.[13]

It is difficult to assess the total represented by all tax exemptions due to lack of detailed information, but a study in 1967 calculated that in that year tax exemptions amounted to some Ptas 27,000 billion.[14] Tax exemptions and subsidies to private industry together totalled over Ptas 72,000 billion in 1970, a figure representing nearly one-fifth of central government expenditure. The creation of the development poles, joint-action plans and other government schemes stimulated the increase in such assistance. This rapid growth has not however resulted in a more flexible approach towards the use of different types of subsidy. Subsidies in connection with the development poles, for example, are available only through annual *concursos* and a change-over from one type of subsidy to another involves the transfer of budget allocation between government departments which constitutes a strongly inhibitory factor to change. Again, the criteria by which certain projects are accepted for inclusion in the development poles or joint-action schemes and others rejected do not always appear to be strictly economic. The widespread use of subsidies and tax exemptions appears to have developed in a fairly haphazard fashion since the early 1960s. The policy is open to criticism on the grounds that there has been no apparent interest in relating costs to expected benefits and, as the Third Plan suggested, certain types of subsidies and exemptions are allowed to continue when the need for them has passed.

Increased expenditure must be financed by one method or another. In Spain, the ratio of taxation to GNP is low. In 1971 this ratio, whether or not social security contributions were included, was one of the lowest of the OECD countries. Table 7.1 sets out fiscal receipts as a percentage of GNP for various countries in 1971.

Taxation in Spain has traditionally been regressive. Despite a reform to spread the tax base in 1940, the essential characteristics of the system remained unchanged from the end of the nineteenth century until 1957. In 1957 and 1964 reforms simplified and improved the tax structure as well as substantially raising levels of collection.

TABLE 7.1   Fiscal receipts as a percentage of GNP, 1971

|  | *Including social security* | *Excluding social security* | *GNP per head*[a] |
|---|---|---|---|
| Denmark | 43·99 | 40·19 | 3530 |
| Sweden | 41·80 | 34·28 | 4397 |
| France | 35·62 | 20·71 | 3170 |
| Germany | 34·46 | 22·80 | 3549 |
| Italy | 30·92 | 19·20 | 1831 |
| Greece | 24·54 | 18·17 | 1088 |
| Switzerland | 23·97 | 18·27 | 3781 |
| Japan | 20·06 | 16·04 | 2163 |
| Spain | 20·02 | 12·01 | 1070 |

[a] In $ US.

Source: OECD, *Economic Surveys. Spain, 1974* (Paris) p. 36.

Over the 1960s taxation accounted for some 60 per cent of central government revenue and social security contributions for some 30 per cent.[15] With the increase in social security contributions at the beginning of the 1970s, these accounted for 40 per cent of total current revenue in 1974. In the 1960s indirect taxes remained stable, accounting for 36 per cent of total revenue in 1960 and 1972 and 65 per cent of all taxation. This is now changing slowly. The reduction of taxes on petroleum products in 1974 and the reduced rate of increase in the yields of turnover tax (because of the slowing down in business activity), in conjunction with a rise in the revenue from direct taxation, has produced a slight fall in the share of indirect taxation. Over the previous decade the most rapid increases were in turnover and excise taxes, which yielded approximately 50 per cent of indirect taxation in 1975. The remaining 50 per cent comes from luxury taxes, fiscal monopolies, transaction taxes and stamp duties.

Direct taxation amounted to just over one-third of all tax revenue at the beginning of the 1970s.[16] The most important sources of direct taxation are taxes on wages and salaries and corporation tax which respectively accounted for 37 and 28 per cent of total direct taxation in 1975. Personal income tax is chargeable on all incomes above Ptas 200,000 a year (Ptas 300,000, if total income is derived from personal services) at basic rates ranging from 15 per cent to 56 per cent. Personal income tax remained at about 1·4 per cent of total tax revenue throughout the 1960s, despite increases in income levels. The standard rate of corporation tax was 30 per cent until 1975, although the effective rate has been slightly higher. Taxation on dividend income is 15 per cent taxed at source. While basic rates are not high compared with other European countries, revenue collected is lower still. One reason for this is the widespread practice of tax evasion which in Spain has not, until very recently, been a criminal offence and is common on both a personal and company basis. On a company basis this is usually effected by the under-reporting of sales and entails keeping more than one set of books. As mentioned earlier, this affects the ability of smaller companies to raise equity capital. Differing stances on taxation have often been a source of friction in companies with a combination of Spanish and foreign interests. One difficulty is that a foreign firm with interests in a Spanish concern cannot repatriate profits which have not been declared, as this would constitute a criminal violation of foreign exchange-control regulations. On the other hand if full tax declarations are made, the company may become a less attractive proposition to the Spanish shareholder.[17]

Another reason for low levels of tax collection has been the global system of assessment which was first introduced as a temporary expedient in 1957 and confirmed in the tax reform of 1964. Under this system a company's tax liability was not related to its individual profits but to the total amount of profit attributed to all companies in a particular industry, within a specified geographical area. The aim of global assessment was to cut down tax-collecting costs and tax evasion. Collection costs may have been cut, but it is widely believed that effective rates of taxation have been considerably lower under the global system. An added disadvantage of the system was that forward planning was often difficult, in particular for smaller companies, as tax liabilities could not be estimated in advance. In practice, it also meant that the largest companies did not always have the largest tax burden. In 1969 a large proportion of companies was taken out of the global assessment system, which is currently being phased out. However, its existence undoubtedly contributed to the small share of corporate taxation in total taxation in the 1960s.

Recent efforts have been made for a further reform of the taxation system. Failure to declare taxable income is now an offence which carries a heavy fine and the number of people expected to pay income tax has been enlarged. More emphasis has been placed on the use of the *signos externos* or outward signs of wealth in assessing personal income-tax liability. Capital gains tax, first authorised by the Cortes in 1964, was given fresh impetus by legislation in November 1973. Attempts to reform company taxation are centred on the phasing out of the global quota system and on a new general accounting plan which sets out to rationalise the current systems of book-keeping. So far, the accounting plan is not compulsory and is therefore unlikely to be adopted by many. Any Finance Minister attempting to introduce fundamental taxation reforms has always met with severe resistance. Prior to any radical reform, a tax amnesty on both a company and a personal basis would almost certainly have to be granted. One problem to be overcome in improving the efficiency of the taxation system is the inadequate machinery for collection. There are not enough inspectors and, as different taxes are policed by different inspectors, it is difficult, for example, for tax inspectors to make any comprehensive assessment of a company's position.[18] This has sometimes led to arbitrary demands for supplementary taxes by inspectors to 'compensate' for unproved but suspected tax evasion. Although revenue from taxation has increased in absolute terms, the share of taxes in relation to total revenue has scarcely changed since the late 1960s. In 1974 direct and indirect taxes accounted for 57 per cent of total revenue. At the beginning of the 1970s it was clear that expenditure could not be maintained at the desired level without renewed recourse to public debt and in 1971 some Ptas 20,000 billion-worth of public debt was issued. Further issues of public debt were made in following years. The debt, however, has remained at a moderate level. Budget deficits have also been offset by borrowing from the Bank of Spain. Public expenditure will probably continue to rise in the coming years and current revenue-raising mechanisms are not at present adequate to finance increased expenditure. While increased expenditure can be financed by increased borrowing, the narrowness of the long-term capital market would mean that increased government borrowing of this kind would create difficulties for firms already competing for such funds.[19] If the Spanish government is to carry out its stated intention of allocating more public money to social purposes, such as social security payments and education, in the long-run some fundamental changes must be made in the taxation system.

The commitment of the government to spend more on social activities prompts the question : How far have taxation policies and government expenditure patterns resulted in a redistribution of income? The answer, as far as taxation is concerned, is very little. The heavy weight of indirect taxes in total taxation makes for lack of progressivity. Moreover, a large proportion of indirect taxes fall on food and clothing items. The idea that progressivity was a desirable feature of direct taxation was reflected in the Carner Law of 1932 but its application has been limited. The yield of personal income tax remains low and, while in principle taxation rates rise in step with rising incomes, widespread tax evasion is often more effective at higher income levels. The general ignorance about the distribution of income in Spain arises from the paucity of information on the real state of individuals' tax liabilities. Since these are lacking, figures on income distribution are based on various surveys, which serve to indicate a broad outline but cannot claim anything like total precision.

It is difficult to assess the redistributive effects of government expenditure. Expenditure which might be expected to have such effects has increased considerably since the early 1960s, when it was negligible. Social transfers from government agencies increased from Ptas 38,000 billion in 1960 to Ptas 189,000 billion in 1972, of which the greater part (91 per cent in 1972) was made up of social security transfers. The extension of social security schemes and transfers was commented on in Chapter 4. From the point of view of redistribution of income, the running down of surpluses in the schemes at the end of the 1960s and the increase in receipts from other central government bodies would appear to imply an element of redistribution.[20] This is question-able, however, when account is taken of the structure of taxation in Spain and does not necessarily imply that transfers are being made from the better- to the less well-off members of the community. More-over, the percentage of State support to the financing of social security remains very small, in the realm of 5 per cent. Given that contributions are by far the most important source of finance for social security, they are central to the question of whether or not social security transfers can be considered as redistributive. As long as contributions remain based on the 'theoretical' wage, transfers cannot be considered to fulfil a redistributive function. The 'theoretical' wage is formally in process of being phased out, but because of the deterioration in the economic situation this reform has not yet been fully implemented. Until this happens increases in social security operations cannot be regarded as indicative of income redistribution on a progressive basis.

Looking more generally at government expenditure, it is true to say that expenditure on social activities has risen substantially. In 1962 expenditure on social activities accounted for 27 per cent of the central budget, while in 1976 this represented 40 per cent of government spending. Education has benefited particularly from this increased expenditure and, while the objectives of the Education Law of 1970 are far from realised, the widening of secondary school facilities has benefited the poorer members of society. How far expenditure on 'pro-tected' or official housing schemes has involved a redistribution of resources to the benefit of the less well-off is doubtful, since government plans in this respect, as discussed in Chapter 5, have not necessarily resulted in the provision of low-cost housing. While government ex-penditure on social activities has to some extent acted as a redistributive agent, this has not been a primary function of such expenditure.

In the 1960s much less use was made of fiscal than of monetary policy in attempts to regulate demand. The deficiencies of the taxation system have by and large precluded the widespread use of changes in the level of taxation as an instrument of macro-economic policy, although the weight of indirect taxes has to some extent acted as a stabiliser, due to the close links between business trends and total tax revenue.[21] Taxes which have been most subject to changes have been those charged on specific articles such as tobacco, petroleum and luxury items. In the 1960s fiscal policy was broadly confined to expanding and curbing the level of public expenditure. Curbs in expenditure levels effectively proved practicable only in relation to investment expenditure which accounted for some 25 to 30 per cent of total public expenditure. Spending by the autonomous agencies has proved particularly difficult to control since, while in principle a fairly rigorous system of control over expenditure by these agencies exists, in practice there is little vigour in application.[22] Changes in public expenditure could more often be described as reflecting economic conditions than in shaping them.

Minimum monetary control became possible at the end of the 1950s with the ending of the issue of long-term debt by the government in the form of long-term securities which could be automatically discounted with the Bank of Spain. During the 1960s, monetary policies were not only more frequently used than fiscal policies in regulating demand, but also tended to be more effective. Monetary measures in the 1960s tended to be unsophisticated and until the end of the decade, when more use was made of changes in interest rates, consisted largely of attempts to set quantitative limits on the amount of credit advanced by the banks. Credit restrictions were frequently applied as cure rather than prevention, as the authorities, aware of the damage that could be wrought on the many firms dependent upon short-term loans, were reluctant to apply severe restrictions until it was considered absolutely necessary.[23]

The following paragraphs give a brief summary of the main cyclical movements in the economy since the Stabilisation Plan and an outline of developments in the use made of monetary and fiscal policies.[24]

The Stabilisation Plan itself included curbs on public expenditure and restrictions on credit. As described in Chapter 3, the collective impact of the various measures which made up the Stabilisation Plan was severe and its effects protracted. In the middle of 1960 rediscount rates were lowered and this was followed by a moderate rate of credit expansion. Fiscal policies were not used to reactivate the economy. Towards the end of 1961 domestic demand rose as a result of easier credit conditions and at the same time demand for exports also increased. Private consumption, investment and construction also showed signs of expansion and the upswing was confirmed in the fall in unemployment, especially in the construction industry. These trends continued throughout 1962 and into 1963. With expansion, however, came a renewal of inflationary pressures. While the Stabilisation Plan had succeeded in improving the balance of payments position, prices had proved less amenable to control. In the second half of 1963 various measures were imposed in an attempt to reduce the inflation rate. These were mainly aimed at controlling the construction of luxury housing and keeping food prices down. At the same time, following the Banking Law of 1962, a liquidity coefficient for the banks was introduced. The coefficient had a perceptible initial impact and, within the first five months of its inception, the level was raised from 10 to 13 per cent. The rate of expansion of bank credit contracted and did not rise again until well into 1964. The coefficient did not however develop into a regular instrument of monetary policy, partly because the coefficient included non-liquid items such as non-pledgeable 'public funds'. These were not of great importance in 1963 but later on became so, and the banks in time covered the whole of the coefficient by holding investment bonds. The size of the coefficient, moreover, was not altered by the authorities in response to increases or decreases in liquidity and was not strictly enforced after the initial months. It was finally abandoned in 1971.

The years 1964 and 1965 were times of expansion and inflation. Controls continued over the construction industry but to little effect. Imports of food products continued on an appreciable scale in the hope of restraining food prices. As mentioned in Chapter 2, the agricultural sector was not (nor is it now) geared to responding swiftly to changing patterns of demand. Moreover, the exceptionally bad harvest of 1964 raised prices further. In 1965 it was not only food prices that were rising. Prices in other sectors showed the same tendency and the balance of payments was in deficit for the first time since the Stabilisation Plan. In response, import duties were lowered and some imports were freed of quantitative controls. Neither in 1964 nor in 1965 were constraints placed on the level of public expenditure and this continued to rise at the rate of 20 per cent per annum. By the end of 1965 it was clear that policies which affected comparatively small sections of the economy were inadequate to the situation and a more comprehensive approach was adopted. The major aim of the programme was the restriction of the growth of credit to an annual rate of 17 per cent.[25] This maximum limit applied both to banks and savings banks, while the official credit institutions were subject to a maximum permitted increase in absolute terms. The banks experienced a credit expansion of only 14 per cent in 1966.

Neither the savings banks nor the official credit bodies, however, complied with the restrictions. As in 1959, credit restrictions were accompanied by a host of supporting measures. Wages were allowed to rise by a maximum of only 8 per cent. Taxes on luxury goods were increased by 10 per cent and an attempt was made to curb current accounts of public expenditure. This, however, did not prove successful. Moreover, public investment expenditure increased by 17 per cent in marked contrast to the restrictive stance adopted in monetary policies. The effect of credit restrictions was more dramatic than intended and during 1966 the authorities switched to regarding 17 per cent growth as a target rather than a ceiling. For the first time the granting of discount lines with the Bank of Spain played a significant part in monetary policy.

By the end of 1966, despite efforts on the part of the monetary authorities to expand credit and reactivate the economy, recessionary tendencies prevailed. Order books fell and stocks accumulated. The index of industrial production also fell and unemployment rose. Prices continued to rise. Moreover, although the trade deficit on the balance of payments diminished, reserves fell sharply, due mainly to short-term capital movements. In 1967 the peseta was devalued,[26] and the devaluation was accompanied by a variety of restrictive measures. These included a wage freeze and a price freeze for public sector goods and services. Price increases for goods produced by the private sector were subject to severe controls. A whole range of investment incentives was introduced. The use of fiscal policies was limited. In 1968, a year of recession, the increase in public expenditure was only 12 per cent, a rate considerably below that experienced in previous years. Apart from raising some interest rates by 0·5 per cent in November 1967 and broadening the scope of selective rediscount facilities, an active monetary policy was not pursued in this period. (The rôle of special rediscount facilities with the Bank of Spain in financing exports was referred to in Chapter 3.) The expansion of these facilities was so rapid that by 1970 the Ptas 63 billion disbursed through these channels was three times as great as that allocated under the Bank of Spain normal discount lines. To some extent this was caused by the banks switching from ordinary rediscount lines to the special ones, since rates of interest were usually lower and conditions more favourable under the latter.

The rising importance of rediscount lines can be seen in relation to commercial bank deposits. In 1960 rediscount lines amounted to 5·1 per cent of deposits of which 1·2 per cent was accounted for by special lines. In 1970 the proportion was 10·7 per cent of which 7·8 per cent were special lines. In 1970 and the beginning of 1971 special rediscount lines were expanded, in some degree to compensate for the cessation of export credit from the Industrial Credit Bank following the Matesa scandal. The law on Official Credit in 1971 abolished the special rediscount lines and they were replaced by an obligatory investment coefficient. The large sums of credit disbursed under the special rediscount lines made it extremely difficult to control liquidity and this had an effect on the economy similar to that produced by the automatic discount arrangements for public debt in the 1950s.

Towards the end of 1968 demand revived both internally and

externally and investment levels recovered. In the first few months of 1969, although unemployment was still high, the upswing was well under way. The balance of payments registered a surplus for the first time since 1964. By the middle of 1969, however, the familiar signs of disequilibrium were in evidence and steps were taken to halt the very rapid increase in bank credit. Banks were to allow credit to rise by only 18 per cent in the course of the year. Meanwhile the rediscount rate was raised from 5 to 6 per cent. Ordinary rediscount lines were cut and short-term Treasury bonds were issued. These measures were only moderately successful. While ordinary rediscount lines were cut back, the special lines continued to expand, effectively negating the intention of mopping up liquidity. Banks responded to the measures by further reducing their liquidity ratios, which were already low. As in 1966, the 18 per cent credit limit did not in practice apply to all credit institutions and was not always strictly complied with where it was applicable. It was interpreted 'more as a counsel of prudence than an order'.[27] In the same year interest rates were linked to the base rate and (as mentioned in Chapter 6) various reforms were introduced in order to simplify the structure of interest rates. Long-term interest rates were freed and rates between banks, savings banks and credit co-operatives were also released from official control.[28]

In the 1960s the power of the Bank of Spain to initiate changes in monetary policy was extremely limited. Control over monetary supply and policy lay in the hands of the Treasury and the Bank of Spain was considered as an executive organ for carrying out decisions made by the Treasury. Moreover, the instruments of control were clumsy. None of the main instruments – rates of interest, banks' coefficients, rediscount lines, debt policies – permitted a flexible response to short-term economic conditions. Until the reforms of 1969, changes in interest rates constituted a small although growing part of monetary policy. Use was made of changes in prescribed interest rate in 1966 and again in 1967, but since before 1969 rates were not linked to the Central Bank rediscount rate, changes in interest rates were sparingly used and limited in effect. While in theory the maintenance of cash and liquidity coefficients was obligatory for the banks and savings banks, coefficients were not strictly enforced in the 1960s. The cash coefficient for commercial banks, stipulated by the 1962 law, did not for instance come into operation until 1970. Reference has already been made to the rapid expansion of special rediscount lines and the inflationary effect this had on the economy. Over these lines the Bank of Spain had little control. Special rediscount lines were fixed by the Treasury and their distribution between banks was also subject to ministerial orders.[29] These lines of credit showed, as we have seen, expansionary tendencies even in periods of official credit restraint.

Ordinary rediscount lines, while subject to more control, were far from perfect instruments of control. One restricting factor was that it was not possible to reduce a particular line once its use had been authorised. Moreover, as far as the industrial banks were concerned, ordinary rediscount lines were linked to the size of their resources and could therefore be expanded without the specific sanction of the Bank of Spain. For most of the 1960s the Bank of Spain's rôle in the management of the National Debt was minimal and it was not until 1968 with the issue of the Deuda Universitaria that the Bank was allowed a certain flexibility with regard to placing the issue. This particular issue also marked the beginning of a trend towards issuing debt at more attractive rates, in this case at 5·5 per cent.

In the 1960s instruments for dealing with variations in liquidity were not sufficiently flexible to achieve the desired objectives, especially in periods of rapid expansion and excess liquidity, and monetary policy relied heavily on overall restrictions on credit. Since these were not always enforced on the savings banks and official credit institutions, the burden of these restrictions fell on the banks, which are the major providers of finance to the private sector, and by implication the burden fell heavily on their less favoured customers. (While restrictions were also applicable to hire-purchase companies, these were not an important source of credit in this period.) Unwilling to apply policies which would reduce investment possibilities, credit restrictions were usually applied as a last resort in a deteriorating situation. Because restrictions were often applied belatedly, they tended to be harsh and the effects protracted. Moreover, official credit institutions, while not always directly affected by the imposition of restrictions, were not immunised from cyclical fluctuations and consequently were not always able to respond to specific projects in the way intended by the government. Periods of rapid expansion were all too often followed by sharply recessionary phases.

By the end of 1969 the balance of payments situation, which had been deteriorating since the middle of the year, showed the largest deficit of the 1960s and an import deposit scheme was introduced for a period of six months.[30] This was the start of a new phase in monetary policy. After 1970 more emphasis was placed on the effective control of liquidity and new instruments were employed to this end. In March of the same year the rediscount rate of the Bank of Spain was raised one point to 6·5 per cent and, as a result of the interest rate reforms of the previous year, this caused other interest rate changes in its wake. This time the changes in rates extended to the savings banks and, with certain exceptions, to the official credit institutions. In December 1970 the cash coefficient of the commercial banks was finally instituted. 1971 was a year of restricted activity and GNP grew by only 4·5 per cent in real terms.[31] Restrictive measures, however, had a salutary effect on the balance of payments and large surpluses on current account were recorded until the end of 1973, although this in its turn created problems in the economy. Once the import deposit scheme had ended, the banks increased their use of the special rediscount lines, interest rates were lowered slightly, and credit facilities once more expanded. Recovery was aided by a deliberate expansion of public expenditure in conjunction with the introduction of a 7 per cent investment tax credit for industry, although due to certain difficulties in execution the effects of these expansionary measures were somewhat delayed. Towards the end of the 1960s attempts to regulate the level of public expenditure concentrated on investment rather than current expenditure and this was to prove more efficacious.[32]

With the economy once more in expansionary phase, in 1971 the authorities were faced once again with the problems of excess liquidity. While this in itself was not novel, the extent of the surpluses on current account greatly exacerbated the problem. To the cash coefficient of the banks, which varied between 6 to 9 per cent, was added a similar coefficient for the savings banks (initially 4 per cent). Following the 1971 law on Official Credit, special rediscount lines were brought to an end and replaced by an obligatory investment coefficient which compelled the banks to invest partly in public funds and partly in sectors previously covered by the special rediscount lines.[33] Ordinary discount lines were reduced. Ptas 20,000 billion of longer-term public debt was issued in two instalments in 1971 with the combined aim of financing the budget deficit and mopping up excess liquidity. A further Ptas 16,000 billion of public debt was issued in 1972. In the course of 1972 the government appeared to be succeeding in its efforts to reduce liquidity and the liquidity ratio of the banks dropped slightly in December. In January 1973, however, the banks' liquidity ratio increased by two points within a single month and it became clear that the measures already in force were inadequate in the face of strongly expansionary forces. Throughout 1973 the demand for credit was sustained at a high level and rates of growth of credit on occasion neared 40 per cent.[34] As the OECD put it, 'A sharp increase in deposits and a strong demand for cash connected with the rise in money wages and the high level of domestic activity, led to a growth of liquid resources that was clearly incompatible with monetary stability.'[35] The restrictive stance of the previous year was intensified with the aim of reducing the rate of growth of liquid assets from 30 to 18 per cent. The discount rate was raised and banks were required to maintain their cash ratios on a daily basis, whereas before this had only been required three days a month. Three-month Treasury bills were issued on terms that became more flexible as the year progressed and after

March 1973 the Bank of Spain intervened daily in the money market.[36] Rediscount lines were also cut.

Since the market in Treasury bills is still quite small, cash is the main form of liquid asset and banks complained that making up the required sum by borrowing overnight was an expensive method of keeping within the law. In February 1974 the ruling was changed and a ten-day average is now required. In 1974 fears of the deflationary effects on the economy of the rise in crude oil prices caused a reversal of attitudes by the monetary authorities. Targets of growth in liquid assets were set at 20 per cent in the first half of the year and 18 per cent in the second half.[37] In fact, bank credit expanded rapidly at the beginning of 1974[38] and restrictive measures were again adopted. Liquidity ratios were raised. This caused a sharp increase in inter-bank rates and in mid-1974 a new instrument for controlling liquidity was used. Short-term credits, usually for one week, were allocated to the banks in proportion to their deposits by the Bank of Spain. No new instruments of monetary policy were added in 1975 but management of bank liquidity progressed more smoothly in a year which was characterised by conflicting trends.

Fears of the damaging impact of the oil crisis caused budgetary and fiscal policies to be used with greater frequency in economic management. An innovation in 1974 was the creation of a short-term intervention fund of Ptas 10 billion to be used selectively to counteract unemployment. This fund was doubled to Ptas 20 billion in 1975 and raised to Ptas 25 billion in 1976. In 1974 taxes on petroleum products were reduced in an attempt to curb inflationary pressures caused by the rise in oil prices. Moreover, the State financed the improvements in social security benefits for the period April to June 1974 in order to keep costs down for firms, many of which were already experiencing financial difficulties. Budgetary and fiscal policies have, like monetary policies, become more flexible. Thus, while the 1975 budget was prepared on the basis of providing a slight stimulus to the economy, the expansionary element was to some extent counteracted by measures passed in April 1975, by which time restrictive policies seemed more appropriate. Company taxes were then raised by an average of 6 percentage points, although the effect of this was somewhat blunted by the concession of tax credits for investment.

In the first half of 1976, both monetary and fiscal policies were more widely used with the aim of regulating short-term economic trends. Fiscal policy has gained in importance, especially since 1974. With the maintenance of minimum cash and investment ratios by the banks and the expansion of operations in Treasury bonds and personal credits, the authorities' control over bank liquidity has been much increased. Control has also been made more effective by the ending of the special rediscount lines. The linking of most interest rates has made it possible to achieve wider-reaching results by changes in rates. The authorities are now equipped with a wider and more flexible range of instruments with which to conduct monetary policy and this has been evident in economic management in the middle 1970s. Monetary policy is still, however, subject to certain limitations. Despite the freeing of long-term lending and borrowing rates, the majority of interest rates are still controlled, but not varied with any frequency. Nor has a substantial money market developed. A fundamental difficulty which inhibits the development of greater flexibility in the execution of policies is the uneasy division of responsibilities between the Bank of Spain and the Treasury. While the Bank of Spain now has greater freedom in some respects, for example in reselling Treasury bills at rates of interest which the Bank determines, its powers of decision are limited.

It is the Treasury which effectively decides on exchange rate policy and objectives for the size of the money supply. The rôle of the Bank of Spain is confined to a limited control over open-market operations and short-term credits. Conflicts can and do arise, over exchange-rate policy, the amount of money in circulation and the further freeing of interest rates, as well as over methods of financing public debt. Not only does the division of responsibility cause friction, it can also delay the implementation of swift and decisive action.

# 8 Foreign Trade and Internal Commerce

Spain's balance of payments position in the early 1970s was such as to give rise to some complacency in the early stages of the economic recession which began to affect Europe towards the end of 1973. This was due in part to the high level of reserves of gold and foreign currency, which amounted to $6799 million at the end of 1973, and partly to the healthy inflow of payments from tourists and workers abroad on current account which, between 1970 and 1973, amply covered the chronic trade deficit. A country's trading position is, however, a function of economic conditions prevailing externally as well as of the state of the domestic economy. Recent developments in the outside world have made heavy inroads on the strong balance of payments position enjoyed for several years by Spain. It can no longer be assumed that tourism and workers' remittances from abroad will offset the trade deficit, especially as the latter has been rapidly inflated by the rise in the price of crude oil. This chapter looks at the chief components in the balance of payments, with the exception of foreign investment which was discussed in Chapter 3, and considers Spain's position *vis-à-vis* her most important trading partner, the EEC. The second part of the chapter examines the structure of domestic trade and the two main methods of freight transport, road and rail.

Balance of payments figures for 1960 and 1973 show that the trade deficit increased steadily over the decade of the 1960s from a position of very slight surplus in 1960 to a deficit of $3545 million in 1973.[1] In 1960 receipts from tourism amounted to $296 million. By 1973 they totalled $2878 million. In a similar manner workers' remittances rose from $55 million to $913 million. The other two items which grew in a spectacular fashion over the 1960s were foreign investment and reserves of gold and foreign currency, which from a negligible base at the beginning of the 1960s increased to $6000 million in the early 1970s.

Since 1960 both exports and imports have grown rapidly. In the years of economic autarky preceding the Stabilisation Plan the predominant aim had been to promote a policy of import substition. Until 1948 trade was almost entirely controlled by a rigorous system of export and import licences, heavily biased in favour of the 'industries of national interest'. After 1948 bilateral agreements were introduced which, through the use of quotas, made trading arrangements even less flexible, and multiple exchange rates were also used. It has been argued that the policy of import substitution at least led to a greater diversification of industries within Spain. On the other hand, it is at least equally tenable that autarkic policies produced inefficient and uncompetitive industrial practices. The period of autarky certainly did not encourage the growth of exports. In some cases, as for instance in the textile industry, a traditional exporting sector, exports actually fell. Over the period 1951–2 to 1958–9 the annual rate of growth in exports in value terms was 0·8 per cent.[2] The Stabilisation Plan of 1959 and the attendant relative liberalisation of trade were dramatically reflected in the rate of growth of exports which, between 1958–9 and 1969–70, grew at an annual rate of 15·7 per cent.[3]

The immediate impact of the Stabilisation Plan on the trade balance was on imports. In the first instance 54 per cent of trade in private hands (taking 1950 as the base year) was freed and a further 35 per cent was placed under a system of global quotas.[4] The initial impulse towards freer trade was not sustained with equal vigour over the decade. The last significant gesture towards freeing imports from quotas of one kind or another were made in 1966. Currently some 70 per cent of Spanish imports are not subject to quantitative restrictions. In 1973, 71 per cent of Spanish imports were freely imported, 5·9 per cent fell under bilateral agreements, 8·2 per cent under State agreements, 5·1 per cent under global arrangements and the remainder were imported under 'special' quotas.[5]

The structure of imports has not changed significantly since the early 1960s. In 1973 raw materials and semi-manufactures represented 48 per cent of total imports, food products 16 per cent and capital goods some 27 per cent, the balance being accounted for by imports of consumer goods. This represented a slight gain in the percentage share of consumer goods, which accounted for only 4 per cent in 1963, at the expense of food imports, which represented 21 per cent of imports in 1963. Raw and semi-manufactures and capital goods accounted for very nearly the same proportion of imports in 1963 as in 1973. The freeing of many imports from the rigid quota system was accompanied by Spain's adoption of the Brussels Tariff Nomenclature.[6] The aim of this change was to move towards a simplified tariff structure.[7]

The simplicity of the tariff structure of 1960 was not destined to last. Since the initial publication of the tariff over 500 decrees have intervened, causing modifications and changes. The gamut of import duties covers fixed tariffs (*derechos definitivos*), temporary tariffs, sliding-scale tariffs, regulatory tariffs, compensatory tariffs (as well as a special system created for capital goods in 1965). Provision is made for temporary suspension of import duties and special treatment for imports destined for favoured industrial sectors or development regions. The tariff as originally set up in 1960 represented a fairly high nominal rate of protection, the average being over 12 per cent. This fell steadily until 1965, when the average rate was 8·82 per cent. Between 1965 and 1973 the average nominal tariff rate fell only to 7·47 per cent.[8] In 1964, the Fiscal Tariff of 1960 was replaced by the Impuesto de Compensación de Gravamenes Interiores a la Importación (ICGI), an internal adjusting tax designed to equate the prices of imports with those of competing domestic production.

The ICGI varies from product to product, but tends with a few exceptions to be levied at the same level as the *desgravación fiscal* or tax rebate for exports. ICGI levels rose from 1961 to 1966, after which they fell slightly, but in 1973 the average rate of this type of import duty was higher than it had been in 1961.[9] In terms of *nominal* rates, the Spanish tariff is high. This is not entirely surprising as domestic producers tend to predominate in the various procedures by which an application for changes in the tariff structure (which is usually for added protection) is brought to the point of decision. The existing Spanish tariff structure tends to reflect the strength of particular pressure groups as much as any overall strategy on the part of authorities to protect any particular sector on the grounds of a wider national interest.

The rate of *effective* protection afforded by the Spanish tariff system is higher than most developed countries but less than the majority of developing countries.[10] A sector which in 1966 showed an especially high rate of effective protection was that of food-processing. Between 1962 and 1968 some rates of effective protection changed considerably. In the manufacture of cars and the transformation of plastic materials the rate of protection fell steeply, while in other sectors, such as iron and steel, the effective rate of protection rose sharply between 1962 and 1968. In general, the rate of effective protection tends to be highest for intermediate products. Between 1962 and 1968 effective rates of protection fell on industrial products. The protection afforded to industrial products is, however, greater than that enjoyed by the Common Market countries, a fact which underlies Spain's ambivalent attitude towards freer trade with her largest trading partner. While measures at the beginning of the 1960s freed trade in relation to the preceding period, the movement towards greater freedom from quota restrictions was (as noted earlier) not sustained in the second part of the decade and, while fixed tariffs have often been lowered, the effect has frequently been negated by the imposition or increase of a different species of tariff. Protection has lessened but at a slower pace since the middle of the 1960s.

The rate of growth of exports in the 1960s was remarkable, showing an annual rate of growth of 15.7 per cent over the decade compared with 0·8 per cent in the 1950s.[11] While Spain's rapid export growth is mainly a reflection of an increase in exports of manufactures, agricultural exports remained the most important group in value terms until 1968. In 1962 agricultural exports, of which fruit was and is still the most important component (particularly citrus fruit), represented over 55 per cent of total exports.[12] This fell to 45 per cent in 1967 and had fallen to 27 per cent by 1973. While fruit has maintained its dominant position in agricultural exports, accounting for nearly 30 per cent of such exports in 1972, other components have changed in relative importance. Fish has become a more important export, accounting for 9·7 per cent of exports of agricultural products in 1972 (4·5 per cent in 1963). The share of canned fish and prepared fish products also rose, from 2·4 per cent to 4·4 per cent of agricultural exports. On the other hand, exports of vegetables and vegetable oil have declined quite substantially. Given the large proportion of agricultural exports in total exports in the first few years of the 1960s, it is hardly surprising that fluctuations in the rhythm of exports were strongly correlated to failures and successes of successive harvests. Since 1967 export growth has been less erratic, and the annual rate of growth has accelerated. Between 1962 and 1967 exports as a whole grew at an annual accumulative rate of 13·5 per cent. In the period 1967–72 the rate increased to over 20 per cent.

The spectacular growth in exports which was noticeable after 1964 was caused by the rapid increase in the export of manufactured goods. Exports of capital goods, consumer goods and intermediate products all expanded rapidly. Most striking was the diversification of heavy industry and the greater variety of consumer goods. Exports of manufactures which represented approximately 54 per cent of total exports at the end of the 1950s accounted for over three-quarters of all exports a decade later. Exports represented 2 per cent of industrial production in 1958–9 and 13 per cent in 1970–1.[13] Growth was especially dynamic in transport equipment and other machinery, chemical goods and shoes.[14]

The main method of stimulating exports in the agricultural sector has been through La Ordenación Comercial by which groups of firms representing at least 80 per cent of the export value of the sector must combine together in order to qualify for various credit facilities. The export incentives available to industry were referred to in Chapter 3. These include fiscal rebates on import duties paid on imported materials, which are used for export goods and generous export credit facilities. Export controls can sometimes cause delays, and slowness in obtaining permits is a frequent ground for complaint.[15] Although no systematic information is available on the distribution of export subsidies, the impression is that subsidies are conceded on a case-by-case basis rather than in relation to any broader strategy.

The rapid growth of Spanish non-agricultural exports has been reflected in Spain's increasing share of the world market for such products. Spain's share rose by an annual average of 9 per cent in the period 1962–73,[16] although it should perhaps be borne in mind that, as the OECD points out, an important reason for this exceptional growth was 'the comparatively recent date of the Spanish industrialisation and the small importance of Spanish exports in world trade at the start of the period'.[17] The rate of growth of a country's exports must depend to a considerable extent on economic conditions obtaining in its main markets. The economic growth experienced by the rest of Europe in the 1960s was clearly a significant factor in Spain's export performance. Spain was, however, able to compete successfully in various sectors on world markets for a variety of reasons. In some sectors, such as shipbuilding, considerable underutilisation of productive capacity was a spur to exporting efforts in the 1960s. In others, such as the chemical industry, Spain benefited from the existence of various raw materials such as deposits of pyrites, potash and mercury which led to a competitive price position. Perhaps the chief advantage which Spain has held over competitors has been the abundance of cheap labour available. Spain has not perhaps made as much use of this asset as it might have done and the government has failed, as mentioned in Chapter 5, to provide adequate training facilities for the creation of a skilled and mobile labour force. The competitive position of the Spanish labour force is being fast whittled away in the mid-1970s by rapidly rising wages. Wage levels are now much closer to those of Europe generally.[18]

Over the decade of the 1960s the share of the EEC countries as purchasers of Spanish exports fell from approximately 38 per cent in 1962 to 27 per cent in 1968 and then rose again to close to the 1962 level at the beginning of the 1970s. Over the same period exports to the USA fell, although with fluctuations, from 25 per cent of total exports in 1962 to approximately 18 per cent in 1972 and to some 10 per cent in 1975. Exports to Latin American countries reached a peak in 1966, accounting for some 17 per cent of total Spanish exports. After 1966 the Latin American share fell away and by 1975 it was close to 11 per cent, which was similar to the share at the beginning of the 1960s. Exports to EFTA countries rose from just over 10 per cent to 16 per cent between 1962 and 1972. The underlying trend is to an increase in Spain's exports being taken by developed countries. Although in the early part of the 1960s exports to the more industrialised nations fell away as Spain fostered trade relations with Latin America and to some extent the Arab countries and Eastern Europe, the latter two groups still account for a very small percentage of total Spanish trade.[19] In 1966 exports to the developed countries had declined to two-thirds from the three-quarters share in 1962. By 1972, however, the share of exports to developed countries had risen to over 71 per cent and this trend will probably continue in the foreseeable future, despite the recent economic recession in Europe and Spain's endeavours to promote trade with the Arab countries and strengthen trade links with Latin America.

A striking feature of Spain's trading position has been the dynamism of trade with the EEC countries since the late 1960s. In 1962–8 the average annual rate of growth of Spanish exports to the Common Market countries was 8·7 per cent. In 1969–72 this average leaped to 28·6 per cent. In 1972 nearly 40 per cent of Spain's capital good exports went to the Common Market countries. Four years earlier 70 per cent had been absorbed by the Americas (54 per cent to Latin America).[20] In 1975 the EEC bought 44 per cent of Spanish exports and supplied 34 per cent of Spain's imports. The future of Spain's relations with the EEC is therefore of considerable importance.

Spain's dealings with the Common Market have been protracted and, although results have so far been meagre, the subject has given rise to much emotion and debate within Spain. The economic advantages and drawbacks of any association have at times (particularly in the early 1960s and again, following the death of Franco, at the end of 1975) been heavily overshadowed by the political aspirations of those who felt that greater contact with the Common Market countries would have a decisive effect on the evolution of Spanish politics, whether for good or ill.[21] In 1962 the Foreign Ministry officially requested the opening of negotiations with a view to examining the possibility of Spain becoming an Associate Member of the EEC. It was not, however, until five years later that a negotiating mandate for a preferential trade agreement was issued and agreement on this basis was not reached until March 1970.[22]

Over the years the area to be covered by any agreement diminished. The major diminution in scope came when it was clear that the Common Market countries would not tolerate any agreement which would directly lead to closer political association as long as Spain's political system remained unchanged. The area of agreement on economic matters was limited. The 1970 agreement consisted almost entirely of arrangements for the reduction of specific tariffs on industrial goods. Very little provision was made for agricultural products and there was no reference to the movement of labour, foreign investment or to more general policies of economic harmonisation. The 1970 agreement in principle covered two phases, although there was to be no automatic transfer from the first phase, scheduled to last six years, to the second phase. Under the first agreement, the EEC offered a 60 per cent reduction on the tariff of industrial goods which could be raised to 70 per cent at a later date, if Spain were willing to make counter-concessions. This reduction did not apply to a list of exceptions for which the tariff reduction was either excluded altogether or was smaller (40 per cent) and scheduled to take place over the six years. As far as agricultural products were concerned, concessions could only be granted when Spanish prices would not undercut price levels agreed by the Community. This has meant, for example, that in the citrus season preferential facilities are frequently withdrawn for periods of varying duration until Spanish and EEC prices are realigned. In return Spain promised three categories of tariff reductions also based on 1968 figures. Tariffs on goods falling under List A were to be cut by 60 per cent and those in Lists B and C by 25 per cent in a series of gradual reductions.[23] Spain also offered a list of exemptions covering a fairly wide range of goods, including certain steel and chemical products, machinery and cars. Spain, in addition to tariff concessions, undertook to increase the quantity of goods imported under quota arrangements from the Community at a rate of 13 per cent a year.[24] Various undertakings were also made by Spain in relation to the purchase of EEC dairy products.

The negotiations and the final 1970 agreement gave rise to much speculation and discussion as to its merits and disadvantages.[25] In general, it was felt that after so many years' waiting the lion had brought forth a mouse. On the other hand, it should be remembered that many Spanish businesses still fear further concessions on imports of industrial goods, which would expose inefficient and highly protected firms. No detailed study has been made of the effects of Spain's concessions to the EEC, although it has been claimed[26] that, by basing the cuts on temporary rather than fixed tariffs, Spain's offer was more generous than it at first appears, as temporary duties tended to be appreciably lower than fixed ones.[27] Despite this, Spain does not seem to have been unduly affected by the tariff cuts already made on imports from the EEC.[28]

Following the expansion of the Common Market to include Britain, Denmark and Ireland, arrangements were made to adjust Spain's preferential trade agreement. This was to be done within the framework of an EEC mandate which included other Mediterranean countries despite Spain's preference for separate agreements. Negotiations again proceeded very slowly. Spain was anxious to see more favourable terms introduced for agricultural exports and to ensure that further dismantling of Spanish tariffs on industrial goods should take place over a fairly long transitional period. Slowness in progress was in part due to internal tensions within the EEC and the difficulties of reconciling Mediterranean interests which include Arab countries as well as Israel, and partly to substantial differences between the negotiating positions of the Common Market and Spain. In the course of 1974 it became clear that the Common Market was not prepared to offer any concessions on agricultural produce, nor to reduce tariffs on certain 'sensitive' Spanish products, including some steel products and footwear, before 1980. On the other hand, the EEC wished to see nearly all barriers to EEC industrial exports dismantled by 1980. Spain felt unable to grant the concessions required by the EEC, especially in view of the tough stance adopted by the Common Market on Spanish 'sensitive' industrial goods and farm produce, and early in 1975 the negotiations reached a stalemate.

Early in 1976 talks were resumed on updating the 1970 agreement.[29] Spain has indicated willingness to grant certain concessions in the industrial sector in return for better terms on agricultural products. Terms of access for agricultural products constitute a delicate and difficult topic as Spanish produce will compete directly with many French and Italian agricultural products. Despite Spain's Foreign Minister making it clear that Spain desired full membership with the Common Market as soon as was practicable, talks have been restricted to trade negotiations and there is no suggestion that the conclusion of a new agreement carries overtones of full membership in the near future. An application for membership is unlikely to be given serious consideration in advance of extensive changes in Spain's political life.

Despite Spain's good export performance since the early 1960s, the pace of growth has ensured that imports have also increased substantially. The ratio of exports to imports has rarely risen above 50 per cent and the trade deficit is a long-standing feature of the balance of payments. The increases in workers' remittances from abroad and the enormous growth in tourism, however, enabled substantial surpluses to build up on current account between 1970 and 1973.

The idea that tourism could be beneficial to Spain and should be encouraged took root under Primo de Rivera's dictatorship when the first State-controlled hotels, the *paradores*, were inaugurated. At the beginning of the 1950s, tourism began to increase in an appreciable fashion. The real breakthrough took place, however, after 1959, the year in which entry visas were abolished for tourists from Western Europe. In 1959, 2·8 million tourists went to Spain. By 1960 the number had already risen to 4·3 million.[30] All through the 1960s tourism was the boom industry *par excellence*. In 1965 there were 11 million tourists and by 1970 over 21 million. In 1973 the number had risen to 34 million and receipts from tourism at $2.8 billion covered over 80 per cent of the trade deficit. Between 1960 and 1973 the number of beds available in hotels and more humble establishments increased from 150,821 to 699,440. Additionally, in 1973 camping sites provided another possible 211,631 places and beds available in apartments, villas, chalets, etc., rose to over 2 million by 1973.

Throughout the 1960s Spain extracted full benefit from its national climatic advantages by its cheapness in relation to other Mediterranean competitors and by catering for the mass market. In 1967 OECD figures showed that Spain was a very close second to Italy in the league of tourist earnings. The apparently limitless flow of tourists set up a wave of speculative building and development, especially along the eastern and south-eastern coastline. While the government lays down strict maximum and minimum price ranges for different categories of hotels, in other respects the development of tourist facilities has been practically unbridled. The need for some sort of control to check the worst excesses of hasty development was recognised in the late 1960s, but this has had few practical consequences.[31] In 1966 the Costa del Sol was declared *de interés turístico* but to little effect. The government has influenced the development of tourism through the allocation of credit to hotels and, less directly, though decisively, through the financing of infrastructure projects, but in the Second Plan, of total investment envisaged in the tourist industry, only 20 per cent was to be undertaken by the public sector. Private interests were encouraged to provide accommodation and other amenities subject to virtually no control.

At the beginning of the 1970s there were stirrings of doubt as to whether the very great dependence on mass-market tourism was advisable. Average expenditure per tourist was declining in real terms and Spain was also facing increased competition for this type of tourism from Greece, Yugoslavia and various North African countries. Possibly an attempt at greater diversification should be made and a larger part of the tourist industry be developed to attract higher-spending visitors. One disadvantage of the way in which tourism has developed is the heavy concentration of tourists both in geographical and seasonal terms. Accommodation figures for hotels and pensions show that the Balearic Islands alone provide almost one-third of this type of accommodation. Two-thirds of hotel and pension accommodation is concentrated within six provinces.[32] Nearly 40 per cent of all tourists visit Spain in July and August, which causes severe seasonal employment difficulties.

The government has made some attempt to counteract this by providing financial backing for setting up ski resorts in the principal mountain ranges. So far, while growing in popularity, the Spanish resorts do not constitute any real competition to other established European winter sports centres. Attempts at a wider seasonal spread have also been made by encouraging conferences in the major cities in off-peak seasons (this is done extensively in Madrid) and in promoting cheaper off-season package tours.

Such expedients, while beneficial, cannot provoke any fundamental changes. Tourism has developed in Spain in the way it has because Spain could provide sunny coastal holidays which large numbers of people wanted and at prices which they could afford. A wide range of cultural and sporting activities exists in Spain, but despite the opportunities available for diverse types of recreation, the fact remains that it is the coastal areas, ironically now the least 'Spanish' areas of Spain, which attract the overwhelming majority of tourists. Three-quarters of nights spent by tourists in Spain are in the coastal resorts. The success of any effort to spread tourist amenities must be largely determined by whether there is a corresponding change in tourist attitudes. Moreover, while in theory it might be desirable for Spain to be less dependent on package tours and low-spending tourists, arrangements have been built up over years between tour operators and hotels and it is unlikely that hoteliers, despite periodic disputes with the agencies, would welcome any wholesale reversion to individual arrangements. Concentration on the cheaper end of the market has had an effect on the relative development of different types of accommodation. Between 1962 and 1973 3-star hotels and 2-star pensions showed by far the greatest rate of growth, both categories increasing capacity by over 400 per cent. The most expensive (i.e. 5-star) hotels and (3-star) pensions showed the slowest rates of growth. Reversing the trend would be an expensive activity.

The shock caused by the number of tourists actually falling by 12 per cent in 1974 and the consequent problems experienced by the tourist industry have probably put an end to any ambitious plans aimed at attracting higher-spending tourists in large numbers in the near future. In 1975 Spain proved anxious to remain attractive to the mass tourist market and hotels were allowed only small price increases, despite strong pressure from hoteliers.[33] The bankruptcy of several tour agencies and the collapse of the real estate company, Sofico, brought home the fact that tourism, like other business, is dependent upon factors outside Spain as well as within. It is unlikely that the phenomenal rate of growth of tourism can be repeated. On the one hand the most popular areas are close to saturation point. On the other, Spain now faces far more price competition from other countries.[34] This should be seen in perspective. While tourist figures for 1975 at

28 million had dropped to the levels of 1970–1, Spain still in 1974 earned more in gross terms than any other European country from tourism. Spain is fortunate in that tourism by no means depends exclusively on any one country. The greatest numbers come from France, Britain and the Federal Republic of Germany, but Spain is also popular with Switzerland and the Scandinavian countries and groups of tourists are beginning to arrive regularly from Eastern Europe. The tourist market is unlikely to show a long-term decline. What will be smaller is the rate of increase. Tourism will no longer be easy money.

One of the questions which tourism raises is how much impact the influx of so many people and so large an inflow of money has actually had on the Spanish economy and more specifically on the everyday life of the mass of Spaniards. Unfortunately it is a question which can be answered at best impressionistically. Even the crudest assessment as to how much of the money spent by tourists in Spain actually remains in the country is impossible to answer with any precision due to the lack of relevant figures. It can only be assumed that some portion of tourist receipts is spent on imports and some goes to non-Spanish owners of tourist facilities

As regards the secondary effects of tourism, these may not be as beneficial as one might at first sight suppose.[35] Moreover, in coastal areas a big tourist industry inflates prices, affecting those in the sur- rounding areas as well as in the towns. Nevertheless, despite the feeling difficult to resist in Castilian *pueblos*, not an hour's drive from Madrid, and in villages in the hills of Extremadura, that little has changed, this is an exaggeration. What have changed radically, above all in the south, are employment opportunities and the possibilities of earning a reasonable wage, even if only on a seasonal basis. In Ronald Fraser's description of the village of Tajos, in the province of Malaga, he details the tangible evidence of increases in living standards : 'In 1957 there were two lorries, two taxis, one motor scooter and no private cars. There was no public transport and mail arrived by donkey from Casas Nuevas each night. Television was unknown, only the better off owned radios and about a dozen newspapers were sold every day.' He goes on to say that in 1971 the vehicle park amounted to more than twenty lorries, five (modern) taxis, approximately ninety cars and 'a swarm of small, noisy, motor cycles'. Buses go to Casas Nuevas each hour and twice a day to Malaga. Television is universal 'and 125 news- papers are bought daily'.[36] The apparent wealth of consumer goods and indeed of bathrooms is also of recent origin. And the source of this change? The fact that the coastal resorts provide employment for 70 per cent of the population of the village of Tajos.

An aspect of the impact of tourism which is often overestimated is the change which it has supposedly brought about in the Spanish out-look and habits of thought. While the change is undoubtedly real as regards the opportunities available in employment in relation to oppor-tunities only thirty years earlier, the concurrent assumption that contact with foreigners has made a deep impact on the Spanish character seems unjustified. Frequently contact is so superficial and the foreigner at his or her least appealing that contact, in the sense of any real ex-change, is minimal and often serves merely to confirm previously held prejudices. Spaniards returning from work abroad are far more likely to be deeply influenced by foreign contacts. The wider social effect of the impact on Spaniards of working in other countries is a subject which merits more attention.

Remittances from Spaniards working abroad trebled between 1967 and 1973, totalling $913 million in 1973, equal to just over 30 per cent of receipts from tourism. While the number of workers leaving Spain each year fluctuated, the level of remittances rose steadily except in 1967 and 1968, years in which employment opportunities were low in Europe and few Spaniards therefore sought work abroad.[37] These official figures probably do not represent the total of such remittances, but they give a fair approximation of the sums involved. This source of income directly affects large numbers of Spaniards and the fact that emigration has continued whenever exterior economic circumstances permit shows that it is a profitable exercise, a fair proportion of savings from abroad being put towards buying a house or small business in Spain on return. Since 1974 Spaniards have found it increasingly hard to find work abroad. In 1975 some 80,000 emigrants returned to Spain, while those leaving Spain to seek employment elsewhere numbered only about 100 a month. The level of remittances fell in 1975. More-over, a large part was made up of severance payments and savings, rather than current earnings. 1976 shows no improvement in the situa-tion. Unlike the recession of 1967–8, the recession initiated by the rise in oil prices at the end of 1973 holds long-term implications for the prospects of Spaniards wishing to work abroad and therefore also for the Spanish economy. With unemployment high in 'host' countries and no prospects that levels will fall substantially in the near future, it will be a long time before Spaniards can hope to find employment outside Spain on any appreciable scale. The consequences of the in-ability of Spain to rely on exporting labour in the near future are considered in the next chapter.

At the beginning of the 1970s the strength of the balance-of-payments position was impressive compared with a decade earlier. Although the trade deficit had worsened, inflows from tourism, workers' remittances and foreign investment provided ample coverage. Moreover, reserves of gold and foreign exchange increased substantially after 1970. The rise in oil prices was, however, to transform the situation in a matter of months. Table 8.1 shows that the trade deficit doubled to $7 billion in 1974 (nearly two-thirds of the increase was caused by the rise in oil prices). Moreover, in the same year earnings from tourism and workers' remittances fell slightly. After a build up of surpluses on current account in the period 1970–3, a deficit of $3 billion was registered in 1974. Inflows from foreign investment also declined in 1974 and 1975, reflecting the international economic climate and also uncertainties about Spain's political future. As the level of reserves has long been a sensitive political issue,[38] the deficit has mainly been financed by borrowing. Borrowing from abroad both by the business community and the government has shown a marked increase.

TABLE 8.1   Balance of payments, 1968–75
(US $ million)

| | 1968 | 1969 | 1970 | 1971 | 1972 | 1973 | 1974 | 1975 |
|---|---|---|---|---|---|---|---|---|
| Imports (fob) | 3,242 | 3,865 | 4,357 | 4,577 | 6,236 | 8,912 | 14,334 | 15,067 |
| Exports (fob) | 1,667 | 1,994 | 2,483 | 2,978 | 3,920 | 5,367 | 7,265 | 7,789 |
| Trade balance | −1,575 | −1,871 | −1,874 | −1,599 | −2,316 | −3,545 | −7,069 | −7,278 |
| Foreign travel | 1,111 | 1,195 | 1,543 | 1,878 | 2,230 | 2,878 | 2,807 | 3,095 |
| Other services | −226 | −250 | −249 | −191 | −209 | −189 | −96 | −439 |
| Workers' remittances | 319 | 400 | 467 | 548 | 599 | 913 | 860 ⎱ | ⎰ 1,164 |
| Other private transfers | 129 | 150 | 192 | 224 | 276 | 508 | 370 ⎰ | |
| Official transfers | — | −18 | — | −5 | −9 | −7 | −8 | −19 |
| Total services and transfers | 1,333 | 1,477 | 1,953 | 2,454 | 2,887 | 4,103 | 3,933 | 3,801 |
| Current balance | −242 | −394 | 79 | 855 | 571 | 558 | −3,136 | −3,477 |
| Private long-term capital | 436 | 481 | 698 | 601 | 934 | 814 | 1,427 | 1,814 |
| Official long-term capital | 145 | 25 | −27 | −103 | −2 | −46 | 53 | 612[a] |
| Total long-term capital | 581 | 506 | 671 | 498 | 932 | 768 | 1,480 | 2,426 |
| Basic balance | 339 | 113 | 750 | 1,353 | 1,503 | 1,326 | −1,656 | −1,050 |
| Short-term capital, errors and omissions | −268 | −343 | 66 | −98 | −135 | 231 | 857 | 957 |
| Monetary movements (increase in assets = −) of which | −71 | 230 | −813 | −1,257 | −1,367 | −1,555 | 799 | 93 |
| Changes in reserves | −46 | 261 | −809 | −1,358 | −1,496 | −1,207 | 821 | 137 |

[a] Includes $581 million drawing on the IMF oil facility.

Source: OECD, *Economic Surveys* (Paris), using Ministry of Commerce figures.

INTERNAL TRADE

In spite of Primo de Rivera's road-building plans, transport and distribution facilities within Spain were minimally developed before the Civil War. Roads were poorly maintained and inadequate for any distributive purpose which required fast transport. The railways, in addition to being virtually cut off from the rest of Europe by the initial adoption of a broad gauge track, by no means covered all parts of Spain. To a large extent it was Spain's terrain which severely limited the development of distributive networks.[39] The large areas of mountainous land, the extremes of temperature do not facilitate or encourage the linking-up of different regions either by road or rail. Galicia, in particular, has always suffered from bad communications with the rest of Spain. George Hills could write, 'Such was the state of communications that in 1959 an orange from Valencia could be shipped to London more easily than by road to Galicia.'[40] Inevitably the destruction wrought by the Civil War made heavy inroads in the total 'stock' of viable road and railway equipment. It was not until the beginning of the 1960s that a conscious effort was made to expand infrastructure in any ambitious sense. Until then money and energy available had been used very largely in replacement of stock destroyed in the Civil War.

The deficiencies in transport and communications in Spain have intensified the natural tendency for commercial relations to remain largely geared to the immediate surrounding area. As Richardson points out, 'The main population concentrations are at least 250 miles apart from each other', and he goes on to say : 'In economic terms this multiple regional disintegration reveals itself in the fact that most industry is oriented to regional rather than national markets and in wide inter-regional differences in incomes, prices and levels of consumer durable ownership.'[41] No exhaustive survey exists on how prices are fixed and of the effects of geography and distribution costs on them. As mentioned earlier in Chapters 2 and 3, however, prices of some agricultural and industrial goods are fixed by the free play of supply and demand, but most are subject to some degree of government intervention. Regional factors give rise to disparities in price and the constant changes in government policy have produced a situation of such complexity that any detailed examination of these factors would lie far beyond the scope of this book. Observations are therefore limited to changes in the structure of wholesale and retail distributive outlets and developments in transportation.

According to the Contabilidad Nacional, retail and wholesale business accounted for 12 per cent of gross domestic product in 1973. In the same year this sector provided employment for approximately 11 per cent of the active population. The overriding characteristic of this sector is the enormous number of small businesses, often on a family basis, which employ very few people per establishment. In the Third Development Plan the number of wholesale establishments throughout Spain was assessed at 38,926 and retail businesses at 391,434. Given the local nature of many transactions, particularly in food products, the large number of retail outlets is not unexpected. What is more surprising is that figures in the Second and Third Development Plans show that the number of such establishments showed a slight increase in the 1960s. The small scale of most retail businesses is demonstrated by the fact that three-quarters of retail establishments provide employment for only one or two people. Moreover, over one-half of retail concerns employ unpaid assistance only, showing the family nature of many such establishments.[42] Because the vast majority of retail outlets are small, the volume of sales is low and consequently mark-up and therefore prices are often high. A study recently carried out on the citrus industry in Spain showed that for some varieties of citrus fruit the consumer was paying often five times the price paid to the farmer.[43] Wide variations in distribution costs on particular products in the different countries make generalised comparison difficult. The margin of difference between prices paid to the producer and paid by the consumer is not, however, uniformly greater in Spain than in the Common Market, according to a study undertaken by the Institute for the Reform of Commercial Structures.[44] On balance Spain's distribution costs, with the exception of transport, were not found to be appreciably higher than in the Common Market countries. Costs were higher for some agricultural products, for example vegetable oils, meat and dairy products,[45] but lower on some industrial products, such as textiles and building materials.

A problem caused by the fragmentation of the wholesale and retail trade is the difficulty of enforcing standards and quality control. This is particularly the case with agricultural products, where producers also tend to work in small units. Where such products are heavily dependent on the export market, and especially if competition is strong, some effort is usually made to enforce a higher degree of standardisation. This has been the case with citrus fruits and tomatoes.

Like many small businesses, retail traders find credit hard to come by and such loans as are made are predominantly on a short-term basis,[46] so that the expansion of an existing business or the merging of different establishments is no easy matter.[47] While there is no evidence that the number of retailers is diminishing, in some sectors of the wholesale trade, namely in food products, pharmaceutical products and textiles, there is some evidence of a desire to combine into larger units.

In the early years of the 1960s, the government, apart from *ad hoc* responses to particular pressures, paid little attention to domestic trading arrangements. As the decade progressed the authorities showed some interest in providing for the construction of modern centralised markets. In the Third Plan provision for financing wholesale markets accounted for well over 60 per cent of the total earmarked for domestic trade purposes. Some provision was also made for retail 'markets' and 'markets of origin'. Government interest seems to have been stimulated by increasing concern about prices for, while the labour-intensive nature of many distribution outlets helped to keep costs down when labour was cheap, the situation has now changed. Direct action by the government has for the most part been concentrated on the organisation of the marketing of foodstuffs. In 1968 all price intervention in the agricultural sector was brought under FORPPA's auspices,[48] in an attempt to co-ordinate agricultural price policies. A State company, Mercados Centrales de Abastecimiento SA (MERCASA), was set up under the aegis of CAT[49] to promote the building of new central markets. Later, in 1971, Mercados de Origen SA (MERCORSA) came into being with the aim of arranging collective marketing by producers. MERCORSA is dependent for 51 per cent of its finances on the Ministry of Agriculture and 49 per cent on CAT and until now has been primarily geared to the more efficient marketing of agricultural crops. Inclusion of livestock products is now under study. These schemes are only in their infancy and the number of 'markets of origin' for farm produce was only fifteen in 1974. Observation suggests that, while the number of intermediaries between producers and consumers has been diminished, prices have not always been correspondingly affected.

The government has also produced legislation on restrictive practices which should, in theory at least, affect domestic trade. In 1963 the Ley de Represión de las Prácticas Comerciales y Restrictivas de la Competencia was passed. Between 1963 and 1970 the Tribunal de Defensa de la Competencia had passed sentence on some seventy cases, most of which dealt with trivial infringements.[50] The consumer in Spain has generally had very little opportunity to make his views felt. Even now, when some consumers' associations have been formed, their rôle is negligible. This is in part because any such association has had until very recently to act in accordance with the Ley de Asociaciones of 1964 and this called for registration and subsequent operation under government auspices. Matters are not helped by the fact that the two consumers' societies which act on a national level have been controlled by the Movement. These various controls have ensured that the associations cannot be independent of the government and have therefore attracted few members. In 1974 there were twenty-eight consumers' associations and ninety housewives' societies.[51]

While the government began to show interest in exercising greater influence over domestic trading arrangements through the installation of central markets (again, as with other planning devices, on the French model) in the late 1960s, a more comprehensive approach was not thought necessary until late in 1973. At this point the necessity of trying to control inflation led the authorities to reorganise the Ministry of Commerce's responsibilities in this field. Until the autumn of 1973 responsibility for domestic trading arrangements was shared by the CAT and the Dirección General de Comercio Interior, both of which were dependent upon the Ministry of Commerce. In November 1973 the rôle of the CAT was redefined. While the Commissariat remained in theory an autonomous body, it was in fact placed under the jurisdiction of the Dirección General de Comercio Alimentario. At the same time an Institute for the Reform of Commercial Structures was created and, within the Ministry of Commerce, a new sub-secretariat 'de Mercado Interior' was put in charge of all the existing sections within the ministry which already dealt with various aspects of domestic trade. Moreover, the sub-secretary of this new section was also *ex officio* made president of the Junta Superior de Precios, a body set up with extensive powers over price control. This showed most clearly the identification of the government's increased interest in domestic trading arrangements with its anxiety over price increases. Further reorganisation has taken place in the Ministry of Commerce since 1973. A Dirección General for consumers has been set up and the Junta Superior de Precios has also undergone changes. As with many developments in Spain, it is impossible after such a short time to gauge what has actually been achieved by successive institutional changes and how much change is effective only on paper. One of the drawbacks of the current reform is that the Ministry of Commerce still has little working contact with the Ministry of Agriculture on a day-to-day basis, which slows down procedures and can lead to deadlock over particular issues. From the increase in self-service shops and the introduction of hypermarkets in 1973,[52] it is evident that the structure of the commercial sector is changing. To date the pace of change has been gradual.

The high cost of transport in distribution costs was referred to above. During the 1940s and 1950s the government's approach to transport was piecemeal. Roads were by and large neglected and government attention focused mainly on re-equipping the railways. In 1941 the Red Nacional de Ferrocarriles Españoles (RENFE) was established as a result of the government revoking most of its railway concessions.[53] RENFE was set up as an official monopoly and since a reorganisation in 1961 has enjoyed a considerable degree of independence. The transport sector as a whole grew at approximately the same rate as GDP throughout the 1960s and represented 5·6 per cent of GDP over the decade. In the 1960s the planning of transport investment was in the hands of different government agencies (i.e. RENFE) and there has been no attempt to provide an all-embracing transport policy, or to evaluate competing road and rail schemes in relation to each other. A ten-year modernisation programme was launched by RENFE in 1964. Three years prior to this a twelve-year national road-building and reconstruction programme was set up under government auspices but there is little evidence of any desire to ensure that the two programmes were complementary in aim or that they bore any relation to the other components or overall strategy of the development plans. Over the 1960s there was a noticeable shift in passenger traffic from the railways to the roads and to air transport. The main growth in freight traffic took place on the road (the share of road transport in the total of rail and road transport increased from 65 per cent in 1960 to 70 per cent in 1970)[54] and in coastal shipping.[55]

The modernisation programme undertaken by RENFE in 1964 (financed in part by the World Bank) aimed at a thorough overhaul of existing track, modernisation of rolling stock, a pruning of personnel and a revision of the structure of rates and fares. The programme was implemented with thoroughness and the quality of service improved. Nearly 3000 kilometres of railway track were renewed in the first six years of the programme, some uneconomic lines were closed and diesel engines have increasingly replaced steam. Between 1964 and 1970 manpower was reduced by 27 per cent. RENFE was still, however, the largest employer in Spain in 1974, with 72,934 employees.[56] In the initial four years after the programme's inception the deficit on operating account increased. However, in 1969 the deficit was smaller and had practically disappeared by 1970. Measures have recently been considered which would allow RENFE's management greater flexibility in relating rates and fares to costs and thus to sustaining the improved financial position. Despite these improvements RENFE still has to contend with a system which is in many ways deficient. The problem of long stretches of single-track line has been mitigated by the installation of sophisticated control-systems, but only 15 per cent of all lines are double-track and the continued existence of single-track lines means that traffic is slow. A fundamental difficulty with which RENFE contends in international passenger and freight traffic is the difference in the width of track *vis-à-vis* the rest of Europe. Tests have been made on a train which would automatically adjust from one width to another on crossing the border, but this is not yet a viable commercial proposition.

Given the costly nature of any radical changes in the Spanish railway system due to the mountainous and rocky nature of much of the country, it is not surprising that other forms of transport should have grown more rapidly in the 1960s. Despite the poor state of most roads at the end of the 1950s, freight and passenger traffic both increased at an annual average rate of 11 per cent over the decade of the 1960s. This was partly due to the improvement of the basic road network under the 1961 road-building and reconstruction plan which was divided into three four-year phases. The road network in Spain is, like the railways, a radial system centred on Madrid. In 1974, 78,659 kilometres were the responsibility of the central government and 64,034 kilometres fell within the orbit of the local authorities. The roads maintained by the central government have benefited most from expenditure both under the general terms of the plan and under the special plans, i.e. Red de Itinerarios Asfálticos (REDIA) 1967–72, which set out to improve conditions on some 5000 kilometres of major roads with high traffic density, and Programa de Autopistas Nacionales Españolas (PANE), which has undertaken the building of motorways on a toll basis, aiming at 3000 kilometres in twelve years. In 1974, 738 kilometres of motorway had been built and a further 1399 kilometres were under construction. Despite the emphasis on improving the condition of roads, under 30 per cent of roads maintained by the central authorities in 1969 had modern surfacing and even those which have been widened and resurfaced are often still inadequate for the increasing load of heavy traffic.[57]

The number of trucks in use trebled in the period 1964–74. However, in 1970 over 90 per cent of trucks engaged in freight transport were still owned by firms or individuals with a maximum fleet of two trucks (many with only one). The growth in trucks has been stimulated by liberal credit arrangements on behalf of truck manufacturers to small truckers.[58] Between 1965 and 1974 the total number of coaches, cars, buses and trucks trebled, reaching over 6 million in 1974. While the original plan for improving the road network was quite ambitious in terms of road conditions in the early 1960s, it proved inadequate to the needs of the early 1970s, though this has to some extent been overcome by the addition of the plans, REDIA and PANE. Motorways, even at competitive prices, are not cheap to build and increased expenditure on *autopistas* has necessarily entailed less spending on minor roads. Although Spain undoubtedly needs better major roads, the price seems yet again to entail the neglect of the poorer regions.

Coastal shipping is an important element in domestic freight transport, accounting for some 30 per cent of total traffic. Approximately one-third of Spain's seaborne external trade is carried in Spanish bottoms. Maximum tariffs are imposed on domestic freight charges and on imported goods which fall in the category of 'State Commerce'. Apart from these restrictions, traders may follow international tariffs or come to private agreements.[59] The shipping trade still attracts a large number of small entrepreneurs. At the beginning of the 1970s there were more than 320 businesses of this kind and 85 per cent of these had fleets registered at less than 5000 Gross Registered Tonnage. Many of these small owners possess just one ship and are unable to meet the cost of replacement, so that a sizable proportion of the fleet, especially in coastal shipping, is of considerable age. Nearly 60 per cent of total shipping tonnage is handled by seven ports,[60] although along the length of the Spanish coastline there are some 200 ports. The twenty-six largest ports enjoy semi-autonomous status, while the rest are under a centralised port administration, La Comisión Administrativa de Grupos de Puertos, which is under the aegis of the Ministry of Public Works.

Air transport grew rapidly in the 1960s and domestic air traffic grew by 14 per cent per annum. Air freight has grown at the expense of rail freight. Both Iberia and Aviaco are owned by the INI and these two airlines have a monopoly on domestic flights which has proved profitable.[61] There are currently forty-eight civilian airports in Spain, of which the most used are Madrid, Palma de Mallorca, Malaga, Barcelona, Las Palmas and Santa Cruz de Tenerife.[62]

In all probability the trend evident in the 1960s towards greater use of road and air transport at the expense of the railways will continue despite the greatly increased cost of crude oil. Spain is geographically more suited to road or air traffic and it is almost certainly uneconomic to improve railway stock and track sufficiently to make it a competitively viable alternative. In domestic trade, the distances served only by single track are a serious obstacle to big increases in traffic and, in international terms, the difference in track gauges over the Pyrenees is an expensive difference to cater for. Coastal shipping will probably continue to hold its own, although it is difficult to foresee any significant increase in its share in domestic trade. While on the face of it the large number of enterprises engaged in road transport and coastal shipping might appear to be economically inefficient, fragmentation in this sector does not seem to be a particular disadvantage. (It could be said that the most efficient distribution service in Spain is the overnight transport of fresh sea fish to Madrid from Galicia.) While so much of Spanish industry remains on a small scale and physically widely dispersed, it is probably as efficient to have transport organised on a similarly small scale. The one major drawback which faces the small entrepreneurs in coastal shipping is shared with other small businesses (although not with small-scale truckers), and that is the difficulty of obtaining credit. If this situation persists, then it is likely that the small-scale coastal trader will gradually be forced out of business and this sector will eventually become concentrated in fewer hands.

# 9 Perspectives

This book has been concerned with changes and developments in the Spanish economy since 1959. Areas where little has changed have been indicated as well as those where much has altered. This has not been in order to belittle undoubted achievements but because emphasis on 'successful' developments in the economy and, in particular, overall rates of growth has too often led to an uncritical assumption of equal progress on all fronts.

It would of course be unrealistic to expect a wholesale transformation in so short a period. A history of autarky in industrial and agricultural practices and the circumscribed geographical nature of most commercial dealings were not legacies which could be discarded in a decade. In addition, the Spanish authorities have had to cope with an unprecedented flow of labour from the countryside into the towns. Providing adequate housing, education and social services facilities for so many people in such a short space of time was a Herculean task, particularly given the minimal bases on which these could be grafted. Nevertheless, while it would be naïve to expect any early or comprehensive transformation, the still substantial pockets of poverty indicate that there is scope for further change. Despite much greater affluence, the long hours worked, the prevalence of moonlighting, cramped living conditions and inadequate municipal and social services for many point to the fact that concentration on macro-economic growth rates can be misleading.

What rôle has the government played in economic developments? The Spanish economy is a mixture of State and privately run business. In this it is not different from other West European countries, although proportions vary. The most direct routes of influence open to the government have been through the activities of the INI companies (which account for approximately one-quarter of industrial investment), through price controls and through subsidies to both the industrial and agricultural sectors. Agricultural subsidies were estimated at some Ptas 80 billion in 1974. Despite the publication of the three development plans, evidence of any cohesive economic strategy remains elusive. The practice of simply cataloguing projects gives little indication of government priorities. Under the plans, the onus of industrial development was placed on the private sector. This has not meant, however, that private industry has been exempt from government controls. While the private sector suffers from few restrictions on standardisation of procedures or products and enjoys considerable privileges as regards taxation, it is hemmed in by endless petty controls, licences and red tape. *Papeleo* – paperwork – invades every activity. Government influence is felt through a series of controls ranging from regulations affecting the size and location of factories[1] to price controls. The application of some measures, such as the granting of credit or export facilities, while selective, conveys no impression that their concession is based on criteria connected with any overall policy nor indeed on the merits of a particular project. In many cases one suspects that *enchufe* remains as important as ever.

Three factors have militated against the government adopting a more defined approach towards the public companies or a more co-ordinated approach in relation to the private sector. First and foremost is the structure of the Cabinet and the Civil Service. Since the early 1960s the Cabinet has been composed of men of very differing political views and ideologies. This was the result of Franco's practice of keeping different and even opposing political forces in check by having them represented at Cabinet level.[2] When one group appeared to be getting too powerful, a shift in numbers or personalities served to adjust the balance. This in itself led to difficulties in producing a cohesive view on economic policy at any given moment, let alone over a period of time. Franco's policy of awarding ministerial posts largely on the basis of balancing political forces also increased the difficulty of achieving co-operation between ministers.

The effects of this would have been less far-reaching if the Civil Service had been organised on a less fragmented basis. Civil Service hierarchies are based not simply on a particular ministry but on a large number of different and often competing corps.[3] The Civil Service contains over 200 corps. This has resulted in rivalries and can cause one group in a government department to disregard work carried out by another. The overlapping of work and frequent contradictions in ministerial publications, as well as the spoken word, act as a very real obstacle to coordinated thought or action. Moreover, there have been cases where certain corps seem to have exerted influence in pursuit of a particular policy on grounds in no way related to any wider economic strategy.[4] Methods of employment also contribute to confusion in the Civil Service bureaucracy. Competing agencies recruit employees regardless of overall needs. 'Indeed, not even the Government itself is quite sure how many persons it has in its employ.'[5] Once employed, prospects depend largely on the prestige and political influence of the particular corps in question; so does pay, as there is in practice no unified system by which wages are paid according to age or qualifications. Attempts have been made to reform the corps system and in 1965 a law was passed providing a unified pay structure for all civil servants.[6] Reform, however, has been slow and in many cases new names have simply served as a cloak for old practices. The corps system is still very much in evidence, despite the vaunted 'new look' of the technocrats.

A further factor which has militated against the implementation of integrated economic policies has, paradoxically, been the degree of centralisation. This has resulted from the development of provincial offshoots of central government departments which have little contact with local institutions and equally little with similar bodies from different central government departments or even from within the same ministry.[7] The proliferation of central government representatives in the provinces is shown by the fact that approximately only 14 per cent of central government employees work in Madrid.[8] The sheer number of government agencies linked to the parent body in Madrid rather than with complementary bodies in the same provincial town makes the enforcement of any policy subject to numerous interpretations. Moreover, the lack of any genuine working contact between local and central government also hinders attempts at co-ordination.[9] The reluctance of the government to allow local institutions any real power often makes it extremely difficult for the authorities to impose a particular policy. Even if the policy itself does not arouse resentment at local level, the institutional structures necessary for its implementation often simply do not exist.

The government has thus been hampered in the formulation and the execution of economic policies by the unco-ordinated nature of the administration. It has also been hindered by the desire of the government, on the one hand, to encourage free enterprise, and the conflicting fear of the political consequences which might follow in the wake of greater freedom from government regulation and control.

Government policies have influenced development but not primarily within the framework of the development plans. Even in the public sector, where objectives laid down in the plans were supposedly binding, targets were seldom met. Both in the public and the private sector, priorities remained vague. Since the decision at the end of the 1950s to open Spain's frontiers to the outside world, the government's stance has encouraged economic expansion. Interest rates were kept low and exports and other sectors, shipbuilding for example, have been helped by various subsidies and incentives. If the government had not taken a more positive attitude towards expansion there would have been no 'miracle'. On the other hand, government policies specifically designed to promote economic development have been fairly haphazard, both in conception and execution. The impetus to growth has come from a variety of sources. Spain's industrial development benefited enormously in the 1960s from the substantial imports of capital goods. Nor can the effects of the economic growth experienced in Europe over most of the 1960s be discounted. Rising prosperity in Europe provided tourists in increasing numbers and also an expanding market for Spanish exports. The abundance of cheap labour made it possible to exploit to the full the benefits of tourism and also of foreign investment which was forthcoming from Europe and the USA. The era of growth in Europe provided employment for literally hundreds of thousands of Spaniards in the 1960s. This had the double advantage of exporting unemployment and creating a flow of remittances into Spain.

Spain's vulnerability to the international economic climate was clearly shown in 1974. While affected rather later than other Western European countries, by the end of 1974 Spain, too, had become acutely aware of the economic difficulties which had affected other countries earlier in the year. The widening trade deficit caused by the rise in oil prices, the cash-flow problems faced by many firms, the rising number of bankruptcies and the especial problems faced by the textile, construction and shipbuilding sectors all echoed the earlier experience of neighbouring countries. Before looking more closely at the impact of the recession and future prospects of the economy, a brief indication of the importance of oil to the economy is necessary.

ENERGY AND OIL

Spain was particularly badly hit by the rise in oil prices in 1973 because, although a relatively small consumer of energy,[10] Spain depends on crude oil for nearly 70 per cent of its energy needs. This heavy dependence on oil is a comparatively recent development. In 1960, 47 per cent of primary energy consumption was made up of solid fuels, mainly coal, 28 per cent of petroleum and 24 per cent was hydroelectric energy. By 1974, 67 per cent of primary energy requirements were met by petroleum, 14 per cent each by solid fuels and hydroelectric energy, nearly 3 per cent by nuclear energy and the remainder by natural gas. With the quadrupling of electric energy output between 1960 and 1974, dependence on oil increased markedly. In 1960 the electricity system was based almost entirely on hydroelectricity. By 1973, thermally-generated power was the chief source and approximately one-half of electricity supplies came from oil. Since 1970 a nuclear power programme has been under way.

Not only does Spain depend on oil for over two-thirds of its energy requirements, but nearly all oil is imported. The search for oil deposits both on the peninsula and off-shore has to date not been very rewarding. In 1974 production from the Ayoluengo field near Burgos and the Amposta offshore field accounted for under 5 per cent of domestic demand and no large increase in production can be expected from Amposta. In 1975 the search for oil was stepped up and the INI has a large investment programme earmarked for this purpose in the period 1976–81. While little oil has so far been found in Spain, oil refining capacity has grown rapidly. The Spanish government has exercised varying degrees of control over the distribution and refining of petroleum products since 1927 when the Monopolio de Petróleos was formed. The aims of the Monopoly were twofold : first, to derive fiscal benefit from the traffic in oil and, second, to acquire greater control over the oil sector by buying up deposits abroad, by building a fleet of tankers and by developing a refining industry in Spain itself. The Monopoly is a State organisation, attached to the Treasury, which controls imports, distribution and sales of petroleum all over Spain,[11] and is run by la Compañía Arrendataria del Monopolio de Petróleos SA (CAMPSA), of which 30 per cent of the capital is held by the State. The government is responsible for fixing the prices of various types of petroleum products and for authorising refining and distilling. Of its original aims, CAMPSA has fulfilled only the first, through its control over distribution either directly or through concessionaries. In so far as controlling the various stages in the industrial processing of oil is concerned, CAMPSA has made little impact. There is little sign of a Spanish tanker fleet, nor of Spanish purchase of foreign deposits and, while oil-refining capacity has grown fast, the influence of CAMPSA has been small. Refineries represent a mixture of Spanish and foreign interests, and State participation is carried out through INI as well as CAMPSA holdings. Since 1967 refining capacity has been comfortably higher than domestic demand and, by 1980, refining capacity should amount to nearly 87 million tons, providing ample coverage of domestic demand and a surplus for export, as well as facilitating the expansion of the chemical industry.

At the beginning of 1974 Spain appeared not to take the higher prices of crude oil unduly seriously. This may have been due to hopes that traditional good relations with the Arab countries would soften the blow. In the event good relations served to ensure supply but not to bring about price reductions. While attempts are being made to attain greater self-sufficiency in oil supplies, prospecting to date has yielded meagre results and more effort is currently being expended on accelerating the development of alternative sources of energy. In 1975 a national energy plan was published, outlining government objectives for 1985. Since coal supplies are dwindling and of poor quality, it is forecast that gas will provide an appreciably larger share of the primary energy sector. Heavy reliance is to be placed on the use of nuclear energy for electrical power. It is estimated that nuclear energy, which currently provides 2 per cent of total energy needs, will account for over 23 per cent by 1985. In accordance with the plan, various targets for electrical power have been fixed and electricity companies which are prepared to join the *acción concertada* will be eligible for fiscal benefits. Whether the incentives offered will be sufficient to achieve the shift away from the high degree of dependence on oil remains to be seen. Fulfilling the targets will be no easy task. Increases in natural gas will depend largely on developments in production and liquefying facilities in Algeria, while technical difficulties in the production of nuclear energy still remain to be solved. The ambitious scope of the nuclear programme will make it a costly exercise. In the short run at least, there is little opportunity for a major reduction in the oil import bill, barring a fortunate discovery of substantial oil deposits on Spanish territory.

RECESSION AND FUTURE PROSPECTS

Between 1961 and 1973 GNP increased at a rate of over 7 per cent per annum in real terms. In 1974, the rate of growth was 4·5 per cent. A year later growth in GNP was under 1 per cent and industrial production fell. In 1975, for the first time since the early 1960s, active population figures failed to show an increase, reflecting employment difficulties.[12] Since 1974, the government has been treading a difficult path, attempting to stimulate the economy by various public expenditure programmes and thereby reduce unemployment, while at the same time trying to curb inflation by selective (and often not very effective) methods of control. A policy of more active economic management has resulted in the greater use of fiscal and monetary instruments. Nevertheless, growth with low rates of inflation has proved as difficult to achieve in Spain as elsewhere.

Spain's economy in the 1960s and early 1970s was characterised by cycles of a stop-go nature and it would be possible to argue that the problems which stand out sharply in the latest recessive phase are by no means new and could be regarded as in earlier cycles as transient difficulties. While it is true that the problems of inflation, unemployment and a balance-of-payments trade deficit are by no means novel features of the Spanish economy, there are fewer grounds for optimism than on previous occasions of a speedy return to fast rates of growth. The recession which began to affect Spain in 1974 has been prolonged and few of the associated problems are capable of any rapid solution. An additional factor is that an era of European growth comparable to that experienced in the 1960s cannot be readily anticipated in the next few years. This, too, is bound to have an effect on Spain's economic development.

Some sectors, such as shipbuilding and the construction industry, have been particularly badly hit by the recession. The collapse of the tanker market has wrought havoc in the shipbuilding yards and, while the government has provided assistance, this cannot in the long term compensate for shrinking order books. The construction sector will also have difficulty in making any full-scale recovery in the short term. The bankruptcy of various real-estate companies has had a sobering effect on the property market and it is questionable whether the heady days of the 1960s will return to real estate. Moreover, the likelihood that tourist numbers will increase only slowly precludes another boom in tourist infrastructure. Buildings of a different type, such as offices and warehouses, may become more important.

Since 1974, rates of inflation have been appreciably higher than in earlier years. In 1974 the official cost-of-living index rose by 17·4 per cent. In 1975 the rise was under 15 per cent but reached close to 20 per cent in 1976. Since these figures are based on an outmoded 'shopping basket', it is probable that inflation has in fact been running at a higher rate. Price controls, which include limits on commercial margins, have not proved especially effective. Indeed it appears that in 1976 prices subject to varying degrees of surveillance actually rose faster than those which technically were free. Despite the linking of wage increases to the cost-of-living index (plus 2 per cent), the labour force's disregard of the ruling and the reluctance of the government (for political reasons) to enforce it, resulted in wage increases in the region of 25 and 30 per cent in 1974 and 1975, either overtly or through concealed bonuses. It is highly unlikely that any effective wage restraint could be introduced prior to recognition of the 'unofficial' trade unions and far from certain thereafter.

A distinctive feature of the recent recession has been the high level of unemployment. In 1967–8, also a time of recession and high unemployment, numbers affected were only one-half as high as in 1976, when by official reckoning unemployment was close to 5 per cent and probably closer to 8 per cent of the workforce. Not only are far more people out of work, but the prospect of their finding employment in the near future is limited. Few of the European countries to which Spaniards have gone to seek work will wish to employ foreign labour until domestic unemployment levels have fallen substantially. This will be a slow process and even then for a variety of reasons 'host countries' are unlikely to encourage large influxes of foreign labour. Unemployment levels remained low, officially below 2 per cent, in the 1960s and early 1970s because Spain was able to export large numbers of workers abroad. Over the 1960s the government was able to assume, if not explicitly, that a constant outlet existed abroad for surplus labour. It is not likely that more than a small proportion of the unemployed can be absorbed once recovery is under way. The return of former emigrants and the inability of potential emigrants to leave has created a large pool of 'extra' labour. Moreover, the most successful parts of industry in the past few years have been those which have been capital- rather than labour-intensive. Investment patterns show that this trend is likely to continue. This poses a problem for the government. Should it, through the concession of official credit and subsidies, favour capital-intensive enterprises or will it feel obliged to foster more labour-intensive industry in order to reduce unemployment? Since the early 1960s the expansion of employment opportunities in industry has not been sufficient to absorb the increase in the active population. Many sought and found work abroad and large numbers of others found employment in the service sector, especially in the rapidly expanding tourist industry. Slower growth in the tourist trade will mean that here, too, employment opportunities will be limited. It is a striking feature of the economy that in the last few years employment opportunities have scarcely risen in industry and it is the service sector that has provided employment opportunities.

The balance-of-payments trade deficit is unlikely to be reduced for some time. In the absence of a fortunate oil strike, Spain is likely to continue heavily dependent on oil imports for energy needs. The rise in oil prices was not passed on to the Spanish consumer as rapidly as in many other countries and the amount of oil consumed in 1976 showed an appreciable increase over consumption figures a year earlier. The trade deficit cannot, however, be wholly blamed on the rise in oil prices. The agricultural trade deficit of $1 billion in 1975 reflects a structural maladjustment which can only be rectified by the government's adoption of very different agricultural policies. Nor is it probable that the trade deficit can be substantially reduced by increases in exports. While Spain's export performance in manufactured goods has been extremely good since the mid-1960s, it will be difficult for Spain to maintain the previous high rates of expansion. The volume of world trade is unlikely to increase at rates comparable to those of the late 1960s and early 1970s. Moreover, while Spanish labour costs are still cheaper than comparable costs in most of Western Europe, the margin is fast being eroded by the size of wage increases since 1973. Since earnings from tourism and workers' remittances are likely to increase only slowly, the deficit on current account will probably not fall below $3 billion in the near future. Rising labour costs and political uncertainties are also affecting Spain's attraction for foreign investors. Given the increasing volume of trade between Spain and the Common Market countries, the result of negotiations will be of considerable importance to those who favour Spain as an export base. The problems outlined above give ground for caution in assuming that once the international economic climate has improved Spain will automatically once again experience rapid rates of growth.

It may seem grudging to dwell on these problems in the light of growth rates achieved over the 1960s and early 1970s. Present difficulties will, however, influence future development and, while growth has been impressive over the last decade, it must be remembered that the 'starting-off' base was a low one. On the positive side Spain is reasonably well-endowed with natural resources. Iron ore and coking-coal are available, though in limited quantity and poor in quality, and coal is available for thermal power. While Spain's hydroelectric capacity is not infinite, thermal power has been extended with ease and Spanish uranium deposits will facilitate the expansion of nuclear energy. In so far as energy resources are concerned, crude oil constitutes the most glaring deficiency. Spain has the world's largest deposits of sulphur pyrites. Copper, lead, tin, zinc, mercury, wolfram and manganese are mined, although in quite small quantities. Raw materials for textiles, for instance wool and cotton, are also available, although the emphasis in the textile industry is increasingly on man-made fibres.

Spain also derives benefit from a hard-working labour force. While government programmes have done little to provide training in new skills, workers returning from abroad from diverse types of employment have contributed to the development of a more highly skilled workforce. On the demand side the latent market, in particular for consumer durables is substantial. Purchases of such products have grown rapidly since the early 1960s, but there is still a large untapped market for such goods.

The fact remains that, in addition to the most immediate problems posed by the 1974 recession, the Spanish economy, despite the 'miracle', is still characterised by anomalies remaining from earlier epochs and these are likely to assume greater importance in less propitious times. The failure of agricultural production to respond to new patterns of demand, the protection afforded to much of Spanish industry which results in costly products in terms of international prices, as in the case of steel, are obvious examples. Another is the erratic way in which official credit has been made available. With the projected expansion of official credit facilities, particularly in the financing of energy and steel projects, this factor will become increasingly important. The next few years will show clearly how far the Spanish miracle has been based on a real transformation of the bases of the economy.

Throughout this book little mention has been made of the inter-relationship of political choices and economic decisions. The question of Spain's political evolution is, however, bound to affect the bias of future economic policy-making. First in a negative way, a prolonged period of unease and indecision makes the prospect of a more co-ordinated approach to economic policy and planning a distant one. The harmful consequences of indecision were clearly shown in the delay in implementing the measures supposed to accompany the devaluation of the peseta in February 1976.[13] Second, once in power, one political group would emphasise policy which another would deem unimportant. Under what group would the public sector be most likely to expand? Who would, in practice, favour and possibly implement a radical tax reform? More fundamental, perhaps, than the espousal of any economic ideology is the attitude which the ruling group adopts towards the organisation of the administration. As long as the means of implementing policy remain so diverse and fraught with rivalries, any government will have difficulty in taking a more active part in shaping the evolution of the Spanish economy. The 1960s and the early 1970s have seen the development of a more scientific approach to economic policy but the gap between theory and realities remains wide.

# Postscript

Since the death of Franco, there have been many – and widely publicised – political changes. Meanwhile, preoccupation with politics seems to have precluded the development of a coherent economic policy to deal with the problems referred to in this book. Indeed, in the absence of any such policy and with the gradual loosening of the authoritarian framework, the economic situation has deteriorated.

In recent weeks, however, two institutional changes have been announced which could have important implications for the structure of Spanish economic life. First, the Movimiento has been formally disbanded. Second, the right to form independent trade unions has been recognised by the government. These developments should pave the way for a more realistic approach to labour relations. Without this, other necessary policies seem unlikely to be workable for long.

It remains to hope that the June elections will produce a government which feels sufficiently secure to come to grips with the pressing economic problems.

*May 1977*

# Notes

1   The Stabilisation Plan is referred to in more detail in Chapter 3.
2   Spain became a full member of the OEEC in 1959 (later known as OECD).
3   This depends largely on what years are chosen for comparison and, since figures, especially for the 1950s, are notoriously unreliable, this is not discussed more fully here. For an interesting discussion of comparative increases in national income at different periods, see Chapter 1 of *Política económica de España*, ed. Luis Gamir (Madrid, 1972).
4   See Raymond Carr, *Spain 1808–1939* (Oxford, 1966) for a comprehensive background up to the end of the Civil War.
5   The active population has remained low partly because of the demographic age structure and partly because as yet few women are in paid employment. In 1965, the Spanish level of female participation in the active population was lower than in France, Italy, Greece, Portugal and Yugoslavia: see Fundación Foessa, *Informe sociológico sobre la situación social de España 1970* (Madrid, 1970).
6   Large numbers, especially in the early part of the 1960s, went to work abroad without any government assistance.
7   For more detail on internal migration, see especially Alfonso Barbancho, *Las migraciones internas españolas* (Madrid, 1967) and Asociación Española de Economía y Sociología Agrarias, *Reunión de estudios sobre los problemas de la movilidad de la mano de obra agrícola en España* (1967). Also Fundación Foessa, *Estudios sociológicos sobre la situación social de España 1975* (Madrid, 1976) Chapter 1.
8   See Chapter 2.
9   Victor Pérez Díaz, *Estructura social del campo y exodo rural* (Madrid, 1966).
10  Overseas emigration is still predominantly male.
11  Foessa, *Informe sociológico 1970.*
12  In Barcelona the comparable density is already over 500.
13  See Amando de Miguel, *Manual de estructura social de España* (Madrid, 1974) Chapter 2.
14  For a survey of political events in Spain in this period, see George Hills, *Spain* (London, 1970); also Max Gallo, *Spain Under Franco* (London, 1973) and publications by Ruedo Ibérico, Paris.
15  Bank of Bilbao, *Informe Económico 1972*, p. 78.

168   *Notes*

1   See Xavier Flores, *Estructura socio-económica de la agricultura española* (Geneva, 1967) for a clear and short description of regional variations in physical and climatic conditions.
2   Lucas Mallada, *Los males de la patria y la futura revolución de España* (Madrid, 1890).
3   Ministry of Agriculture and Syndical Organisation, *Censo agrario de España 1972*.
4   See Edward Malefakis, *Reforma agraria y revolución campesina en la España del siglo XX* (Barcelona, 1971) for a historical perspective on the development of types of land-holding in Spain. Also Gerald Brenan, *The Spanish Labyrinth* (Cambridge, 1943).
5   OECD, *Les Faibles revenus dans l'agriculture* (Paris, 1964).
6   Bank of Bilbao, *Renta nacional de España y su distribución provincial*, various years.
7   See J. Manuel Velasco, 'Situación y perspectivas de la actual crisis y política agrarias', *Información Comercial Española* (Madrid: July 1975).
8   Now the Instituto Nacional de Reforma y Desarrollo Agrario (IRYDA).
9   By 1969 the total number of farmers resettled on new land (both dry and irrigated) was 50,000.
10  See Miguel Siguan, *Colonización y desarrollo social, Estudio en el marco del Plan de Badajoz* (1963). Also author's conversation with settlers in Castile and Badajoz.
11  The first law on *concentración parcelaria* was passed in 1952 on an experimental basis. This was confirmed and expanded in a second law in 1962.
12  The process is a lengthy one. A thorough description is given in *Legislación y procedimiento de concentración parcelaria* (Ministry of Agriculture, Madrid, 1963) Serie Monografia No 5.
13  See IBRD, *The Economic Development of Spain* (Baltimore, 1963) Chapter 14, for a description of legislation covering all aspects of farming at the beginning of the 1960s.
14  See Rafael Martínez Cortiña, *La ganadería vacuna en la economía española* (Madrid, 1969).
15  Joint-action plans are referred to more fully in Chapter 3.
16  See Ramón Tamames, *Sistemas de apoyo a la agricultura: España y los países de la Comunidad Económica Europea* (Madrid, 1970) for a detailed account of policy measures affecting different sectors.
17  The Tabacalera holds that it is necessary to mix Spanish and foreign-produced tobacco to achieve a better quality product, while Spanish growers contend that the quality of Spanish tobacco is capable of considerable improvement given the right incentives.
18  Ministry of Agriculture, *Plan de Intensificación de Producciones Deficitarias*, 1974.
19  Confederación Española de Cajas de Ahorros, *El mercado del crédito agrario en España* (Madrid, 1971) Vol. 1.
20  Formerly called Servicio Nacional de Crédito Agrícola, set up in 1925.
21  This is based on calculations made by J. Rodriguez de Pablo in an article,

'Los problemas de financiación del sector agrario', in the Ministry of Commerce publication *Información Comercial Española* (April 1963). These differ very considerably from Ministry of Agriculture figures.

22  See *El mercado de crédito agrario en España*.
23  E. Castelló Muñoz, *El papel del crédito en el desarrollo agrario* (Madrid, 1970).
24  See Chapter 6.
25  In 1970 production was valued at Ptas 11 billion, of which 36 per cent was exported.
26  This is referred to in more detail in Chapter 5.

CHAPTER 3

1  See Raymond Carr, *Spain 1808–1939* (Oxford, 1966) Chapter VII.
2  The railways were not wholly financed by foreign capital but Spanish companies were frequently bought out by the larger foreign concerns; for example, in 1860 the French Norte Company bought out a line financed by Catalan capital.
3  See Carr, *Spain 1808–1939*, p. 407.
4  Ramón Tamames, *Estructura económica de España* (Madrid, 1970 and other editions) comments on the specialisation of industry which took place between 1881 and 1914; for example, Vizcaya became primarily a producer of iron, Asturias of coal (though expensive), the cotton industry was concentrated in Barcelona and the wool industry in Sabadell, Tarassa and Bejar, the paper industry in Guipuzcoa.
5  In 1906 Spain had the highest tariffs in Europe. The most notable laws on protection before the Civil War were those of 1907, 1917, 1918, 1922, 1924 and 1927.
6  'Thus the Spanish economy fell into the hands of committees regulating everything from hydroelectric power to the rabbit-skin industry' (Carr, *Spain 1808–1939*, p. 580).
7  24 October 1939, Protección y fomento de la industria nacional; 24 November 1939, Ordenación y defensa de la industria nacional.
8  For a full description and discussion of these laws and the extent of control exercised, see Tamames, *Estructura económica de España*, Chapter 12, and IBRD, *The Economic Development of Spain* (Baltimore, 1963) Chapter 15.
9  This led to a situation in which some firms in a particular branch of industry could be considered of national interest and others not, depending on whether they had INI connections or not.
10  For a description of this, see Arthur P. Whitaker, *Spain and the Defense of the West* (New York, 1961); Benjamin Welles, *Spain: The Gentle Anarchy* (London and New York, 1965).
11  In 1959 Spain abolished entry visas for visitors from Western European countries, all of whom reciprocated except Great Britain. In 1959 there were 4·2 million tourists.
12  Income per head did not recover its pre-war level until 1954.
13  The trade balance, in surplus at the beginning of the 1950s, was transformed into a deficit of $360 million in 1958 and official reserves registered a $4 million deficit in the same year.

14   In addition to the disquieting economic facts, the government was no doubt influenced by the wave of unrest and strikes in 1958 which led to the temporary suspension of the Fuero de los Españoles; see Max Gallo, *Spain Under Franco* (London, 1973) Chapter 4.

15   Some measures were taken in 1957 and 1958, i.e. the rate of exchange was stabilised at Ptas 42 to the dollar in April 1957, but the majority followed in 1959.

16   Base year 1950. The rest remained in bilateral quotas.

17   Spain became a member of the United Nations in 1955.

18   The cost-of-living index had risen by 16 per cent in 1957 and by 10 per cent in January to May 1958.

19   IBRD, *The Economic Development of Spain*, p. 98. The Report also drew attention to the list of products whose prices were fixed by the government, a small but significant number, in addition to a far larger number of products under 'supervised freedom'.

20   George Hills, *Spain* (London, 1970) p. 315.

21   GDP at factor cost. See Bank of Bilbao, *Informe Económico 1975*, p. 100.

22   Bank of Bilbao, *Informe Económico 1975*, p. 180.

23   For figures in late 1960s, see OECD, *L'Industrie sidérugique en 1967 et tendence en 1968* (Paris, 1968).

24   For a detailed analysis of intersectoral changes, see O. Fanful, F. Maravall, J. M. Pérez Prim and J. Segura, *Cambios en la estructura interindustrial de la economía española 1962–1970: Una primera aproximación* (Madrid, 1974).

25   Based on Bank of Bilbao, *Renta nacional de España y su distribución provincial* (1964 and 1973).

26   GDP at market prices in current pesetas. Figures for 1973 and 1974 include variations in stock levels. Bank of Spain, *Informe Anual 1974*. Comparisons over various years are difficult because the Spanish national accounting system has recently been revised. It is now much closer to the European system of integrated economic accounts.

27   Cf. levels of 56 per cent in the UK and 68 per cent in the USA.

28   Until 1937 foreign investment in Spain was almost entirely free from regulations.

29   See *American Investments in Spain*, Studies by Stanford Research Institute (International) and Data SA (Madrid, 1972) Table 6.

30   In 1960 the figure was $10 million.

31   *American Investments in Spain*, p. 17.

32   11 October 1973, Decree No 24 95/1973. Reorganisation under Decree No 17 94/1973 of 26 July set up the Dirección General de Transacciones Externas at the Ministry of Commerce, to control Spanish investments abroad (which are still small) and foreign investment in Spain.

33   Decree No 2343/1973.

34   Investors complain of a lack of detailed information which makes it difficult to comply with regulations, in addition to confusion caused by bureaucratic tangles.

35   Article 135 of Ley de Reforma Tributaria of 26 December 1957.

36   Four main types of import duty refunds exist but these are of lesser importance.

37   Two lines covering pre-financing activities and large-scale capital goods

were granted exclusively to the industrial banks; the remaining lines were shared between the industrial and commercial banks.

38 This is referred to more fully in the section on official credit in Chapter 6.

39 This figure includes 'commercial services abroad'.

40 Its subsequent development has not borne much resemblance to that of IRI, particularly in regional development.

41 In the 1940s and 1950s annual investment by the INI amounted to approximately 15 per cent of all Spanish investment.

42 'Industries of national interest' were primarily INI firms. Up to 1959 only thirty industries had been allowed these privileges, of which twenty were owned wholly or in part by the INI. See Charles W. Anderson, *The Political Economy of Modern Spain* (Wisconsin, 1970) p. 42.

43 Extracting coal from the mines is expensive. In 1970 by unofficial calculations it cost Ptas 1306 to produce a ton of coal, compared with a sale price of Ptas 762. See 'Between Past and Future. A Survey of Spain', *The Economist* (19 Feb 1972).

44 Self-financing of INI companies reached 27 per cent in 1974; see Economist Intelligence Unit's *Quarterly Economic Review*, No 2 (1975).

45 See Miguel Boyer, 'La empresa pública en la estratégica industrial española: el INI', *Información Comercial Española* (April 1975).

46 This was in large part due to political factors. In the 1960s the INI was a stronghold of the Falangists, while the predominant force in the government was the Opus Dei.

47 See Amando de Miguel and Juan Salcedo, *Dinámica del desarrollo industrial de las regiones españolas* (Madrid, 1972) Table 34, p. 282.

48 71 per cent of Enpetrol is owned by the INI, 22 per cent by Chevron/ Texaco and the rest by banks and industrial groups.

49 OECD, *Políticas Nacionales de la Ciencia: España* (Madrid, 1971).

50 In 1969 twenty-four projects were approved with a total value of Ptas 153 million.

51 Kenneth Medhurst, *Government in Spain* (Oxford, 1973).

CHAPTER 4

1 Except in the most general sense of bolstering the Spanish government's desire for economic self-sufficiency.

2 The Second Plan was not in fact put into action until February 1969.

3 The *comisiones* corresponded roughly to the syndical organisations.

4 Kenneth Medhurst, *Government in Spain* (Oxford, 1973) p. 99.

5 E.g. RENFE's ten-year modernisation plan began in 1965.

6 See K. Medhurst, *Government in Spain*; also Salustiano del Campo and Manuel Navarro, *Crítica de la planificación social española 1964–75* (Madrid, 1976).

7 In 1974 the signals of alert were replaced by a bi-monthly report on the economy by the Minister of Finance.

8 '1968, el año de la austeridad', *Gaceta Ilustrada*, 10 December 1967, quoted in Luis Gamir (ed.), *Política económica de España* (Madrid, 1972) Chapter 11.

9 See Charles W. Anderson, *The Political Economy of Modern Spain* (Wisconsin,

1970) p. 231: 'In Plan II there is a certain symbolic quality to the emphasis on the social factors in developments.'

10  Growth was highest 1961–6 (with the slight drop of 1964). 1967–71 showed a relative decline.

11  See *III Plan de Desarrollo Económico y Social 1972–1975* and Ramón Tamames, *Introducción a la economía española* (Madrid, 1972) p. 520 *et seq.* for a summary.

12  Medhurst, *Government in Spain*, p. 176.

13  See Luis Gamir, ed., *Política económica de España* (Madrid, 1972) p. 252.

14  H. Richardson, 'Regional Development Policy in Spain', *Urban Studies* (London: February 1971).

15  Ibid., p. 47.

16  The Badajoz and Jaen Plans, which should have ended in 1967 and 1968 respectively, were extended until 1975. The others are *sine die*.

17  Guadalajara, Alcazar de San Juan, Aranda de Duero, Toledo, Manzanares. Three more have been added: Talavera, Tarancón and Aranjuez.

18  Aranda de Duero, Alcazar de San Juan, Manzanares.

19  This is mostly due to the 'failure to insulate the Bank of Industrial Credit for monetary movements in the economy as a whole' (Richardson, *Regional Development Policy in Spain*, p. 45).

20  Ibid., p. 45.

21  IBRD, *The Economic Development of Spain* (Baltimore, 1963).

22  See Richardson, *Regional Development in Spain*.

23  See C. Anderson, *The Political Economy of Modern Spain*, p. 173: 'It appears that the policy-makers intended their participatory apparatus primarily for co-ordination and, in a secondary sense, consultation.'

24  K. Medhurst, *Government in Spain*; see his Chapter 8 on Local Administration for a clear account of the working of local government in Spain.

25  Social conditions and government policies during the three development plans are discussed in Chapter 5.

26  For further reference to the government's rôle in the economy, see Chapter 9.

27  In France the comparable figure is over 30 per cent.

28  1970 figures from the Encuesta de Población Activa and not from the Censo of the same year, which has rather different figures.

29  For instance, the Indicadores Económicas and the Encuesta de Población Activa, both published by the Instituto Nacional de Estadística, show considerable variations.

30  This is referred to more fully in Chapter 5.

31  According to the Indicadores Económicas of the INE. According to the Encuesta de Población Activa, also of the INE, the index rose steadily throughout.

32  See, for example, figures given in the Encuesta de Población Activa, the Oficina de Encuadramiento y Colocación of the Ministerio de Trabajo and in the various development plans.

33  Publication of unemployment figures began in 1964.

34  OECD, *Economic Surveys: Spain* (Paris, 1975) p. 10.

35  OECD, *Development Study – Andalusia* (Paris, 1967).

36 Roy Bradshaw, 'Internal Migration in Spain', *Iberian Studies*, Vol. 1, No 2 (1972).
37 OECD, *Economic Survey: Spain* (Paris, 1976) p. 12.
38 Fundación Foessa, *Informe sociológico sobre la situación social de España 1970* (Madrid, 1970) p. 1056.
39 The earlier survey referred to, i.e. 1966, confirms a greater tendency to multiple employment in Madrid; this reflects the greater employment opportunities in Madrid than in many places.
40 Foessa (1970), see note 38, p. 1077.
41 K. Medhurst, *Government in Spain*, p. 110.
42 Long hours are not necessarily due to multiple employment. Taxi-drivers with one job, for instance, in Madrid, frequently drive fourteen hours a day, despite recent changes in the law.
43 Instituto de Estudios Sindicales, Sociales y Co-operativos, *Estudio sociológico sobre el trabajador y su medio en la ciudad de Barcelona* (1969).
44 Foessa (1970), see note 38, p. 1056.
45 For greater detail on the beginnings of the INP and social insurance schemes, see Felipe Soler Sabaris, *Problemas de la seguridad social española* (Barcelona, 1971).
46 Various National Funds are still in existence, of which the most important are the Fondo de Principio de Igualdad de Oportunidades and the Fondo Nacional de Protección al Trabajo.
47 In 1975 for the first time pensions were granted to war veterans who fought on the Republican side.
48 See OECD, *Economic Surveys: Spain* (Paris, 1975).
49 See J. Jané Solá, *El problema de los salarios en España* (Barcelona, 1969) p. 136. The sectors affected included public utilities, banks, mining, wool, leather, textiles and others.
50 See J. Jané Solá, *El problema de los salarios en España*, p. 103.
51 This originated from the Ley de Reglamentación, October 1942. In 1956 the law was altered so that employers were free to pay more if they so wished.
52 See Ronald Fraser, *The Pueblo* (London, 1973) p. 72. The author argues that this was a deliberate policy pursued by the government to subdue the working class.
53 See J. Jané Solá, *Los condicionamientos del mercado de trabajo y el crecimiento económico español de los años sesenta* (Madrid, 1975).
54 For various aspects of salaries in Spain, see J. Jané Solá, *El problema de los salarios en España*; J. C. Linz and A. de Miguel, 'Los problemas de la retribución y el rendimiento vistos por los empresarios españoles', *Revista de trabajo*, No 1 (1963); A. Nieto, *La retribución de los funcionarios en España* (Madrid, 1967).
55 Bank of Bilbao, *Renta nacional de España y su distribución provincial* (Bilbao, 1964 and 1973).
56 Low compared, for instance, with Germany, France, Britain, Italy, and also, of course, the USA.
57 At factor cost. Bank of Bilbao, *Informe Económico 1975*, p. 105. The INE figures are higher. In 1974, according to the INE figures, the share of wages including social security was equal to 63·8 per cent. The discrepancy

is due to differing calculations of national income, lower in the case of INE.

58   INE, *La renta nacional en 1974 y su distribución* (Madrid, 1975).
59   K. Medhurst, *Government in Spain*, p. 114.
60   J. Jané Solá, *El problema de los salarios en España*, p. 130.
61   See the Stanford Report, which indicates that many companies use a two-envelope system of paying wages which not only avoids taxes but is also used as a method of sacking people when a 'crisis' has not been declared. When a person is to be dismissed, the envelope containing the undeclared pay is withheld. This also adds a further degree of complication in assessing wage levels actually paid.
62   No new wage agreement could be negotiated in 1968.
63   The nuances of correlation between the original Falange conception and the actual evolution of the *sindicatos* are not discussed here. An excellent account of this is to be found in J. Amsden, *Collective Bargaining and Class Conflict in Spain* (London, 1972), who gives a clear and full description of labour relations in Spain, to which I am much indebted.
64   The Falange became known as the Movimiento in the early 1940s.
65   Quoted from *Pueblo*, 13 December 1969, by Jordi Estivill and Ignasti Pons in *Apuntes sobre el trabajo en España* (Barcelona, 1971) p. 150.
66   Iglesias Selgas, 'Los sindicatos en España: origen, estructura, evolución', quoted in J. Amsden, *Collective Bargaining and Class Conflict in Spain*, p. 75.
67   In order to intervene in collective bargaining on a company basis, it is necessary to be on the *jurado de empresa*.
68   J. Amsden, *Collective Bargaining and Class Conflict in Spain*, p. 99.
69   A. de Miguel and J. Linz, *Los empresarios ante el poder público* (Madrid, 1966).
70   José María Maravall, *El desarrollo económico y la clase obrera en España* (Barcelona, 1970) p. 96.
71   Reference to the recognition of the right to strike was made in 1974 by the then Minister of Syndical Relations, Señor Fernández Sardo, but in vague terms.
72   For a full description of the law, see J. Amsden, *Collective Bargaining and Class Conflict in Spain*, p. 130 *et seq.*
73   The fourth type is not in fact used.
74   J. Amsden, *Collective Bargaining and Class Conflict in Spain*, p. 150.
75   The question of the provenance of assessors has been a particularly bitter one and there have been repeated efforts in the past by workers to be allowed to choose assessors from outside the syndical framework.

CHAPTER 5

1   See especially the national income calculations of the Bank of Bilbao and the Instituto Nacional de Estadística. Prior to 1965, see also figures of the Consejo de Economía Nacional.
2   Bank of Bilbao calculations, taking into account differing exchange rates for the peseta/dollar. At factor cost, the $500 line was crossed in 1964.
3   Bank of Bilbao, *Informe Económico 1975*, p. 320.
4   In 1971, there were 132 television sets per 1000 inhabitants and in 1970,

151 telephones and 71 passenger cars per 1000 inhabitants. Comparable figures for France were 227, 185 and 245; Britain, 298, 289 and 213, and Italy, 191, 188 and 187. OECD, *Economic Survey: Basic Statistics: International Comparisons* (1974).

5 In 1970, 40 per cent of the family budget in Spain went towards food. In France the comparable figure was 25 per cent, in Britain 23 per cent, in Denmark 20 per cent and in Italy 35 per cent.

6 Taken from national accounts of OECD countries.

7 Ministry of Agriculture, *La Agricultura Española*, in various years. OECD figures coincide for some years but differ in others, e.g. the calorie level is put at 2813 by the Ministry of Agriculture in 1967–8, whereas the OECD places it at 3100 in 1968.

8 INE, *Encuesta de Presupuestos Familiares* (May 1975).

9 Bank of Bilbao, *Renta nacional de España y su distribución provincial* (Bilbao, 1973).

10 E.g. Alfonso Ferres and Armando López Salinas, *Caminando por Las Hurdes* (Barcelona, 1960 and 1974); Ramón Carnicer, *Donde Las Hurdes se llaman cabrera* (Barcelona, 1963); Antonio Pintado and Eduardo Berrenchea, *La Raya de Portugal* (Madrid, 1972); Juan Goytisolo, *Campos de Níjar* (Barcelona, 1960); Jesús Torbado, *Tierra mal bautizada* (Barcelona, 1968); Alfonso Comin, *España del Sur: Aspectos económicos y sociales de desarrollo de Andalucía* (Madrid, 1965); Juan Martínez Alier, *La estabilidad del latifundismo* (Paris, 1968).

11 J. Martínez Alier, *La estabilidad del latifundismo*. Chapter 2 points out how little expenditure on the basic necessities of bread, oil and chickpeas fell between 1903 and 1965 in relation to the daily usage in the province of Cordoba.

12 E.g. the Bank of Bilbao's *Informe Económico 1972*, p. 61, points out the contradiction in figures published for prices in the agricultural sector in different Ministry of Agriculture publications.

13 INE, *La renta nacional en 1973 y su distribución* (Madrid, 1974). For 1973 and 1974 actual figures are not given, only percentage increases. These show, however, that the trend continues.

14 I.e. Huelva, Jaen, Malaga, Cordoba, Granada.

15 Census of 1970.

16 Schemes such as *concentración parcelaria* are only tangentially concerned with improving living standards and in any case affect a small number of people.

17 OECD, *Development Study on Andalusia* (Darmstadt, 1964).

18 There are also sizable shanty towns in Granada, Tenerife, Cordoba and Cadiz.

19 See *Cambio 16*, 6–12 January 1975 (Madrid).

20 INE, *Encuesta de Presupuestos Familiares* (Madrid, 1964 and 1965).

21 See J. Estivill and J. Pons, *Apuntes sobre el trabajo en España* (Barcelona, 1973) p. 102.

22 For greater detail, see Julio Alcaide Inchausti's article 'La distribución de la renta: ¿Cómo se reparte el dinero de los españoles?', in *Los domingos de ABC* (23 November 1975).

23 E.g. certain maternity and children's services, cancer clinics, etc.

24   INE, *Estadística de establecimientos sanitarios con régimen de internado* (Madrid, 1972).

25   Studies of WHO and the International Federation of Hospitals.

26   Kenneth Medhurst, *Government in Spain* (Oxford, 1973) p. 95.

27   Hospital beds for use by the military totalled 13,023 in 1972.

28   See the statement of the Minister of Labour in 1970 on this point in F. Soler Sabaris, *Problemas de la seguridad social española* (Barcelona, 1971) p. 126.

29   The number of those insured under social security schemes and unable to get help in treatment for a particular illness has been put as high as one-half of the total insured; see *Triunfo* (13 November 1971).

30   The highest ratios of doctors and numbers of beds to population are in the north, north-east and Madrid.

31   This is in no way meant to imply that there are not outstanding doctors and hospitals in Spain. The general standard, outside the private clinics, is not, however, conducive to confidence.

32   In 1931 rent control was applied to the whole country.

33   Houses built under official schemes reached 30,658 in 1951; 45,721 in 1955; 77,726 in 1956 and 127,518 in 1960. Private interests supplied more houses than State interests at the beginning of the 1950s. By 1960 housing undertaken by private individuals had fallen in absolute terms and in relative terms to about one-tenth of all new housing. See Second Development Plan, 'Comisión de Vivienda'.

34   It is impossible to get strictly accurate figures and approximate estimates have to be used.

35   See Luis Gamir, ed., *Política económica de España* (Madrid, 1972) p. 326.

36   This covers very inadequate housing in addition to a shortage of houses.

37   Confederación Española de Cajas de Ahorros, *Demanda y acceso a la propiedad de viviendas* (Madrid, 1969).

38   OECD, *Economic Survey of Spain 1974*, p. 30. A footnote adds that house-building loans financed by official bodies specialising in this form of lending have levelled off since 1967.

39   See Gamir, *Política económica de España*, p. 326. Statistics on private sector housing are even more fallible than on government sponsored housing, but the trend is undeniable.

40   In 1960, 349,987 houses were registered as empty. In 1970, this had risen to 1,137,742.

41   A landlord will usually find a way round fixed rents by imposing various supplements.

42   See A. Santillana, *Analisis económico del problema de la vivienda* (Barcelona, 1972).

43   See Ramón Tamames, *Estructura económica de España* (Madrid, 1970) p. 387.

44   Ley del Régimen del Suelo y Ordenación Urbana.

45   OECD, *Economic Survey of Spain 1974*.

46   See IBRD Report, *The Economic Development of Spain* (Baltimore, 1963) Chapter 18.

47   In 1960 the *sindicatos* ran four centres under the Formación Profesional Acelerada scheme.

48   Max Gallo, *Spain Under Franco* (London, 1973) p. 91.

49 Ibid., p. 194. The IBRD report of 1963 refers to the 'welcome increase in secondary education in general' but estimated that 'only about 15 per cent of children of secondary school age are currently at school', p. 393.

50 The Mediterranean Regional Project based on manpower planning includes Greece, Turkey and Spain.

51 In 1964 there were fewer State secondary schools than in 1935; see Medhurst, op. cit., p. 169.

52 North Castile, despite no background of affluence, has a tradition of high educational standards.

53 Fundación Foessa, *Informe sociológico sobre la situación social de España 1970* (Madrid, 1970) p. 862.

54 Quite apart from cost it is customary for the private secondary schools which comprise most of the secondary education sector to take their pupils from private primary schools.

55 In 1967–8 there were 326 centres available for *bachillerato laboral* and 471 for industrial training, compared with 2599 centres for the *bachillerato general* (Ministerio de Educación y Ciencia, *Datos y cifras de la enseñanza en España*, 1969).

56 Ley General de Educación y Financiación de la Reforma Educativa, 4 August 1970. The law in any case represents a watered-down version of the *Libro Blanco* in many respects.

57 See Amando de Miguel, *Manual de Estructura Social de España* (Madrid, 1974) p. 476.

58 IBRD Report, cited in note 46, p. 395. In the periods 1952–3, 1954–5 the average number of students registered in science faculties was 12,600, but numbers graduating in 1957–8 and 1958–9 were only 475 and 565 respectively. In 1972, out of a total of 56,038 registered pupils in the Escuelas Universitarias de Ingeniera Técnica, only 6067 finished the course. See INE, *España Anuario Estadístico 1974* (Madrid, 1974) p. 347.

59 Ministerio de Educación y Ciencia, also INE, *Datos y cifras . . .*, 1969; *Anuario Estadístico* (1971).

60 *L'Observateur de l'OECD* (June 1966).

61 The proportion spent by Spain is similar to Greece and Portugal.

62 It is estimated that only 6 per cent of Spanish firms spend anything on research and development and that the total proportion of private earnings spent in this way is not above 0·05 per cent (*Economist Survey*, July 1972, p. 25).

63 See J. Jané Solá, *El problema de los salarios en España* (Barcelona, 1969) p. 257. The same problem also affects the labour institutes.

CHAPTER 6

1 See for example Juan Muñoz, *El poder de la banca en España* (Madrid, 1969); Ramón Tamames, *La lucha contra los monopolios* (Madrid, 1970).

2 See R. Trias Fargas, *Las fuentes de financiación de la empresa en España*, 2nd edition (Madrid, 1972) Chapter 5, to which this historical summary is indebted.

3   R. Trias Fargas, *El sistema financiero español* (Barcelona, 1972) p. 189.
4   IBRD, *The Economic Development of Spain* (Baltimore, 1963) p. 125.
5   Ley de Bases de Ordenación del Crédito y de la Banca, 14 April 1962.
6   This was lowered to 45 per cent in 1967 and later to 40 per cent.
7   Reglamento de las Bolsas Oficiales de Comercio, 30 June 1967.
8   For a fuller description of the law, see especially R. Trias Fargas, *Las fuentes de financiación de la empresa en España*, and R. Martinez Cortiña, *Crédito y banca en España: Analisis y estructura* (Madrid, 1971).
9   Small banks can fetch grossly inflated prices in these circumstances.
10  The Banco Urquijo.
11  I.e. laws of 9 April 1926, 21 November 1929 and 14 March 1933.
12  The 1962 law laid down that the savings banks were expected to carry out the instructions of the Treasury.
13  It is arguable that throughout the 1960s the Instituto was a less forceful body than the Confederación General de Cajas de Ahorro.
14  The other 50 per cent of the surplus goes into the reserves as there are no shareholders.
15  Confederación Española de Cajas de Ahorro.
16  Ptas 750,000 in 1972.
17  In 1966 the Cajas de Ahorros were subject to a limit of 17 per cent on credit, but this was not complied with (the official credit bodies did not keep within this limit either). At the beginning of 1971 the Cajas de Ahorros were affected by the rise in the basic interest rate and the new allied rates. (Official credit rates were also affected, with certain exceptions.)
18  Roger Matthews makes this point in 'Slow progress in bank reform', *Financial Times* 'Survey of Spanish Banking and Finance' (30 March 1976).
19  Ley de Crédito a Medio y Largo Plazo.
20  Only the Banco Exterior de España was not included in nationalisation procedures. The Instituto Nacional de la Vivienda, Servicio Nacional del Trigo, Instituto Nacional de Industria, etc., which were not primarily financial bodies but provided finance, often quite large sums, were not nationalised either.
21  Which replaced ICMLP in 1971, although with reduced powers.
22  Ministerio de Hacienda, *ICMLP Memoria* (Madrid, 1970) and the *Informe Anual 1975* of the Bank of Spain (Madrid, 1976).
23  Finance for shipbuilding was increasingly provided by special rediscount lines.
24  Until 1969 the official institutes did not pay interest on Treasury disbursements and were also exempt from taxes.
25  Organización y Régimen del Crédito Oficial, 19 June 1971.
26  Funds to public credit institutions as in the past were to come mainly from the Treasury, but some also from direct borrowing in domestic and foreign capital markets which could be guaranteed by the Instituto de Crédito Oficial.
27  Other minor sources of credit are credit co-operatives and hire-purchase companies. The former came into existence following a law of 1942 and the latter followed the laws of 1962 and 1964. There are also specialised

savings institutions such as the Cajas Postales, but they do not constitute important sources of credit.

28 In both cases the banks were allowed to raise the coefficient slowly over the year in order to arrive at the appropriate figure by the end of the year.

29 In February 1974 the investment coefficient for the industrial banks was raised to 18 per cent.

30 OECD, *El mercado de capitales en España* (Madrid, 1972).

31 See the Bank of Spain's estimates in the *Informe Anual* of various years.

32 Banks were also allowed to offer 'preferential' terms to established customers of good credit, but there has been little evidence of customers benefiting from such terms.

33 The dependence on short-term loans as well as being costly in these circumstances also induces a feeling of uncertainty for the firm concerned.

34 Assistance to medium-sized and small firms is one field where some degree of decentralisation is taking place.

35 Prior to this foreign companies were often able to get round the restrictions on medium- and long-term loans by obtaining short-term loans with a guarantee from the parent company or a foreign bank, which meant that short-term loans were easily renewed and were little different in practice from long-term ones.

36 This figure obviously varies from year to year but only three times since 1964 has it been lower than 20 per cent.

37 Angel Lascunción Goni, 'Stock market still has its limitations', *Financial Times* 'Survey of Spanish Banking and Finance' (30 March 1976).

38 Market capitalisation in 1975 was $21 billion in Spain, $27 billion in France, $41 billion in the Federal Republic of Germany and $122 billion in the UK. Figures for the Netherlands, Belgium and Italy were $13 billion, $11 billion and $8 billion respectively (Banif SA Investment Bulletin, quoted in *Financial Times* 'Survey' (30 March 1976) ).

39 See Roger Matthews, 'Stock exchanges fail to yield long-term capital', *Financial Times* 'Survey of the Spanish Capital Market' (13 February 1974).

CHAPTER 7

1 In order to make this comparison, both sets of figures include the social security family allowances, which were in fact not included in public sector accounts until 1967.

2 See OECD, *Economic Surveys: Spain* (Paris, 1974) p. 32.

3 This is partly because of the size and number of agencies; see Kenneth Medhurst, *Government in Spain* (Oxford, 1973) p. 162, for an example of this: the Agriculture Ministry has over twenty dependencies whose total expenditure is larger than the supervisory ministry.

4 For an account of the very great autonomy enjoyed by the agencies prior to 1958, see the IBRD report, *The Economic Development of Spain* (Baltimore, 1963).

5 Ramón Tamames, *Estructura económica de España* (Madrid, 1970) p. 700.

6   Ministerio de Hacienda, *Liquidación de los Presupuestos de los Organismos Autónomos de la Administración* (Madrid, 1975).
7   See OECD, *Economic Survey* (1974) p. 33.
8   Central government transfers to local authorities rose from Ptas 0·2 billion to 30·3 billion in 1971. See OECD, *Economic Survey* (1974).
9   Borrowing by local authorities on the long-term capital market has, however, increased from an average of Ptas 1·0 billion in 1966–8 to an average of Ptas 3·0 billion in 1969–71. (Until 1967 local authorities sold land to raise money but have since become net purchasers of land.) See OECD, *Economic Survey* (1974) p. 33.
10   In principle central control over local taxation is limited but in practice this has not always been observed, see Medhurst, *Government in Spain*, p. 203.
11   See OECD, *Economic Survey* (1974) p. 34.
12   The OECD 1974 *Survey* makes the point that despite the drop in government financed investment, public enterprises were able to increase their investment at a higher rate than the private sector as a whole.
13   3 per cent in 1962 (OECD, *Economic Survey* (1974) p. 35).
14   Study by the Instituto de Estudios Fiscales, directed by Félix de Luis.
15   The remainder was covered by charges for postal services, lotteries and income from property.
16   For the reasons mentioned in connection with indirect taxation, the share of direct taxation has risen slightly since 1974.
17   Because full information would be made public on dividends and sales and taxation would accordingly be higher.
18   In 1974 the Minister of Finance announced a wholesale reorganisation of the tax-collecting corps which should result in a unified structure and more efficient collection methods.
19   See OECD, *Economic Survey* (1974) p. 38.
20   Ibid., p. 33.
21   Ibid., p. 37. The *Survey* points out that an increase in the relative share of direct taxation would weaken this stabilising influence.
22   Medhurst, *Government in Spain*, p. 163, comments on this aspect of the autonomous agencies in the following terms: '*Post hoc* controls also tend to be ineffective. At worst accounts are not presented and at best they are uninformative.'
23   A consequence of this was that credit restrictions were often applied 'too late' and too harshly.
24   The annual reports of the Bank of Spain and the economic surveys of the OECD provide detailed description and analysis of such developments.
25   In the middle of 1965 bank credit was expanding by 35 per cent.
26   Following the devaluation of the £.
27   *Informe Anual*, Bank of Spain (Madrid, 1970).
28   By an Order of 1964 interest rates between different kinds of financial institutions, i.e. banks and savings banks, were fixed at a maximum rate of 4 per cent.
29   See R. Martinez Cortiña, *Crédito y banca en España: Analisis y estructura* (Madrid, 1971) p. 64.
30   Price controls initiated in 1967 were maintained.

31  In 1967 GNP in real terms had also increased by only 4·2 per cent.
32  The blocking of investment credits from the previous year was for example a restraining factor in 1970.
33  See Chapter 6.
34  See OECD, *Economic Survey* (1974) p. 21.
35  Ibid., p. 21.
36  From March onwards the Treasury sold bills to the Bank of Spain at a rate of 5 per cent, but the Bank could then resell the bills at whatever rate it thought appropriate. The freeing of interest rates on Treasury bills in the second half of 1973 was an innovation.
37  Growth in liquid assets was 17·7 per cent on average from 1961 to 1970 and 23·7 per cent from 1971 to 1973 (OECD, *Economic Survey* (1975) p. 25).
38  34 per cent at an annual rate in March, 40 per cent in April 1974. The increase in bank assets was largely due to the expansion of time deposits which increased very rapidly in the second part of 1974, when rates on borrowing for more than two years were freed: see OECD, *Economic Survey* (1975) pp. 26 and 28.

CHAPTER 8

1  Ministerio de Comercio, *Balanza de pagos en España, 1960–73*, and OECD, *Economic Surveys*. The 1960 surplus is slightly misleading as it reflects the strong impact of the Stabilisation Plan and the trade deficits in 1961 and 1962 were $278 million and $634 million respectively.
2  See Juergen B. Donges, 'La configuración de la exportación industrial española', *Información Comercial Española*, September/October 1973, p. 187. Donges cites this period as illustrative that industrialisation does not necessarily favour a growth in exports.
3  These measures included the abolition of multiple exchange rates and the devaluation of the peseta.
4  This is in striking contrast with the situation before the Stabilisation Plan when 9 per cent of Spanish trade was 'free' and almost all the remainder under bilateral quotas.
5  The 'special' quota comprises four categories, including repatriation of Spanish capital.
6  The Brussels Tariff Nomenclature is a system of classifying goods for the purpose of customs tariffs. It was drawn up in 1955. Spain is divided into three customs areas: (1) the Peninsula and Balearic Islands, subject to normal tariff procedures; (2) the Canary Islands, which enjoy free ports and where import duties are imposed on very few products; (3) Ceuta and Melilla, which are similar to (2).
7  I am indebted to Luis Gamir for discussion about tariffs. See Luis Gamir, ed., *Política económica de España* (Madrid, 1972) Chapters 5 and 6, and 'La política arancelaria española', in *Información Comercial Española* (March 1972).
8  See Gamir, *Política económica de España*, Chapter 6.
9  Ibid.
10  Ibid. Comparisons are necessarily inexact since for some countries quota

G

arrangements are included in calculating the effective rate of protection, and for others not.

11 Juergen B. Donges, *La configuración de la exportación industrial española*, ICE, September/October 1973.

12 In the following section I have drawn on Luis Martínez Arevalo's article, 'La exportación española en los últimos once años', *Informacíon Comercial Espaníola* (September/October 1973) p. 77 *et seq.*

13 Donges, *La configuración de la exportación industrial española*, p. 193.

14 The export of shoes in total exports rose from 2 per cent in 1958–9 to 6·2 per cent in 1967–70, whereas the export of other leather goods fell from 2 per cent to 1·4 per cent in the same period.

15 In January 1971, it became necessary to obtain a special permit for each export shipment. As the IEME also reviews every export application after it has been cleared by the Ministry of Commerce, the total delay incurred may be considerably greater than under the previous global system.

16 OECD, *Economic Survey: Spain* (Paris, 1975) p. 15.

17 Ibid. Spanish products represented 0·5 per cent of total OECD exports of industrial products in 1966 and 1·2 per cent in 1973. Reference is also made to the 'quite small and very erratic' increases in market shares of agricultural food products.

18 In 1970 OECD figures showed that the difference in labour costs in Spain and other European countries was still substantial. These were four times greater in West Germany, three times in Belgium and the Netherlands and about two and a half times greater in France and Italy.

19 Trade with the USSR and Eastern Europe amounted to 1·5 per cent of Spanish exports and 2·1 per cent of Spanish imports in 1973.

20 See OECD, *Economic Survey* (Paris, 1975) p. 16.

21 Despite the oversimplification, it is broadly true that the Opus Dei group were in favour of closer co-operation with the Common Market and the Falangists against.

22 A second negotiating mandate came into effect in October 1969.

23 In the event of the EEC offering to cut tariffs by 70 per cent Spain would be expected to offer cuts of 70 per cent on List A and 30 per cent on List B.

24 The rate of 13 per cent was to cover the increase of imports under all quota arrangements. Each individual quota was expected to rise by at least 7 per cent.

25 For a study of the EEC concessions to Spain, see L. Gamir, *Las preferencias efectivas del Mercado Comun a España* (Madrid, 1972).

26 See Ramón Tamames, *Estructura de la economía española* (Madrid, 1970) p. 762.

27 In 1971 fixed and transitory tariffs were replaced by a unitary system which in most cases is nearer to the transitory tariff level.

28 A curious feature of the trade agreement is that Spain reserved the right to *raise* its tariffs in certain circumstances, which is certainly against the spirit of the treaty.

29 Talks were actually suspended in October 1975 by the Common Market countries in protest at the execution of Basque nationalists.

30 Ministerio de Información y Turismo, *Estadísticas de turismo*. This does not include 'twenty-four hour only' tourists.

31 Despite the existence of a Ministry especially for Information and Tourism, lack of co-ordination between it and the Ministry of Public Works and Housing has led to the usual conflicts and contradictions. It has also led to the slow and inadequate growth in municipal services in relation to the great seasonal increases in population.

32 The Balearic Islands, Gerona, Barcelona, Madrid, Alicante and Malaga.

33 At the end of 1975, however, prices for four-star hotels were freed from any control.

34 Another problem is the conflict in some areas between tourist and industrial interests, which is already evident in the region of Tarragona. Local inhabitants have protested vociferously against the installation of nuclear reactors along the north coast of Spain on the grounds that it would be damaging to the tourist industry.

35 See H. W. Richardson, 'Regional Development Policy in Spain', *Urban Studies* (February 1971) p. 44, for comments on tourism and gross value added in various provinces.

36 Ronald Fraser, *The Pueblo: A Mountain Village in the Costa del Sol* (London, 1973).

37 In 1967 there was a net return of Spanish workers from abroad.

38 In 1976 more use was made of the reserves and there is evidence that the issue is now a less sensitive one.

39 Spain's export trade has long been concentrated in a few coastal areas. Before the Civil War the provinces of Barcelona and Valencia provided 30 per cent of Spain's exports (see Raymond Carr, *Spain 1808–1939* (Oxford, 1966) p. 400). In 1974, 22 per cent of Spain's exports originated in the Catalan region.

40 George Hills, *Spain* (London, 1970) p. 309.

41 Richardson, *Regional Development Policy in Spain*, p. 40.

42 See Angel Luis Lopez Roa and Nieves Esteve, 'Analisis sobre la estructura del comercio minorista', *Información Comercial Española* (February 1976).

43 Study undertaken on behalf of the National Farmers' Association, 1975. The price differential was felt to be particularly bitter in view of the farmers' claim that production costs could not be met on some citrus fruits at current prices.

44 The results of this study, 'Los costes de comercialización en España', are summarised in an article by Ana Maria Portals and Julio Alcaide Guindo in 'Los costes de distribución en España', *Información Comercial Española* (February 1976).

45 In the case of meat and dairy products, distribution costs were higher in Italy.

46 For figures on credit matters, see the survey undertaken by Angel Luis Lopez Roa and Nieves Esteve for Información Comercial Española in February 1976.

47 For details on the structure and geographical location of domestic trade outlets, see the *Anuario del Mercado Español*, produced by the Banco Español de Crédito.

48 See Chapter 2 for a description of FORPPA.

49 CAT is also referred to in Chapter 2.

50 See Ramón Tamames, Alianza edition, *Introducción a la economía española* (Madrid, 1972) Chapter 7.
51 See Francisco Hernandez Sayans, 'Las asociaciones de consumidores', *Información Comercial Española* (March 1974) p. 139.
52 There were nine hypermarkets open by 1973 and thirteen more planned.
53 In 1974 the total railway network was 15,718 kilometres, of which 13,315 is wide-gauge and run by RENFE. The remaining narrow-gauge track belongs to the State and is run by the Ministry of Public Works and private companies.
54 OECD, *Economic Survey: Spain* (Paris, 1974) p. 32.
55 Shipping freight increased from 16,848 billion tons/km to 24,800: see Tamames, *Introducción a la economía española*, Chapter 7, quoting the Dirección General de Transporte 1961–6 and the Comisión de Transportes of the Third Plan for 1967–70.
56 RENFE was followed by the Telefónica, which employed 55,885, and the construction company Dragados y Construcciones, which employed 31,870.
57 Roads in rural districts tend still to be poorly maintained.
58 On the whole these vehicles, usually heavily overloaded, are worn out within a few years.
59 Spanish shipping plays little part in fruit exports due to strong competition from non-Spanish shipping firms: see Tamames, *Introducción a la economía española*, Chapter 6.
60 The ten most important ports are: Cartagena, Santa Cruz de Tenerife, Bilbao, Barcelona, Gijon, Aviles, La Luz, Huelva, Valencia, Seville.
61 Three Spanish charter companies exist but their share in total flying time is very small.
62 Madrid, Malaga and Palma de Mallorca airports cater for over one-half of all tourists arriving by air.

CHAPTER 9

1 In January 1975 a government decree made it possible to waive the authorisation for certain industries.
2 This did not of course embrace all shades of political opinion.
3 The corps is an administrative entity dating from the end of the nineteenth century. See Kenneth Medhurst, *Government in Spain* (Oxford, 1973) Chapter 5, for an excellent description of the corps in the Civil Service.
4 Medhurst gives the example of investment decisions on irrigation as having been sometimes influenced by 'the size of the reward which interested corps could earn in the form of *tasas*'. *Tasas* are 'surcharges levied for services rendered and shares in incoming revenue', and count as income for which officials are not publicly accountable (see Medhurst, *Government in Spain*, pp. 112–13).
5 Ibid., p. 114.
6 Ley de Retribuciones de los Funcionarios de la Administración Civil del Estado, 5 May 1965.

7  There seems extraordinarily little contact between provincial branches of different sections of the Ministry of Agriculture.
8  K. Medhurst, *Government in Spain*, p. 102.
9  An extreme case of this lack of contact was the minimal rôle of the towns concerned in the choice of *polos de desarrollo* in the development plans.
10  Although energy consumption per person grew at an annual average rate of 11 per cent between 1962 and 1971, in 1971 energy consumption per person in Spain was approximately two-thirds that of Italy and similar to consumption levels in Romania and Hungary.
11  It does not operate in Ceuta and Melilla.
12  Since the beginning of the 1970s, the annual average rate of growth of the active population was greater than 1 per cent. The decline in 1975 was not a reflection of changing demographic trends. See OECD, *Economic Survey* (1976) p. 12.
13  In fact the measures, after being delayed in the Cortes for several months, were never implemented.

# Index